THE GREAT SALMON RIVERS
OF
SCOTLAND

Other books by John Ashley-Cooper
A SALMON FISHER'S ODYSSEY
A LINE ON SALMON
A RING OF WESSEX WATERS

THE GREAT SALMON RIVERS
OF
SCOTLAND

An Angler's Guide to the rivers
Dee, *Spey*, *Tay* and *Tweed*

by

John Ashley-Cooper

LONDON
H. F. & G. WITHERBY LTD

First published by Victor Gollancz Ltd 1980
Second edition, with some revision,
published 1987 by
H. F. & G. WITHERBY LTD
14 Henrietta Street, London, WC2E 8QJ

British Library Cataloguing in Publication Data
Ashley-Cooper, John
The great salmon rivers of Scotland: an
angler's guide to the rivers Dee, Spey,
Tay and Tweed.—2nd ed.
1. Salmon-fishing—Scotland
I. Title
799.1′755   SH684
ISBN 0-85493-157-0

Printed in Great Britain by
BAS Printers Limited,
Over Wallop, Hampshire

CONTENTS

The plates of the flies were painted by Tim Havers who also drew the maps and all of the line drawings in the text.

ACKNOWLEDGEMENTS

I am glad to take this opportunity of thanking my publishers for their helpful advice and encouragement, also Tim Havers for his excellent illustrations and maps. I should like too to thank Messrs Malloch of Perth for allowing me to quote from P. D. Malloch's *Life History and Habits of the Salmon*. For the story of Miss Ballantyne's 64-pound salmon, I thank *The Field*. Also, I thank Messrs Longmans Green & Co. for the 'Bishop Browne' story, as well as for that of Mr Craven's great 53-pound fish from the Spey. I am indebted to Messrs E. Arnold for figures of Spey salmon catches, and to Messrs Methuen for Mr Crossley's figures. Mr Thompson of the Tay Salmon Fisheries Company has given me valuable information for which I am grateful. Last but not least, I would like to thank my many fishing friends for their hospitality and kindness, especially the following : Capt. Charles Burrell, Major the Hon. Hew Dalrymple, Major and Mrs Fearfield, Major Derick Foster, Major and Mrs Jepson-Turner, Col. G. Kidston-Montgomerie, the Marquess of Lansdowne, Col. J. P. Moreton, the late Sir Brian Mountain, the late Countess of Seafield, Mrs Stainton, Col. the Earl of Stair, Major Anthony Tabor, the Hon. Aylmer Tryon, Major Sir H. D. H. Wills, and many others. All such kind friends have given me great enjoyment as well as experience, and I shall always be grateful.   J. A-C.

FOREWORD TO FIRST EDITION

An esteemed and knowledgeable fishing friend once said to me, when we were discussing fishing books, 'I don't mind middle-aged fishermen airing their pet theories, which doesn't do any harm, and one needn't pay attention; but I do object to their telling downright lies!' Well, I have tried in this book to maintain strict veracity as best I can, but circumstances change fast. For instance, I have harped on the deterioration of spring fishing for many years past, but after my writing thus during the winter of 1977 what should happen but that the spring of 1978 has produced the best fishing for fifteen years. Perhaps the spring of 1979 will be even better. Such matters are impossible to forecast, so I hope my readers when necessary will make appropriate allowances.

Above all in this book I have tried to steer clear of laying down any law about anything to do with fishing. Any attempt in this direction is doomed in advance to failure; and there are bound to be differences of opinion over fishing matters as there are over everything else. I remember reading some unkind Victorian critic's lampoon about the great Kelson, which started:

> 'Piscator magnus sum,
> Let others all be dumb,
> By Jove, by gum,
> I make things hum!'

and it continued in this vein. Whether it was justified or not is now impossible to say, but the message is clear, and no one would want to emulate Kelson in the way implied.

Let every fisherman therefore follow his own bent, governed only by the letter of the Law and of local rules, and by the effort to cause as little inconvenience as possible to fellow sportsmen. Indeed, help not hindrance should be his motto, and inducement through example rather than arbitrary dogma the guideline for his preceptor, should he seek one.

So whether my readers pay any attention to my theories about fishing in this book, or whether they don't, will be up to them. (One can always put a book, unlike a bore, aside!) I do not seek to force theories on anyone, but will be well satisfied if they merely arouse interest in one way or another. In any case the main part of this book, and certainly the pleasantest part to write, is concerned primarily with a description and history of four wonderful Scottish rivers, apart from the process of fishing them. This surely should not lead to controversy and one would have hoped it would be of interest to most salmon fishermen, wherever they normally fish.

One of a writer's main tasks is to try to bring to view something original; but in this case it is not easy, as salmon fishing as a sport is now over 300 years old and many hundreds of books have already been written about it. One can but try. In any case how much of any subject matter in any book is 'original' thought? Very little, one might say, though much of it might have previously been overlooked or forgotten, which is another matter.

Surely, in this connection, it is part of the useful function of any book to record notable past happenings that are in danger of slipping into oblivion over the passage of time. Hence in this book I have tried to bring into the limelight some little-known facts or incidents such as the former existence of the cruive dyke near Craigellachie with its attendant right of fish spearing; the account of Mr W. G. Craven's landing of the record Spey salmon (53lb) on a No. 4 Carron Fly (with one strand of its gut eye broken) in only fifteen minutes; of Caird Young's loup across the Dee at Potarch; or of the laconic addendum to the Floors Castle fishing record describing Mr Pryor's great catch on October 27th 1886 of fifteen fish, 'biggest $57\frac{1}{2}$ lb'!

Are not all such things matters of note, even though now long past? Or, if something nearer to hand is wanted, what about the astounding exploits of Mr George McCorquodale of Dalchroy, who caught more salmon than any man ever? Are these to be forgotten? Such a list would be endless, and its individual items perhaps only of limited interest, but collectively beyond price.

With advancing years one begins to realize more clearly that the number of one's future fishing seasons is limited, which is an added inducement towards making some attempt to pass on what one has learned to a younger generation of fishermen. Whether they will be as fortunate as us is doubtful. It is obvious nowadays that salmon are decreasing both in size and numbers in most British rivers – so is the available fishing, but in contrast the tally of both fishermen and expenses has increased alarmingly. No one will dispute this. Is it not right then that as complete a record as possible of fishing both in the past and present should be passed on, so that the fishermen in times to come may be able to form a reliable estimate of the sort of sport that we and our fathers and grandfathers have had? Will this not give them some sort of goal to aim at in the difficult task they will undoubtedly face in the protection, maintenance and improvement of the fisheries of the future?

Far from there being too many fishing books, as is sometimes said, I am personally inclined to feel that the opposite is true. I know I buy every book which is published on salmon fishing, and I enjoy them all, whether in agreement or not with their contents. The next best thing to fishing is reading about it. Both reading and writing about fishing help greatly to while away the long dark evenings of the close season. How one regrets that so many of the giants of the past did not record their views and experiences! If only such master-fishermen as Mr George McCorquodale, Mr Robert Pashley of the Wye, or Mr Arthur Wood of the Dee, or Mr Percy Laming of the Dee and Spey had put pen to paper! They are all awa' now, and what a wealth of experience has thus been lost. Others have written about them and their views, sometimes very effectively, but this can never be the same thing.

Too little attention has also been paid towards recording the views of outstanding boatmen or ghillies on first-class beats. Their experiences and opinions would doubtless be an eye-opener to many, both now and in the future.

One thing becomes clearer as one gets older and one's fishing experience increases, and that is the paramount importance of one's fishing companions. In younger days, and I suppose we most of us felt the same, what really mattered was whether one killed fish or not; and if one did, preferably in the largest possible numbers, and by any legal method; little else mattered. How mistaken this outlook was, though it took time to realize it. Of course as in any sport it is the company of one's friends that must come first, and that they should enjoy the whole affair as much or more than oneself. If other considerations are put first, such as the number of fish caught, whether or not the opposite bank catches more, or whether or not one's companions do, or how much fish are worth in the market, surely and inevitably one's enjoyment of this wonderful sport must be undermined.

It has been said that fishing is a way of life. I must admit that it has been largely so in my own case, though I know I am in good company and am thankful for it. When the recording angel makes his inventory, I shall truthfully be able to tell him, if he looks askance, that I have no regrets at this, but in fact only wish that I had been able to fish twice as much.

It is in this spirit, or in sympathy with it, that I hope my readers will bear with my writings in this book.

J. A-C.
Wimborne St Giles 1979

SUPPLEMENTARY FOREWORD

It is now some few years since the first edition of this book was written. Many marked changes as regards salmon fishing and all that goes with it have taken place since then on the four rivers concerned, (as well as elsewhere). Most of these are for the worse, though by no means all.

In 1979 spring fishing was still well worthwhile. 1976 and 1978 for instance had produced spring runs respectable by any standard. Although certain adverse factors were already obviously at work, there was apparently no call for undue pessimism. Since then however a black curtain has inexorably descended on the spring stage. Spey and Tay have now virtually no worthwhile spring catch; Dee and Tweed fare a little better, though they are in no way prolific compared to their past. Every river in fact seems to have suffered a devastation of its spring run, which as generally agreed was formerly the pride of its fishing.

The causes of this collapse are many; and it is no doubt the combination of these, rather than any single one, which is at the root of the trouble. Amongst the main bugbears are Greenland netting, Faroes long-lining (greatly increased since 1979), drift netting off Ireland, illegal offshore drift netting off Scotland, over netting by legal coastal and estuary nets, fresh water poaching and illegal fishing, U.D.N., and Northumberland drift netting (particularly harmful to the Tweed). All these are detrimental to fish stocks, and it is the early fish that appear to suffer worst.

Rod fishing too is not blameless; in some places far too many rods are fishing, not always by creditable methods, for a depleted spring stock. Could not the rod season be ended sooner, at least in the upper reaches of rivers where the stale spring fish late on are to be found? Thus an extra hundred or two potential spawners might survive each year. And could not the 'fly only' rule be more generally introduced after say mid-April, as well as a stricter limit be imposed on the number of rods allowed to fish at any one time? All such limitations would help fish stocks in spring, as well as in summer and autumn.

It has been argued that a change has occurred in the habits of the fish themselves, in that many more fish are returning to spawn after one sea-winter as grilse instead of waiting two sea-winters to return as salmon. It has been argued too that this change is a natural cycle beyond the control of man. This is possible without doubt, but I wonder. . . . Have the offspring of the grilse and summer fish proliferated through lack of competition with the offspring of spring fish which now longer exist *owing to excessive predation in the past by man*, (whether Greenlanders, Faroese, or British)? If so, this cycle is man-made, not natural, and if man-made it could be possible to reverse it.

It is true, as mentioned below, that a remarkable change over the past ten or twelve years has taken place in fish movements during summer in these four rivers. In Spey and Tay the summer run of grilse has steadily increased between early July and September. It is now very large. A copious number of salmon also enter the Tay during these months, though fewer than the Spey. The Tweed lacks a summer run, and any fish that enter then are likely to be caught in nets. But its autumn run in October and November, both of grilse and salmon, is as massive as ever. Even the Dee, formerly considered purely a spring river, is now experiencing (given suitable water) a modest grilse run in summer, with a fair sprinkling of fresh fish entering the lower reaches during September.

Another beneficial feature over these past five years has been evident, that is the increased activity and influence of various Associations devoted to the protection and increase of Atlantic salmon everywhere. Here in Britain, amongst others, we have the Salmon and Trout Association and the Atlantic Salmon Trust. On the other side of the Atlantic we find the International Atlantic Salmon Foundation and the Restoration of Atlantic Salmon in America Inc. There is also the North Atlantic Salmon Conservation Organization, perhaps the most influential of all. All bodies such as these do good work, all are worthy of support, and no one should try to cause division between them; it is labouring the obvious to point out that the combined efforts of a combined team are the factor which leads to victory in a tug of war. So I would ask any reader who scans the text of this second edition to bear in mind the above considerations, and while reading to make allowances for the recent great changes in circumstances.

Reluctantly one must admit that on all counts the outlook for Spey, Dee, Tay, and Tweed spring fishing is a bleak one.

From July onwards howevever the picture changes. Spey and Tay have a prolific grilse run, together with some summer salmon, which has increased over the past five years. This run is now massive, subject to favourable weather and water conditions, although grilse are capricious in their choice of pools and areas of river in which to lie. By September, and often earlier, these rivers hold a huge stock of such fish throughout much of their length, though the greatest concentrations are in the lower reaches.

The Tweed has no sizeable run of grilse or summer salmon that get past the nets until mid-September when the nets are lifted. Thereafter the autumn run of both grilse and salmon is prolific, and fishing is good whenever the river runs at a fair height with water reasonably clear.

Even the Dee is now producing a certain number of fresh-run fish during September, given suitable water conditions; though such fish at present seldom permeate above Banchory.

There would seem no reason therefore why summer fishing on the Spey and Tay from July onwards should not continue to be good or even improve over the next period of years. Tweed autumn fishing also seems set fair for the future. What will happen to the Dee spring fishing is anybody's guess. One can but hope for the best, even if one is apprehensive. The Dee in Victorian times was an autumn river; and it is just possible that in years to come it will revert to that state, though the loss of its magnificent spring fishing would be a catastrophe.

To be more outspoken than the above over future prospects on these four rivers would be a mistake, as in fishing like many other things the unexpected can arrive in disconcerting fashion, whether for better or worse. What is more the above conjectures are based on the present attendant conditions. Should there be radical changes, as yet only imaginary, such as our grilse feeding-grounds being discovered and exploited by long-line or drift net, or our netting season being substantially extended, or North Sea illegal fishing becoming a greater menace than it is at present, or a more virulent form of U.D.N. occurring, a realistic forecast could be much more pessimistic. On the other hand it is possible that artificial rearing of salmon, now so much on the increase, could dramatically benefit angling for salmon through a steep fall in the market value of these fish, with consequent reduction or even phasing out of commercial netting.

Finally, I should like to make it clear that this book is deliberately planned in the form of five sections, the first four mainly in the form of general descriptions and remarks (not always to do with salmon) about the four rivers concerned, and the fifth devoted entirely to the process of fishing them. Any reader primarily concerned with the latter might do worse, therefore, than to turn at once to Chapter 29, and revert later to the earlier sections.

J.A-C.
(1984–5)

PART ONE

The Spey

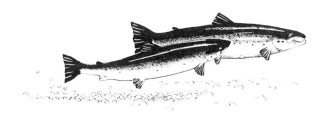

Munro's Killer

Black Pennell

Black Heron

Arndilly Fancy

Delfur Fancy

Black Tosh

Lady Caroline

Gold Riach

Purple King

Tim Havers

CHAPTER 1

General remarks—Character of the Spey—Snowfed—Fast
current—Peatiness—Distilleries—Spates—Gravel

That the Spey is the most magnificent of Scottish rivers few would deny. Its attraction lies mainly in the size and strength of its stream, the rocky nature of its bed, and the wildness and splendour of its surroundings. The view of the upper part of Strathspey looking southwards from near Dulnain bridge towards the Cairngorm hills is breathtaking, particularly in May when snow still crowns the high tops, and when the larch and the broom are newly out, or else in late summer when the heather is in full bloom.

Lower down the river there are also endless spectacular panoramas as the Spey hastens on its course from rapid to pool, and again to rapid, to its final entry into the Moray Firth at Kingston, on Spey Bay. This perhaps is the Spey's unique feature, that nowhere to within half a mile of its mouth does its current relax – there is no slow-running tidal estuary on this river; in fact there is almost no tidal water at all, and in high spate the Spey colours the open Moray Firth brown with peat water for several miles out to sea, almost as far as the eye can reach.

Another interesting characteristic of the Spey is that, alone amongst the sizeable rivers of Scotland, it has no town of any size at its mouth. Fochabers (pop.1200) is five miles upriver from Spey Bay, and only the small villages of Garmouth and Kingston feature near its course below, the latter so-called to commemorate the landing there from France of King Charles II in 1650, at the start of his Odyssey ending in the disastrous Battle of Worcester, and his final escape to France.

One other peculiar feature of the Spey is the great snow reservoir which it possesses high up in the Cairngorms. In early spring most Scottish rivers are to some extent snow-fed, but this seldom lasts elsewhere beyond February or March. Not so in the case of the Spey however, as many square miles of its catchment area on the north and west slopes of the Cairngorms are over 3000 feet in height; and deep snow there, particularly when frozen hard in the corries, can last as late as June. Slowly melting snow thus helps to keep this river running at a fair height right through the spring months, and sometimes into summer, irrespective of whether or not there is rain. The only other river sharing this advantage, though to a lesser extent, is the Aberdeenshire Dee, which drains the south side of the Cairngorms; but all other rivers, being more dependent on rain, can be running low by April or May, while the Spey and the Dee can still be holding to a good height.

There are no falls on the Spey, or rocky linns like the Linn of Campsie on the Tay. This is a pity in some ways, as such falls would be a grand sight, particularly with the river in spate. Nor are there any artificial weirs* or 'caulds', as there are on the Tweed for example. So there is no obstruction, natural or artificial, to the upstream passage of fish.

Even if the Spey is only the third largest river in Scotland (after the Tay and Tweed), with a catchment area of 1097 square miles and a length of just over 100 miles, it is certainly a big river by British standards, and is second to none in grandeur and speed of flow. In high spate the fastest section of the river, from Grantown down, is truly an awesome sight, with all pools and rapids obliterated by a steady torrent of some fifteen knots bearing a succession of tree trunks and branches, drowned animals and debris of all sorts on its surface, hustling them seawards. Even at a normal height the Spey's current is more formidable than that of any other British river, as those who attempt to wade in it, or boat it, soon discover. In fact it has been said that the Spey is the only British river (apart from the Awe, now, alas, denuded of water by the Hydro) which is comparable to Norwegian rivers in this respect.

Nor is the Spey subject to that curse of many sizeable rivers, the presence of a main road with an endless flow of traffic alongside its course, and destructive of that natural peace and harmony which are a salmon river's birthright. On the contrary, for most of its length, and anyhow all along that bottom half of the river where the fishing is best, the Spey has only footpaths or rough tracks along its banks. Such disturbing factors as main roads, railways, airfields, camping sites and the like are still conspicuously absent, nor are there any large towns or

---

*That this was not always the case is not often realized. In the middle of the last century there was certainly a weir or dyke across the Spey a short distance above Fochabers. Its existence is confirmed by Thomas T. Stoddart in his *Angler's Companion to the Rivers and Lochs of Scotland* (1853), in which he refers to 'the cruive-dyke above Fochabers'. A. E. Knox in *Autumns on the Spey* (1872) also refers to this dyke.

Tradition further has it that there was a second dyke across the river half a mile below Craigellachie, near a pool known as the 'Heathery Isle', and one privileged individual had the right to spear salmon as they ascended it. But all traces of these dykes have long ago disappeared.

industrial areas in the neighbourhood. Long may this happy state of affairs last!

There are other features of the Spey, worthy of note, which help to make it different from other rivers. One is the extreme peatiness and acidity of its water. Presumably this arises from the character of its upper course above Grantown, which is comparatively slow-running amid a wide and very peaty valley, and tributaries such as the Dulnain (in itself a sizeable river of twenty-five miles length, rising in the Monadh Liath mountains to the west) bring in a vast amount of peat. Many other tributaries also, such as the Avon and Fiddich and Feshie to name the main ones, although they may be crystal clear (particularly the Avon) in fine weather and with low water, all help to increase the peat content of the main Spey after rain. The final and very perceptible result is that the Spey, although it is clear enough during a spell of fine weather, runs black and peaty for a surprisingly long time after heavy rain, at least for several days. No doubt this natural peatiness is also accentuated by the large amount of artificial drainage in the catchment area, carried out in recent years for the benefit of forestry, or of agricultural land, or of grouse moors – all of them extensive. In former days it was only after rain in summer and autumn that the Spey tended to run really black; but now this happens in spring also, and presumably it is the increased drainage which has made this change. Nor is there any large loch midway down the course of the Spey, which could possibly act as a 'settling tank' for the peat. Compared with the Tay, Ness, or Lochy for example, the waters of which all run through lochs of great size in their middle or lower reaches, the Spey is poorly endowed in this respect, and possesses only the insignificant Loch Insh near Kingussie, too small and too high up to be of any advantage as a filter.

Now, as any experienced fisherman knows, salmon dislike peaty or pronouncedly acid water. Presumably it makes them feel sick, or otherwise uncomfortable, with the result that they take badly or not at all. Any of us who have fished in the Emerald Isle have surely noted the Irish ghillies' lurid curses on the 'bogwater', that comes down after heavy rain there. Maybe the Spey peat water is not quite so devastating in its effect on the salmon, but it certainly does not help, and its presence definitely spells fewer fish on the bank. A pure flow, for example the beautiful clear water of the Dee, is greatly to be preferred; so the Spey thus suffers an inherent disadvantage, so far as fishing is concerned.

Yet, in connection with this peatiness, no description of the Spey would be complete without reference to that unforgettable product, the wonderful Speyside malt whisky. There are at least forty distilleries in Strathspey, working all round the clock, including the one and only Glenlivet distillery of unrivalled fame. Anyone who has not yet quaffed the true Speyside malt, diluted or not as the case may be with a moderate amount of local water, has still something in life to look forward to; and one is told that it is the peculiar quality of this peaty Speyside water which makes the creation of such unrivalled 'Uisge-beatha' possible. No other whisky-producing area in Scotland can compare with Strathspey, either in the quality or quantity of its output. So even if a certain amount of 'burnt ale' does seep its way surreptitiously and illicitly into the river, surely if this is kept within reasonable bounds any tolerant fisherman who enjoys his dram at the end of a hard day will turn a blind eye?

Mention has already been made of the fierce character of the Spey spates, and these are perhaps more sudden and savage than those of most other Scottish rivers. Not only is the natural course of the lower Spey a steep one, with a fall of around 600 feet in forty-eight miles (so that in any case its spates are bound to be impressive), but in addition to this the artificial drainage has resulted in an unnaturally quick run-off of surface water after heavy rain. This in turn results in the river rising much quicker and to higher levels than formerly, which can result in great damage in the way of banks ripped away, boats lost, fishing huts and rod boxes destroyed, and sheep, cattle and other livestock drowned. Subsequently, after the rain has stopped, the high water level is not maintained by rainwater stored in the natural reservoirs of bog, marsh, or undrained ground, but quickly falls away again. From the fishing point of view this is another drawback, and it would be far preferable to have a river that rose and fell more slowly in the more stable way of olden days. However, in these sort of matters, fishermen have to make the best of the inevitable; and perhaps as the large areas of afforestation mature, a better storage of rainwater will evolve.

One certain harmful effect of these rapid rises and falls is the great destruction of salmon fry and parr all up and down the river. At the height of a big flood these little fish come close into the side to escape the force of the main current; and when the peak level has been reached, and the water begins to fall rapidly, they get stranded where the river has overflowed its banks amongst the grass and bushes, and so perish.

This wholesale destruction can be seen by anyone who takes the trouble to investigate after one of the outsize spates of present times; and the mortality must run into millions. The effect on the eventual stocks of adult fish can only be left to the imagination, and one wonders whether any recent decline in their numbers may be in part due to the series of such outsize spates which has occurred in the past twenty or so years.

To digress for a moment, it might here be of interest to give a brief description of the Great Moray Floods of 1829. These were a catastrophe, still referred to locally, which affected not only the Spey but most other rivers in the north-east of Scotland; and which are ably described in detail in the book under that same heading by the Rev. Sir T. Dick-Lauder. So far as the Spey was concerned, it appears that approximately four-and-a-half inches of rain fell generally over the catchment area during one night in early August. Nothing like the result has ever been seen before or since.

The Spey rose generally to around twenty-five feet above its normal level and flooded out indiscriminately over its banks. The whole haugh round Rothes for instance, also past Dandaleith and Dundurcas and Dipple, looked like one vast loch, and Rothes itself was flooded up to the level of the first-floor windows. In several places the river completely changed its course and innumerable sheep and cattle were drowned. It was said that many of the smaller burns entering the Spey were swollen so big as to look like the main river itself at a normal level, and hundreds of acres of agricultural land were temporarily ruined by being covered with gravel and stones. Every bridge on the Spey was washed away, except the bridge at Craigellachie, which exists to this day and which spans the whole width of the river with a single arch. Fortunately human casualties were few, only one poor crippled boy who failed to run clear in time from the Fochabers bridge as it collapsed, and one unlucky victim of the flooded Knockando burn, who was marooned in a treetop by the swollen torrent. Repeated efforts to rescue him were made both by rope and boat; but all failed, and eventually he was swept away and drowned as the water rose.

Apart from such catastrophes, any excessive spate is liable to cause appreciable damage to fisheries by bringing down quantities of gravel (and sometimes sand) which can fill in pools and spoil favoured salmon lies. How often has one heard of this or that noted pool being 'badly gravelled' after some big flood, and no longer holding fish! One wonders where all the gravel comes from, in such massive quantities. Presumably the Spey has been carrying it seawards for the last two million years or so, at a surprisingly fast rate, and one would have thought that by now the supply might have been exhausted. But not at all, if anything it increases.

As regards high spates, not all the entries of course are on the debit side. If they can 'gravel' a pool, they can often 'ungravel' it again, particularly if helped by artificial groynes or, better still, bulwarks, and make it a good holding place for salmon once more. Also high water helps to bring the fish into the river past the nets, and helps them to ascend tributaries to spawn there. It washes the river bed clean and brings an increased oxygen supply to the whole river system.

Every fisherman knows with what exhilaration he welcomes the steady patter of heavy rain on the roof after a period of prolonged drought; and a persistent downpour arouses almost as much anticipation as the actual arrival of fresh fish. In moderation high water at suitable intervals is certain to be welcomed; and it is far preferable to the shrunken flow of continued drought, even in a big river like the Spey which will fish reasonably well at a lower level than most.

CHAPTER 2

Fishing and fish—Speycasting—Grant Vibration rods—Varying weather
Spring fishing—Summer fishing—Pollution—Hatchery—Sea trout

The runs of salmon in the Spey and the quality of its fishing are almost legendary; and one can hardly picture a more ideal setting for this sport. The quick succession of rapid and pool, together with the fast flow of the stream and the rocky nature of the river-bed and banks, provide magnificent fishing water, particularly for fly-fishing. The Spey has given its name, as is well known, to a method of switch-casting which nullifies the obstacle of high banks or rock faces behind; and it is a joy to watch this cast when practised by a skilled exponent, of which there are many in the neighbourhood. A special type of rod has even been designed for perfecting this cast, the renowned 'Grant Vibration' spliced greenheart, which was first produced in the late years of the last century by Alexander Grant of Inverness. Grant, a schoolmaster by profession, and a violinist as well as a fisherman in his leisure hours, was a redoubtable champion in the fishing world of his day. He is recorded as having switch-cast sixty-five yards without shooting any line. Who could do anything approaching this now? Grant Vibration rods, following his prototype patterns, were made till fairly recently by Messrs Playfair of Aberdeen; but now, alas, they have gone out of production, and greenheart is anyhow out of fashion, so these rods have nowadays become something in the way of museum pieces. But they are still a delight to fish with, if one is lucky enough to possess one.

To return to the characteristics of the Spey as a fishing river, it is occasionally possible to fish a Spey pool off the bank, even when the water is low, but pools which can properly be so covered are rare, though more frequent with high water when the fish often come close in to the side. Normally, the fisherman needs long trouser waders, and has to wade deep, while sometimes the use of a boat, particularly on the wide pools of the lower Spey, becomes essential. To be able to throw a long line, the longer the better, ranks high among the Spey fisherman's needs, as does the ability to compete with strong adverse winds. Anyone who fishes the Spey in spring with the icy north-east gales whipping up the Strath off the Moray Firth, unchecked since they left the frozen fjords of Norway, knows well what the prosaic term 'adverse winds' can imply!

By contrast one can meet the soft and balmy breezes of May, or the baking summer glare of July and August, interspersed at times with torrential thunderstorms – even snow in June or July is not unknown. So one gets it all in turn, the only constant weather factor being the great uncertainty.

The early salmon sometimes start to enter the Spey in January, or even December, if the river is running full and not too cold. Usually by the opening of the fishing season on February 11th there are a fair number of fresh fish in the lowest pools from Orton downstream (twelve miles from the sea). After a warm winter fish may even be found as high up as Grantown, fifty miles up-river, on the opening day. Generally speaking however the Spey cannot be classed as an 'early' river, and cannot be compared with the Dee or the Tweed, for instance, in this respect. Only the very lowest reaches have ever been known to produce large bags in February or March, and now even this seems to have become a thing of the past. It is now April or May before the main spring run enters the river.

Every now and then there is a freak winter of exceptional cold, when on the opening day of the season the Spey may be found frozen from bank to bank in the slow-running pools, with the water elsewhere dead low, and full of floating ice or 'grue'. Such winters occur on average perhaps in one year out of twelve, and fishing may be impossible until late March, or April.

But normally in the very lowest parts of the river, from Orton down, March should see the best of the spring fishing; while elsewhere in the river mid-April to mid-May is probably best. June everywhere is frequently a poor month; the spring run of salmon has fallen away, and the summer run of salmon and grilse is only apt to start sometime in early July. During these last ten years or so, sad to say, the former magnificent run of spring salmon has gravely diminished.* It has been reliably commented that there is only one spring fish in the river now for every twenty that there used to be in the 1950s and early '60s. That the same thing has happened, and often to a worse extent, in almost all other rivers is poor consolation; and nowadays the best Spey fishing is usually between mid-July and the end of August. September also can be good; but even so this summer fishing is particularly at risk from the vagaries of the weather. Continuous hot weather, bright sun and low, warm water, or in contrast high, peaty floods, do not spell good fishing conditions; and by September most of the fish are getting unpleasantly red, though fresh ones are still to be found low down the river.

*The 1978 spring run was much better.

The causes of the deterioration of the spring run are no doubt many, and it is almost certainly a combination of these, rather than any individual one, which is at the root of the trouble. In the past sixteen years, have we not suffered for instance from Greenland nets, U.D.N., overfishing by our own coastal and estuary nets, illegal drift-netting off our coasts, overfishing by too many rods in our rivers, pollution, and in the Spey as noted above the destruction of vast numbers of fry and parr after high spates? There may also be other local harmful factors too many to list here. Is it not surprising, in the face of this formidable array, that the stocks of adult fish have not fallen away further than they have? The wonder is that although the spring fish have been decimated the Spey summer fish still maintain their numbers, or perhaps increase. In addition to, or as a result of the hazards above, of which our salmon must now run the gauntlet, it may well be that a change in the normal life-cycle of the salmon is now taking place. Certainly some factor unknown is causing more and more fish to return to freshwater as grilse, or to a lesser extent as small salmon of two sea-winters; while the larger fish of 16 lb or over with three or more sea-winters are becoming ever scarcer. This again is now noticeable in all other rivers, and not only in the Spey. Is it a natural change in the salmon's breeding cycle, or is it because more and more of the potential three sea-winter fish are being caught on the high seas or off foreign coasts by newly devised methods of fishing? At this stage it is difficult to say, but the situation is not a happy one.

On the credit side however it must be admitted that Spey fishing from July to the end of the season is now probably better than it has ever been, particularly in the lower part of the river; even better perhaps than in the golden days of the old autumn fishing in the 1800s and the early 1900s, at least for numbers if not for weights.

Spring fishing, although but a shadow of what it was, does still exist and can be well worthwhile at intervals (for instance the spring of 1975, after a mild winter of high water was quite good by any standard). There is always the possibility that this fishing may once more come into its own again.

Pollution is better checked now than for a very long time past. For example, Rothes, Craigellachie, Aberlour and Grantown all now have efficient sewage disposal plants, instead of their drains running straight into the river, as they once did. Distilleries also have been induced to exercise much greater care over the disposal of their waste products, and the pollution on this score has been agreeably lessened.

One further additional benefit is that the Spey Board for several years has run an efficient hatchery at Knockando and has turned salmon fry by the million into suitable burns or stretches of river. This must help the stock, particularly in years when U.D.N. must have killed large numbers of potential parent fish before they spawned. Net-poaching in the main river, which some years ago was so prevalent, is now almost wholly eliminated, and there is a good team of watchers and bailiffs.

So all in all there are still benefits for which the Spey fisherman should be thankful. The future for the Spey as a salmon river is not without hope, but there is a crying need that excessive netting both in the river and sea (and particularly illegal drift-netting out at sea) should be stopped. Also pollution and poaching must always be kept under control; and too intensive rod fishing both in the main river and tributaries should be checked, so that a plentiful supply of potential spawners is maintained.

But salmon and grilse are not the only fish that ascend the Spey, and some mention should also be made of the extensive run of sea trout. It is not widely known that the Spey is certainly the most prolific sea trout river in Scotland. The net-catch is said to be immense, and certainly runs into many tons; and the rod-catch is also big, though largely unrecorded. Sea trout are caught in numbers by rod over the whole of the middle and lower Spey, from Fochabers up to Grantown; and even at times above Grantown, though fifty miles is a long way upstream for these fish to run. Large specimens frequently reach double figures in weight, and one of 18 lb is on record, taken from the middle Spey.

These big fish start entering the river in April, but June and early July are the best times to fish, when the average size drops to about 2 lb. Undoubtedly the best part of the river for sea trout fishing lies between Ballindalloch and Wester Elchies, Ballindalloch and Pitchroy offering something quite exceptional in this line. The fact that the Avon enters the Spey at Ballindalloch must have a good deal to do with this, because many sea trout go up this sizeable tributary, and are apt to congregate downstream from its mouth while awaiting a spate to attract them into leaving the main river. Yet there are few parts of the Spey below Grantown where sea trout cannot be caught in good numbers, if they are properly fished over at the right time and place. If there is a good spate or two towards the end of May and early in June it is most welcome to sea trout fishers, in that it is likely to bring a big run into the river and past the nets. But the main reason why one does not hear more of the Spey sea trout is that salmon are the most sought-after quarry. Night is the best time to fish for sea trout, and it is impossible for anyone to fish all day for salmon and all night for sea trout, so the latter are usually left for the ghillies and local fishermen, who do not fail to take advantage of them and often get double figures in the night. This is wonderful sport, considering the large size of the fish, but it is not publicized.

CHAPTER 3

Upper Spey from source to Grantown—Source—Headwaters
Water abstraction—Loch Insh—Upper tributaries—Pike

For descriptive purposes, over its 100-mile course, the Spey is best divided into three sections. The first of these is the upper Spey from the source to Grantown.

Rising in little Loch Spey in the Corriearrick Forest of Wester Badenoch, at a height of 1200 feet, and only nineteen miles crow-flight from Fort William, the Spey in its early course has the character of little more than a highland burn as it flows eastward towards Newtonmore, twenty miles downstream. Its main tributaries in this area are the Mashie and the Truim on the south side, and the Calder on the north, none of them of consequence from the angling point of view, though they have a value as spawning streams, as does the upper Spey itself.

The headwaters of the upper Spey, as well as the Truim, are both now subjected to water abstraction for hydro and other purposes. So far this has not reached an extent which can do appreciable harm, and it is to be hoped it never will.

By the time it reaches Newtonmore, reinforced by these tributaries, the Spey has increased to a fair size. The fall in the course of the river has thus far been reasonably steep, i.e. a drop of around 350 feet over the twenty miles. But from Newtonmore downstream past Kingussie, Kincraig, Aviemore, Boat of Garten and so to Grantown, over this further thirty miles, the fall is slightly less than 200 feet (an average of only just over six feet per mile). Most of this fall occurs only a short distance upstream from Grantown. The inevitable, and rather unusual result in the upper course of a highland river, is that the Spey in this area is mostly slow-running and of rather dull character, apart from its magnificent surroundings with the Cairngorms to the east and the Monadh Liaths to the west. At one point near Kincraig, and four miles downstream from Kingussie, the river widens into a shallow and picturesque (though weedy) loch called Loch Insh. This loch is about one-and-a-half miles long and one mile wide, and is said to have been visited by St Columba as long ago as the seventh century A.D. (when he built and consecrated a chapel on an island there). Salmon can be caught in it early in the season before the weed grows up, a fact

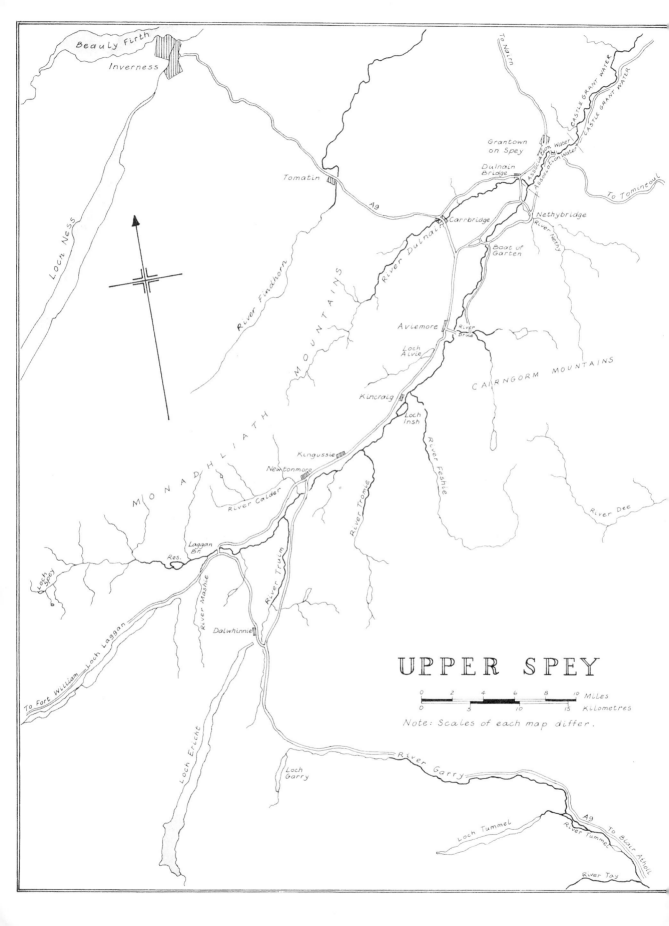

Beauly Firth

Inverness

Loch Ness

To Nairn

Grantown
on Spey

CASTLE GRANT WATER

CASTLE GRANT WATER

Dulnain
Bridge

Association Water

Association Water

To Tomintoul

Tomatin

A9

Carrbridge

Nethybridge

River Nethy

River Findhorn

River Dulnain

Boat of
Garten

MONADHLIATH MOUNTAINS

Aviemore

River Druie

Loch
Alvie

CAIRNGORM MOUNTAINS

Kincraig

Loch
Insh

River Feshie

Kingussie

River Dee

Newtonmore

River Calder

River Truim

River Tromie

Laggan
Br.

Res.

Loch
Spey

River Mashie

To Fort William Loch Laggan

Dalwhinnie

Loch Ericht

UPPER SPEY

0   2   4   6   8   10 Miles
0   5   10   15 Kilometres

Note: Scales of each map differ.

Loch
Garry

River Garry

A9

To Blair Atholl

Loch Tummel

River Tummel

River Tay

that may surprise many of the anglers on the more renowned Spey fisheries fifty miles further downstream.

Below Loch Insh the Spey again resumes its slow-running course, with little to recommend it to the salmon fisher, although an odd fish may be caught here and there, particularly late in the season. Only when it reaches the neighbourhood of Boat of Garten and the area immediately upstream of Grantown (which is fished by the Grantown Angling Association) does the current quicken enough to form good holding pools. A fair number of salmon are caught in this area each season.

The main tributaries on the right bank of the Upper Spey are the Tromie, the Feshie and the Nethy, which flow from the Cairngorms; and on the opposite side, the Dulnain off the Monadh Liaths. These are all valuable spawning streams; and the Feshie, Nethy and Dulnain all provide a certain amount of rod fishing in their own right from May onwards. There are also a host of smaller burns on both sides of the river, which help to swell its flow. They all have the character of mountain spate rivers, which need rain and consequent high water to draw the fish into them, but nevertheless from all points of view they are a valuable asset to the main river, except only that they bring in much peat after rain.

A curious feature of the upper Spey in the Newtonmore and Kingussie area is that in addition to its large stock of brown trout it also abounds with pike. Some of these run to a large size. Readers of Colonel Thornton's *Northern Tour*, published in the 1830s, will remember how the author describes pike fishing with his 'greyhounds' or trout lure baits in Loch Alvie, close to Kincraig. Both brown trout and even more so pike must do great damage to salmon parr stocks, and efforts have been made lately by the Spey Board to reduce the numbers at least of the pike by netting. Pike, in fact, do occasionally drop down to the lower Spey below Grantown, but normally they dislike the fast current there, and prefer to remain in the slow-running upper reaches.

CHAPTER 4

*Middle Spey from Grantown to Rothes—Increased fall
Famous beats—Avon—Big fish—Duncan Grant—George McCorquodale*

In the neighbourhood of Grantown, some forty-eight miles from its mouth at Spey Bay, the Spey changes its character. The fall over these forty-eight miles is some 600 feet, or an average of over twelve feet per mile. Already at Grantown the Spey is a big river, and a fall so abrupt is unparalleled elsewhere in Britain for a river of this size. In fact one might reasonably describe the Spey at Grantown as leaving a plateau over which it has ambled peacefully for many miles and tumbling quickly down to the sea with a never decreasing impetus over half of its long course. This is in curious contrast to most rivers, which run faster in their upper reaches and more slowly lower down. From the salmon fishing angle, it is of course this lower half of the river that holds the main interest. For descriptive purposes in this book a division between middle and lower Spey has been made at Rothes; because above that point (or at least above the mouth of the Fiddich, another sizeable tributary which enters two miles above Rothes) the river is not quite so large. Also from Rothes downstream the valley opens wider, which allows the river to spread; and the banks become less stable, and the main stream less firmly confined; in fact the river below Rothes does tend to change character.

In the course of the so-designated middle Spey, between Grantown and Rothes, such famous fisheries as Castle Grant, Tulchan, Ballindalloch, Pitchroy, Knockando, Carron and Laggan, Wester Elchies, Kinermony, Easter Elchies and Arndilly follow one another in quick succession. Nearly all these beats have both banks for all their length, or at least for most of it; the only exceptions are Wester Elchies, Kinermony, Easter Elchies, and part of Arndilly. From the fishing point of view, as every fisherman knows, to have both banks is a welcome advantage at all times, except when the river is very high.

From a general point of view, these fishings might nowadays be described as the cream of the Spey – a wonderful river, here cradled in an unsurpassable setting. As a rule the valley is deep and steep. High banks tend to enclose the river, sometimes pressing close to the water's edge, sometimes withdrawn a short distance as though to give the river breathing space and to allow the

The Manse Pool and Cromdale Bridge, Castle Grant
A pool on the Spey three miles below Grantown. This part of the river fishes best in May and early June. Although the fishing is not here so prolific as the beats lower down, the scenery and surroundings are unsurpassable.

fisherman a view of the distant Cromdale hills or the nearer Ben Rinnes. Magnificent tree growth in most places along the banks gives shelter and shade and enhances the view. Larch, pine, and Scots fir trees are plentiful. Gean trees (wild cherry) add their wonderful blossom in springtime to the colour scheme, and it is not by accident that so many salmon pools are named after them. Pool follows pool, all good holding water for salmon and affording first class fishing, interspersed with tumbling and rocky rapids. How could any keen fisherman fail to fall under the spell of such surroundings, unspoilt as they are and remote from all forms of outside disturbance?

At Ballindalloch, some eleven miles below Grantown, the Spey is joined by its largest tributary, the Avon, locally pronounced 'A'an'. This in itself is a sizeable river of forty miles length, rising far back in the Cairngorms, and skirting Tomintoul, which at 1200 feet is said to be the highest village in Scotland. Augmented by its own main tributary the Livet burn (of whisky fame), the Avon enters the Spey at the famous Junction Pool at Ballindalloch. Many salmon and sea trout ascend the Avon at any time from May onwards, though they prefer to wait for a spate to help them on their way. Many fish are caught on this river; though the process is not always easy because, except in time of spate, its water is reputed the clearest in all Scotland. Later on, the Avon provides good spawning ground after the fishing season is finished.

To return to the middle Spey, if one was asked to single out any one beat as being of surpassing attraction above all the others, this would indeed be a difficult task. If pressed one might cite Ballindalloch or Wester Elchies as being second to none. Ballindalloch, or its subsidiary Upper Pitchroy, has the famous pool at Blacksboat, where there is a road bridge across the river. This bridge is a popular vantage point for those who want to watch the salmon lying in the pool below, where they often gather in numbers. Blacksboat is so called, incidentally, after the ferry run by the black servant of a former laird of Ballindalloch in Victorian times.

Wester Elchies, five miles further downstream and immediately above the village of Aberlour, has perhaps the finest pools of all, though its fishing is from the left bank only. Such pools as Dailuaine, Pol ma Chree, Dellagyle and the Rhynd, make an unforgettable impression and can nowhere be surpassed.

It is not surprising that epic accounts of struggles with big fish in the middle and lower Spey are numerous. Usually they end in disaster, but occasionally otherwise. Perhaps the best of them is one of the earliest, that taken from William Scrope's angling classic *Days and Nights of Salmon Fishing* (1843). And as it is particularly relevant to the Spey at Wester Elchies, it is hoped that the

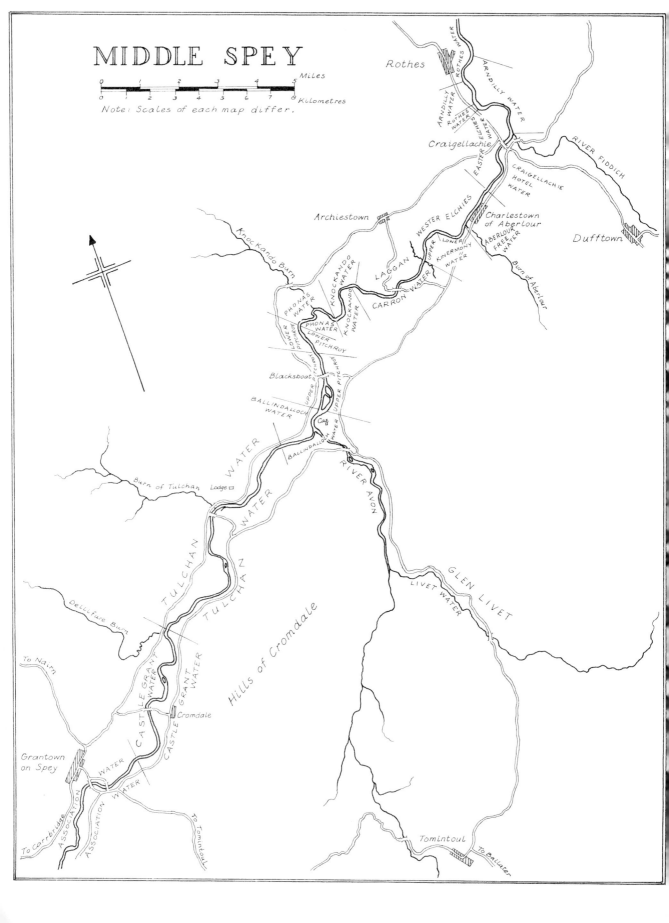

MIDDLE SPEY

0   1   2   3   4   5 Miles
0   1   2   3   4   5   6   7   8 Kilometres

Note: Scales of each map differ.

Rothes

ARNDILLY WATER

ROTHES WATER

ARNDILLY WATER

ROTHES WATER

RIVER FIDDICH

Craigellachie

EASTER ELCHIES WATER

CRAIGELLACHIE HOTEL WATER

Archiestown

WESTER ELCHIES

Charlestown of Aberlour

Dufftown

ABERLOUR FREE WATER

Knockando Burn

LAGGAN

UPPER

LOWER

KINERMONY WATER

Burn of Aberlour

KNOCKANDO WATER

CARRON WATER

PHONAS WATER

LOWER PITCHROY

PHONAS WATER

LOWER PITCHROY

KNOCKANDO WATER

Blacksboat

UPPER PITCHROY

UPPER PITCHROY

BALLINDALLOCH WATER

Cas.

BALLINDALLOCH WATER

RIVER AVON

WATER

Burn of Tulchan   Lodge

WATER

TULCHAN

GLEN LIVET

LIVET WATER

TULCHAN WATER

Dellifure Burn

TULCHAN

Hills of Cromdale

To Nairn

CASTLE GRANT WATER

CASTLE GRANT WATER

Cromdale

Grantown on Spey

WATER

ASSOCIATION

ASSOCIATION WATER

To Carrbridge

To Tomintoul

Tomintoul   To Ballater

reader may appreciate its inclusion here:

In the month of July, some thirty years ago [this would have made the date about 1812] one Duncan Grant, a shoemaker by profession, who was more addicted to fishing than his craft, went up the way from the village of Aberlour, in the north, to take a cast in some of the pools above Elchies Water. He had no great choice of tackle as may be conceived; nothing, in fact, but what was useful, and scant supply of that.

Duncan tried one or two pools without success, till he arrived at a very deep and rapid stream, facetiously termed 'the Mountebank' [not now identifiable. If it was 'two or three pools' upstream from Aberlour, might it be Dellagyle or Dailuaine, or Delbreck?] Here he paused as if meditating whether he should throw his line or not. 'She is very big', said he to himself, 'but I'll try her; if I grip him he would be worth the hauding.' He then fished it, a step and a throw, about half way down, when a heavy splash proclaimed he had raised him, though he missed the fly. Going back a few paces, he came over him again and hooked him. The first tug verified to Duncan his prognostication, that if he was there 'he would be worth the hauding'; but his tackle had thirty plies of hair next to the fly, and he held fast, nothing daunted. Give and take went on with dubious advantage, the fish occasionally sulking. The thing at length became serious; and after a succession of the same tactics, Duncan found himself at the Boat of Aberlour, seven hours after he had hooked the fish, the said fish fast under a stone and himself completely tired. He had some thoughts of breaking his tackle and giving the thing up; but he finally hit upon an expedient to rest himself, and at the same time to guard against the surprise and consequence of a sudden movement by the fish.

He laid himself down comfortably on the banks, the butt end of his rod in front; and most ingeniously drew out part of his line, which he held in his teeth. 'If he tugs when I'm sleeping,' said he, 'I think I'll find him noo'; and no doubt it is probable that he would. Accordingly, after a comfortable nap of three or four hours, Duncan was awoke by a most unceremonious tug at his jaws. In a moment he was on his feet, his rod well up and the fish swattering down the stream. He followed as best he could, and was beginning to think of the rock at Craigellachie, when he found to his great relief that he could 'get a pull on him'. He had now comparatively easy work; and exactly twelve hours after hooking him, he cleicked him at the head of Lord Fife's water; he weighed fifty-four pounds, Dutch, and had the tide lice upon him.

Could any fishing story be more vivid or enthralling than this? Incidentally, it may be mentioned that only five years ago (1974) a forty-eight pounder was killed at Wester Elchies; so some of the big ones are still with us, though scarcer than formerly no doubt.

Turning from Duncan Grant to fishermen of more modern times, no account of Spey fishing would be complete without mention of George McCorquodale of Dalchroy, who fished the Spey from 1891 to 1935. He was probably the greatest salmon fisherman of all time, yet his fame has never been extolled to the extent it deserves. He fished mainly at Tulchan, between Castle Grant and Ballindalloch; but also on that part of the Gordon Castle Water now known as the Brae Water in early spring and autumn. He was a 'fly only' man, and during the above years his carefully kept records show that he killed no less than 8924 salmon and grilse in the Spey alone, including at least three forty pounders. But this was not all, as Mr McCorquodale also fished extensively on other rivers, notably the Shannon, Tay and Helmsdale; but unfortunately he kept no record of his catches there. These, however, must have been numerous, bringing the total well into five figures, and without mentioning names of any other famous fishermen, it seems certain that for numbers of fish killed, as well as for ability and experience, Mr McCorquodale stands on a pinnacle alone.

Carron Bridge

CHAPTER 5

Lower Spey from Rothes to Spey Bay—Larger river—Banks less stable
Bigger pools—Good beats—Spring fishing—Summer fishing—Long season
Big fish—Record Spey fish—Gordon Castle fishing—Netting—Conclusion

Although this lowest section of the river is similar in many respects to the middle Spey from Grantown down, there are a few marked differences, which justify its description under a separate heading.

As might be expected, the river down here tends to become larger, owing partly to the influx of a sizeable tributary at Craigellachie, the Fiddich, as well as other smaller burns, and partly because the whole valley becomes much wider and flatter as the river nears the Moray Firth.* This in turn tends to allow the Spey to widen its bed, hard rocky banks that stand up to spates become increasingly scarce, and more and more the banks are formed of soft shingle, sand, or earth. Unless reinforced artificially they are apt to give way at every big spate, and indeed after such spates, and especially as it nears the sea, the river is often found to have changed its course over sizeable stretches. Also, unless artificially constricted with groynes or bulwarks, pools tend to get filled more and more with small gravel as their banks recede, and the force of the main current, which might otherwise serve to keep them clear, is dissipated. This in turn discourages salmon from resting in them, and thus the fishing is liable to deteriorate.

Tree growth also, in this region of the lower Spey, is noticeably sparser, riverside trees of any size being scarce. This means that there are few widespread tree roots on the edge of the river, which are of such value in strengthening the bank. Bank maintenance in this part of the river is a real problem, and unfortunately a very costly one into the bargain.

As to the pools, as well as tending to become wider, they certainly become longer. Some of them are very long indeed, for instance Cairnty, a famous pool

---

*Riverside farmlands also improve in this area, as recorded by the old rhyme:

> Dipple, Dundurcus, Dandaleith, and Dalvey
> Are the four fairest farms on the banks of the Spey.

Three of these farms are on the lower Spey.

at Orton, is at least 600 yards long, and Two Stones and Beaufort at Delfur are similar. Such pools are far bigger than any pools on the middle Spey.

At the same time, the fisheries in this part of the Spey can be most productive and are famous. One need only quote names such as Aikenway, Delfur, Orton and the Brae Water to make any Spey fisherman give prompt attention. All these beats have both banks throughout their length. Spring fishing down here used to be excellent; February and March for Orton and below, April and May for Delfur and above, were the best months. During the 1950s and early 1960s the catches were phenomenal. Delfur had over 2000 fish one season and other beats killed in proportion. Sad to say the spring run, as has already been noted above, is now but a shadow of what it used to be, though spring fishing still continues on a more modest scale, and is still much sought after.

By contrast, July and August down here, as in other parts of the Spey, have recently become the most prolific months, particularly if there is a good grilse run. Moreover, it is these fish which nowadays tend to make up a large proportion of the bag. September also can produce a lot of fish, given suitable weather.*

Appropriate fishing methods on the lower Spey are no different from elsewhere on the river. There are a great number of streamy pools, not too deep, which give excellent fly fishing. Boats are more frequently used than they are higher up, as it is sometimes difficult to cover these big pools properly without their help; but even so wading is still often adequate.

The late-running fish, already mentioned, in July and August have always seemed to prefer to remain in this part of the river, and even spawn down here – either in the main river if the water is low, or else up one of the numerous tributaries such as the Fiddich, the two Rothes burns, or the Mulben burn, if there is enough water to take them up.

The result is that this lower Spey has an unusually long fishing season, compared to most waters. Fresh fish are found here right at the opening on February 11th, and all the season through, at least until the middle of August, or sometimes thereafter. Even in September fish with sea-lice are still rod-caught in some numbers between Fochabers and Spey Bay, in the part of the river that is previously net-fished. There are few other waters, on other rivers, that can provide productive fishing over so long a period in the legal fishing season.

Another notable fact is that most of the big fish of 40 lb or over have been caught in this part of the river. The term 'smoking-room fish' is believed to have

---

*In these later years (up to 1983) this summer and early autumn fishing has improved yet further, and is now first class.

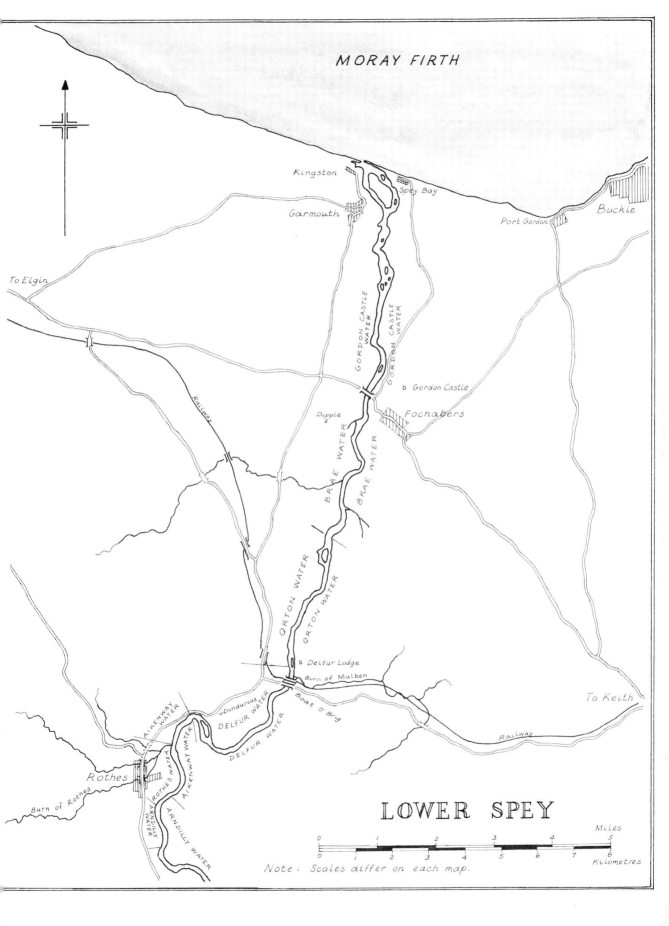

MORAY FIRTH

Kingston

Spey Bay

Garmouth

Port Gordon

Buckie

To Elgin

GORDON CASTLE WATER

GORDON CASTLE WATER

Gordon Castle

Railway

Dipple

Fochabers

BRAE WATER

BRAE WATER

ORTON WATER

ORTON WATER

Delfur Lodge

Burn of Mulben

Dundurcas

DELFUR WATER

Boat o' Brig

To Keith

AIKENWAY WATER

DELFUR WATER

Railway

ROTHES WATER

AIKENWAY WATER

Rothes

ARNDILLY WATER

Burn of Rothes

ARNDILLY WATER

LOWER SPEY

Miles
0   1   2   3   4   5

0   1   2   3   4   5   6   7   8
Kilometres

Note: Scales differ on each map.

originated at Gordon Castle during the last century, where only leviathans of this size were considered fit to be modelled and displayed in that ducal sanctum. There must be scores of such fish on record from the lower Spey by now, and they seem to have been slower to wend their way into the middle or upper river.

The record Spey fish weighed 53 lb and was caught by Mr W. G. Craven on the Gordon Castle Water in 1897. This account of the capture is taken from *The Salmon* (1898), by A. E. Gathorne-Hardy.

Although he fought gallantly [this fish] was killed in a quarter of an hour. Mr Craven, who was fishing the Dallachy Pool, not more than a mile from the sea, with a small No. 4 Carron fly, with lemon body, silver twist and black hackle wing, tied on a double hook, on a double gut cast with four feet of single, observed the fish rising behind a sunken stone and beyond the rapid stream from which he was casting, the rise, as is frequently the case with very large fish, being only indicated by the swirl of the water. From this position he could only reach him by casting his fly into the comparatively slack water beyond the stream, and allowing it to be dragged past his nose in a manner quite contrary to the rules of casting. Three times this was done without success, but on the fourth occasion there was a wave on the water and a hard pull, and in a second away went 40 yards of line downstream. Mr Craven was beginning to think of the boat 200 yards below, when the fish suddenly stopped and gave two or three unpleasant tugs; but being very firmly hooked, he allowed himself to be reeled slowly up, and enabled his captor to get ashore. He then made for his old resting place and began to sulk, but not for long, as he quickly went upstream as fast as he had come down it, and it became a labour of difficulty to keep above him.

At this point a disagreeable grating feeling indicated that the line was rubbing against the edge of the shingle between the rod and the deep water and it was necessary to take to the water again and get the line perpendicularly over him as he again stopped. At this point Mr Craven first realised what a monster he had hooked, for although the rod was apparently pointing directly over the fish, the line suddenly ran out at full speed. This was because having drowned the line under the heavy stream, the salmon was trying to ascend a small 'draw' on the far side of the river and there he showed himself struggling in about eight inches of water. The strong tackle bore the strain well; the sunken part of the line was successfully reeled up, and but for the bend of the rod, the line was once more horizontal between fish and angler. Now a slow, steady pull not only checked his career, but drew him back with a splash into the deep and the line was reeled up short, so that when he had been carried a little way down he came into the slack water, where fisherman and gaffer were waiting for him, but just out of reach. This was repeated twice, but the third time, with two or three more feet reeled up, he came well within reach, and the steel went into him just above the dorsal fin, the left hand came to the rescue of the overtaxed right, and W. Davidson, who had not uttered a syllable during the fifteen minutes contest, broke the silence with the exclamation: 'The biggest fish I have ever taken out of the Spey ...' His length was four feet one and a half inches, and his girth two feet five; a male fish, rather coloured but perfect in shape and condition. The subsequent examination of the tackle showed that the risk of losing him had been considerable as the reel line was cut a quarter through where it had grated against the shingle, and had to be removed as untrustworthy, and one strand of the double gut eye of the fly was severed and standing out at right angles.

So much for Mr Craven's 53 lb autumn fish in 1897. But fifteen minutes! ... A second fish of exactly 50 lb was also landed on the Gordon Castle Water in the Rock Pool by Lord Winterton, one autumn in the 1880s. But there is no record of any other fifty-pounders from the Spey. To land such fish in the strong current of the Spey, particularly if they are hooked on the light tackle which is now generally in favour, is bound to be a task of outstanding difficulty, with the odds heavily in favour of the fish. Time and time again one has heard stories of huge Spey fish played for many hours in this or that part of the river, only for something eventually to go wrong, and for the fish of weight unverified to go free.

As to numbers of fish caught by one rod in a day, although double figures are common, and fifteen fish were once caught by a rod at Delfur, one does not hear of larger numbers. The reason for this is chiefly because of the time taken to play fish, particularly when there are almost certain to be several large ones amongst a big catch. The size and strength of the river is apt to make the playing of a fish, at least of a sizeable one, a lengthy business. On average, for instance, it would take twice as long to kill a spring fish in the Spey as in the Tweed; so big kills on the Spey are less frequent.

No description of the lower Spey would be complete without more detailed reference to the famous Gordon Castle fishings, belonging to the Duke of Richmond and Gordon, at the turn of the last century; and without some record of the wonderful catches then made there, together with catches from beats higher up.

The following Gordon Castle catches are a sample for the six weeks only from

September 1st to October 15th each year. Figures are quoted from Calder-wood's *Salmon Rivers of Scotland* (1909). (Netting ceased on August 26th, and the water was rested for a few days afterwards.)

1890	452 salmon	1895	696 salmon
1891	899 salmon	1896	583 salmon
1892	950 salmon	1897	495 salmon
1893	705 salmon	1898	426 salmon
1894	813 salmon	1899	445 salmon

The fishing then extended from Boat o' Brig at the bottom of Delfur to the sea. So there was at least nine miles of it, and it was normally fished by nine or ten rods . . . some of the best salmon fishing ever known. It comprised what is now divided into Orton, the Brae Water, and the water below Fochabers Bridge; a long stretch, and it could be argued that the above catches might be equalled in the present day on this water between, say mid-August and September 30th, under good conditions (i.e. during a similar period, as fishing now ends on September 30th).

This is perhaps true, so far as numbers alone go. But fishing in Victorian times was carried out under very different conditions from now. In those days, for instance, there would have been only half the number of rods that would be found on the same water now, or fewer; and their tackle would have been less efficient. Then they used fly only, while nowadays this is far from being the case, especially with high water. The size of fish also comes into it; then they averaged 16–18 lb. Thirty-pounders were common and forty-pounders killed almost every year. Now they average barely half the weight and even twenty-pounders are becoming scarce.

As to transport for the fisherman, it was then entirely horse-drawn (if they didn't walk), by wagonette or dogcart; and it would have taken nearly an hour at a smart trot from the front door at Gordon Castle to the furthest part of the fishing at the top of Orton. Admittedly some of the rods whose beat was near at hand might only have had a ten- or twenty-minute walk to the water, but compare all this to the ease and speed with which the modern fisherman reaches his pools in a Land Rover!

Anyone who has been fortunate enough to have been shown the old Gordon Castle Fishing Records will never forget them, particularly the photographs. The ladies wore long skirts, so presumably fished either from boat or bank. The ghillies invariably wore bowler hats, a form of headgear occasionally adopted by the rods also.

More than seventy fish were killed in one day on one occasion, and over eighty on another, with the biggest fish over 40 lb; and one October 210 salmon were taken in the first nine days.

Presumably fishing started somewhere between 9.30 and 10 a.m. after a comfortable breakfast, and it would certainly be stopped by 5.30 p.m. in order to enable the fishermen to be back and changed into evening clothes in good time for dinner. But in spite of all this they still managed to kill that great number of big fish in the six weeks. All things considered, one could well envy the Duke and his guests.

So much for the Gordon Castle fishing in autumn. And what about the spring fishing there? it may be asked. The answer is brief, i.e. until 1904 there was none. The whole water up to Delfur Bridge was netted continuously by some fifteen different crews all through the season from February 11th to August 26th, with a forty-two hour 'slap' at the week-end. The effect of such extensive netting on the spring and summer run can be left to the imagination; but the following salmon and grilse catches from further upstream may help to shed some light:

	Ballindalloch	Knockando	Wester Elchies	Aikenway	Total
1887	47	88	154	136	425
1888	72	66	113	128	379
1889	17	23	77	77	194
1890	21	46	91	72	230
1891	37	88	175	236	536
1892	64	110	157	204	535
1893	74	53	82	97	306
1894	65	122	161	102	450
1895	91	73	135	112	411
1896	136	134	152	105	527
1897	111	52	145	93	401
1898	66	58	139	130	393
1899	71	51	129	48	299

Now these were catches during the whole season, not just autumn, on what nowadays would be classed as some of the best beats on the Spey. (And Aikenway then had a good share of what now belongs to Delfur.)

In the light of later or present-day catches on these beats, compared with the above, the effect of the Gordon Castle nets, operated as they were up to 1903, is obvious. A further comparison between the *season* totals of the four upstream beats and the *six week* totals at Gordon Castle is equally significant, as the reader can no doubt appreciate. So it is not difficult to understand the sore feelings of the then upstream owners at this state of affairs.

But from 1904 onwards all netting above Cumberland Ford,* one mile below Fochabers, ceased; and this has been the upper limit of the netting ever since. With the spring and summer fish thus having a much better chance of getting past the nets, the pattern of the fishing gradually changed. More and more the Spey developed into a spring river, and 1921 was said to have provided the last good autumn. In 1947 the rod season was curtailed by a fortnight, to end on September 30th, a good move as the autumn run had virtually died out. But the spring fishing, up to the middle of June in some years, had become first class.

In the present decade, however, things once again seem to be changing; the spring fish seem to have become far fewer, both for nets and rods, but the summer runs in July and August, especially the grilse, have much increased. There are still a few genuine fresh autumn fish that run during September, but they are seldom caught above Fochabers.

That the net-catch of both salmon and sea trout is still large, no one doubts – although accurate information is hard to obtain. The biggest net-caught fish of recent years is reliably reported to have weighed 58 lb, and no doubt many other monsters have been netted without any disclosure made.

Up to the present no step has been taken to reduce netting beyond the limits agreed under the 1904 settlement, but there are strong feelings in many quarters that the nets catch too large a proportion of both salmon and sea trout, in these days of reduced stocks, particularly during the summer when the water is low.

Conclusion

It is hoped that the above description of the Spey, of its course, characteristics and fish, however limited its scope, will give the reader an idea of the esteem in which Spey fishermen hold their beloved river.

There could be no better testimony to this than the following extempore verses quoted from *Autumns on the Spey* (1872) by A. E. Knox, one of the Duke's guests at Gordon Castle:

*So called because it was here that the Government forces under the Duke of Cumberland forded the Spey in April 1746 on their march towards the battlefield of Culloden, and Inverness.

Oh, tell me, kind angels, why is it,
When hundreds of miles far away,
That often in dreams I revisit
The banks of the glorious Spey?

King David once ruled on the Jordan,
On the Tiber bold Caesar held sway,
But Caesar was 'nocht' to the Gordon,
And Tiber a joke to the Spey.

And the Amazon, Nile and Euphrates,
Are all very well in their way,
And Shannon in land of 'pitatees',
But none can compare with the Spey.

Such fishing! By Jupiter Ammon,
There's nothing like fishing, I say,
And especially fishing for salmon
In the pools of the galloping Spey.

Six weeks from the first of September,
Ever pass like one beautiful day,
'Tis a time I shall ever remember,
A paradise passed on the Spey.

If I've any particular wish,
Since my hair has grown grizzled and grey,
Why it is to be able to fish
Every year till I die, in the Spey.

And when the grim tyrant draws near,
And life's breath is ebbing away,
May all that is left of me here,
Repose on the banks of the Spey!

PART TWO

The Dee

Logie

Blue Charm

Silver Blue

Jeannie

Shrimp Fly

March Brown

Gordon

Akroyd

Mar Lodge

Tim Havers

CHAPTER 6

General remarks—Character and surroundings—Pure water
Lack of pollution—Good spawning grounds

It has been called the 'Silver Dee', and it fully deserves that title. Many would say that it is the most attractive of all the larger Scottish salmon rivers, as well as one of the most prolific in fish. It is a lovely, tumbling, fast-flowing river of crystal clear water, so clear that it is often hard to estimate its depth.

Rising high in the Cairngorms, the upper Dee flows through a fairyland of delightful surroundings, past Braemar, Invercauld, Balmoral, and Ballater. Perhaps the most enchanting view of this part of Deeside is to be obtained on the road which comes from Donside, where it crosses the watershed between Gairn Shiel and Crathie. Here one can look southwards over the Dee valley far below to the huge massif of Lochnagar* and its surrounding hills. To the west lie Ben Avon and the Cairngorms, and to the south-east Mount Keen and the lesser hills towards Angus. All this affords a magnificent panorama, such wonderful heather-covered scenery, with bare rock and patches of snow on the high tops, a home for the grouse and deer as well as for salmon, and 'a vast country of hills', as it has been vividly described.

Another magnificent view of upper Deeside is to be found on the road from Blairgowrie to Braemar, as one descends from the Devil's Elbow, and has one's first sight of Braemar in the Dee valley below and looks across to Ben Avon and Cairngorms beyond. Truly in this part of the Highlands the roads are built over the hills as often as through the glens, and what traveller could fail to appreciate the magnificent spectacle which as a result continually unfolds itself before his eyes?

It is amid such surroundings that the upper Dee pursues its course. At intervals along its banks are lovely woods of birch, fir, and pine; and even if these latter are subject to the dictates of scientific forestry, and are seldom truly

---

*Lochnagar, the 'Loch of Laughter' seems a curious name for a hill. In Gordon's map of 1640 this hill is called Ben Chiocan. There is certainly a small loch at the foot of the main corrie on the east face at a height of 3000 feet. It must be frozen over for months on end in winter, but surprisingly holds good brown trout averaging nearly one pound in weight.

wild, they enrich the scenery and provide welcome shelter for fishermen whenever they approach the riverside. The pleasant scent of pine needles and pine woods is in fact a typical characteristic of the Dee, sufficient when encountered elsewhere to conjure up nostalgic memories of that beautiful river, as it pursues its rocky course from pool to pool along its hill-girt valley.

For the whole of its course the Dee has practically every advantage that could be desired in a salmon river. Like the Spey, it has a snow reservoir in the Cairngorms to feed its source, and to keep a good water running until well into April or May. It maintains a fair streamy flow throughout its ninety miles length, until close to Aberdeen at its mouth. Its fall averages twelve feet per mile in the upper reaches, though somewhat less further downstream; and it has an endless succession of lovely and varied pools, some rocky and some gravelly, intersected by sharp rapids; all forming ideal water for fly fishing, and blessed with a sparkling flow, very seldom peat-coloured. This pure water is indeed an outstanding asset for the fisherman. For some reason the Dee does not become peat-stained to anything like the same extent as its bigger neighbour, the Spey, in spite of the many peat-covered hills which border its course. At low or medium height one can expect it to be gin-clear, and only in spate does it colour to any extent.* Even then it clears far more quickly than does the Spey.

As to pollution, the Dee is remarkably free of this affliction. There is only one distillery on Deeside, so pollution from such a source has never been a serious problem, as it has on the Spey. The only sizeable towns, Braemar (population 1018), Ballater (1000), Aboyne (2270), and Banchory (2429) all now have efficient sewage disposal systems, even if this was not always the case and even if their constantly increasing size does still give cause for anxiety. Aberdeen (182,600) at the mouth is a large city and port, but its sewage and waste products are fairly efficiently dispersed into the sea through a sewer system, clear of the mouth of the river. The large number of ships using the harbour, with the consequent risk of oil pollution, does also give anxiety from time to time, especially when the river is very low. But a close watch is kept on all these possible sources of trouble, and generally speaking it would be fair to say that the Dee water, in comparison with that of many other rivers, is kept remarkably pure, to the benefit of both fish and fishermen.

In its upper reaches and tributaries the Dee possesses a wealth of good spawning grounds, most of them at over 1000 feet, which in spite of their high altitude seem regularly to produce a vast number of parr and smolts. The result

*One tributary, the Feugh at Banchory, brings in a fair amount of peat when in spate.

is that this river still produces an excellent run of spring fish until well into May, while grilse in June or July now also appear to be increasing in numbers. These spawning grounds are well watched during winter, and overland access to most of them is difficult, so that poaching of spawning fish is kept to a minimum, in spite of the efficiency of modern illegal methods.

Old Brig O' Dee

CHAPTER 7

Catchment area—Size of river—Absence of falls—Lochs—Spates

As a spring-fishing river, many would say that the Dee is unsurpassable. Although, with a catchment area of 825 square miles it is the smallest of the four rivers described in this book, many fishermen would again say that this is no disadvantage. It is in fact an almost ideal medium-sized river, often big enough to require the longest caster to open his shoulders and put all he knows into his effort, and often wide enough for hooked fish to run out a long line, well on to the backing. Yet there are only a few pools, and those low down the river, where a boat is needed, while some beats such as Inchmarlo and Cairnton can be fished entirely off the bank or off 'croys', with no more than knee-deep wading.

Naturally, high up, near Invercauld or Balmoral, the Dee is a small river compared to its lower reaches at, for instance, Crathes, or Tilbouries, or Park, forty-five miles downstream – but in general it could fairly be said that for size the Dee is about as big a river as can be satisfactorily covered by wading, if not from the bank; which is surely not a bad criterion for any salmon river?

Of artificial weirs or obstructions the Dee has none, and it has only one natural obstacle to the passage of salmon and that is at the Linn of Dee, some seventy-nine miles upriver from the mouth, six miles upstream from Braemar, and eleven miles down from the source. The linn (i.e. a narrow passage or gorge through a massive outcrop of rock) has a fall near its head. This is not impassable to fish, which can and do jump it, but it does form a definite obstacle which fish seldom ascend before mid-May (see page 66). Nor does the Dee flow through any lochs on its main channel as do the Tay and the Tummel. In some ways this is to be regretted, as sizeable sheets of water at some accessible point on any river's course form a good resting place and to some degree a sanctuary for salmon. That they also form a 'settling tank' for peaty or discoloured water is also an advantage, though this would seldom be relevant in the case of the Dee, with its exceptionally pure water. Right at the headwaters, however, of the main Dee and of its tributaries are to be found mountain pools, or moderate-sized lochs or lochans. Of these only Loch Muick is of any consequence to salmon or grilse. This loch is three miles long and about half a mile wide and lies at 1300 feet above sea level, eleven miles to the south-west of Ballater. This is the largest loch in the Dee catchment area, with its outlet down the Muick river, which joins the Dee at Ballater. The Muick is a sizeable stream which late in the season attracts a fair number of salmon and grilse from the main river. There are falls midway up its course, which formerly were impassable for fish, but lately these have been opened up by the construction of a ladder, so that fish can now reach Loch Muick and the headwaters above it. Neither the Muick river nor Loch Muick are of any significance for angling, as fish do not enter them till so late in the season, but they do give access to some good spawning grounds, formerly unattainable, now that fish can penetrate far upstream.

As to spates on the Dee, these are frequent as on all Scottish rivers, especially on those in hill country. In spring there are frequent big rises from snow-melts rather than from rain; but spring spates are seldom outsize, though melting snow may keep the river running at a high level for weeks on end. It is in the period between July and November, as usual in this part of Scotland, that most of the biggest spates occur, particularly as the result of heavy thunder rain.

The biggest spate of all was in August 1829, simultaneous with the 'Great Moray Floods' which affected so drastically the Spey, the Findhorn, and other neighbouring rivers. Its effects on the Dee were not quite so devastating, nevertheless it is recorded that the streets of Ballater stood five feet deep in water on this occasion, and that the Telford bridge there was swept away, as had already been the fate of two earlier bridges in previous spates. Also the pool on the Dinnet water called 'Twenty-nine' was presumably formed then, or for some other reason commemorates this notable flood.

Other great Dee spates occurred (listed in order of height) in 1937, 1920, 1913, 1928, 1907, 1923, and 1941, to mention only the biggest. There was also a cloudburst on the upper Dee on July 13th 1927, which flooded the Inver Inn, between Invercauld and Crathie, up to the level of the ground floor windows, the modest Inver burn being transformed into a roaring raging torrent. On this occasion the main road between Braemar and Ballater was blocked by floods at this point, which to those who know it will give some idea of the violence of this downpour. So without doubt the Dee, like any other northern river, has had its fair share of big spates and in the last few decades their suddenness and quick run-off has no doubt been accentuated by increased drainage for the benefit of agricultural land, forestry and grouse moors.

As a rule however the banks of the main river are strong and well reinforced by artificial batteries or stone bank facing where necessary. Spates can do little damage to such banks. But they do shift a lot of loose gravel, which can spoil pools if it is allowed to settle where fish like to lie. Until the spawning season approaches fish seldom lie on flat gravel; they prefer shelving rock outcrops, or a broken rocky bottom. So it is important to stop gravel from settling on the bottom of good holding pools, and this can best be done by the firm construction of stone and concrete bulwarks, batteries, or groynes at the appropriate places.

No one will dispute that the unforeseen arrival of sizeable spates can be most aggravating for fishermen, particularly if for example they occur during a short week's hard-earned fishing, remove the resident stock of fish, and fail to replace it with new ones. Or they can make the water so high or coloured as to put a stop to all fishing, perhaps for days on end. Nevertheless a moment's reflection will confirm that spates are essential for the well-being of salmon and salmon rivers. Not only do they bring fish into the river past the nets at the mouth, but they help them on their way upstream, and ease their eventual passage to the spawning grounds. They also keep the bed of the river clean and wash away any foul matter which may have collected there; and in time of hot summer they re-oxygenate the water. Anyone who has not appreciated the full value of natural spates has only to fish on a 'hydro-ed' river for a short time, where the water is kept permanently low and only a small artificial 'freshet' occasionally allowed, for his eyes to be widely opened. Fortunately the Dee is free of all hydro schemes.

CHAPTER 8

The course of the Dee—Upper reaches to Ballater—Middle reaches to Banchory
Lower reaches below Banchory

The true source of the Dee lies in some small mountain pools, known as the 'Wells of Dee', which lie at a height of 4000 feet on the upper slopes of Braeriach in the Cairngorms, and in its topmost reaches the infant river is joined by many burns draining the southern side of those high hills. Its upper reaches therefore lie at a much higher altitude than those of Spey, Tay, or Tweed; indeed the Dee does not descend to 1000 feet until it reaches Invercauld bridge, some twenty-four miles downstream.

For its first eight miles the Dee runs almost due south, through Glen Dee, until it is joined by the Geldie Burn from the eastern slopes of Glen Feshie Forest. It then turns east, and for the rest of its eighty-mile course runs due eastwards except for minor vagaries, through the County of Aberdeenshire all the way, except for a short incursion near Banchory into Kincardineshire; while from Durris downstream for its bottom sixteen miles it forms the boundary between those two counties.

Three miles below the influx of the Geldie, the Dee reaches the well-known Linn of Dee to which reference has already been made. The Linn is a narrow passage of about sixty yards long between sheer rock faces, where an active man, if he so wishes, can jump from side to side in one or more places. It is extremely deep and there is a sizeable fall near the head of it, which ascending salmon must jump. In the potholes below, fish can often be seen lying in layers, a fascinating sight, but an easy target for poachers. A public motor road from Braemar extends as far as The Linn, which is a popular ground for sightseers. Both banks of the river in this neighbourhood belong to Mar Lodge, formerly a royal stalking and fishing residence. The scenery is most attractive with high hills, heather, and pine woods on either side; and although it is small up here, this part of the river holds a great stock of fish from June onwards. Flowing past Inverey and Mar Lodge, and swollen by a number of small tributaries from both north and south, the Dee after a further seven miles reaches Braemar. Here it receives the influx of its first main tributary, the Clunie water, a hill stream from the south, rising near the Devil's Elbow, with a course of some ten miles of rapid fall before reaching Braemar. The Clunie's main merit is that of a spawning stream. There are one or two pools, near its junction with the Dee, where salmon are sometimes caught; but few fish ascend it before October. Half way down its length it is joined by a tributary called the Callater, which runs out of a small loch, one-and-a-half miles long, of that name. This loch for some unknown reason holds pike in numbers, and at a height of 1600 feet it must be the highest loch in Scotland to do so.

Below Braemar the Dee, now a sizeable river, runs past Invercauld, the scene of the raising of the Standard in 1715 by the Jacobite 'Bobbing John', Earl of Mar. This enterprise was to end fatefully on the battlefield of Sheriffmuir, in the Ochils; a savage contest, subsequently described by some northern humorist as:

> A battle there was that I saw, man,
>   And we ran, and they ran,
>   And they ran, and we ran,
>   And we ran; and they ran, awa' man!

It sounds more like a fight with an exceptionally wild fish! Nevertheless the pipe march, 'The Standard on the Braes o' Mar' is inspiring music which won Piper Laidlaw the V.C. at Loos in 1915, in a battle far more bloody than that of Sheriffmuir.

Invercauld is primarily the clan centre of the Farquharsons, who played a prominent part in highland history and who in the eighteenth century were staunch supporters of the Jacobite cause. This they paid for bloodily on the field of Culloden Moor in 1746 under their then leaders Farquharson of Balmoral and Farquharson of Monaltrie.

But to return to the Dee, below Invercauld it passes under the beautiful old 'Brig o' Dee', a Wade bridge of the early eighteenth century, which spans the river with three main arches and two subsidiary ones – a fine structure in a wonderfully picturesque setting. The modern Invercauld bridge carries the Ballater–Braemar road across the Dee 150 yards upstream of the 'Old Brig'.

After a further seven miles the Dee flows past the royal castle of Balmoral, acquired and rebuilt by Queen Victoria and the Prince Consort in 1847. The hand of the Prince Consort is still to be traced in the organized forestry of the area, and in the presence of many cairns on the hill tops, which he enjoyed building, and one of these commemorates the taking of Sebastopol in 1855.

Three miles below Balmoral, on the south bank of the Dee, stands the lovely old keep of Abergeldie Castle, overlooking the river. This was a Gordon family stronghold since mediaeval times, though rented by the monarch from Queen

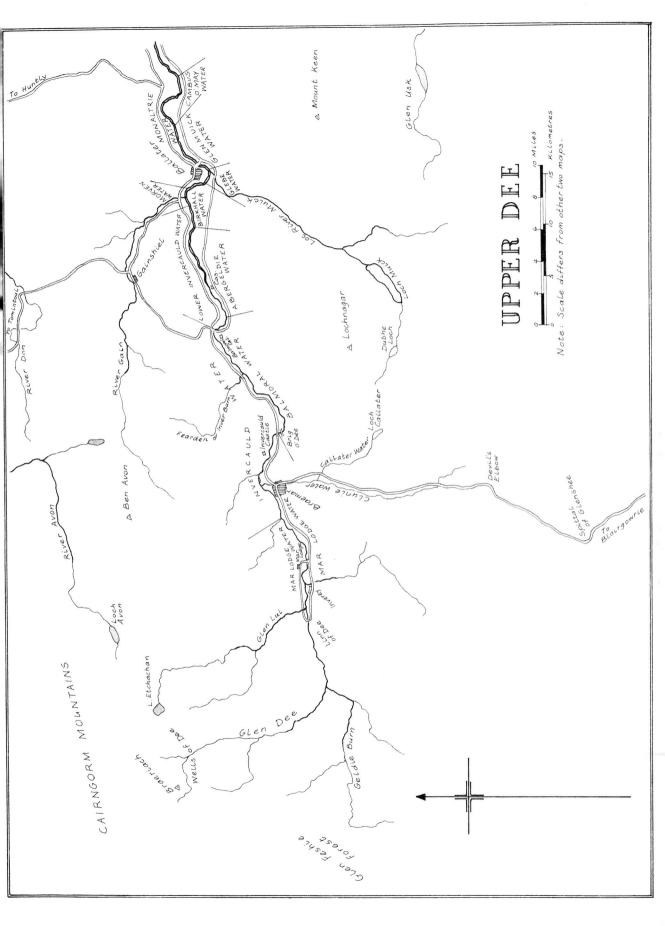

UPPER DEE

Note: Scale differs from other two maps.

Victoria's day until recently. Now a Gordon lives there again. The hill immediately to the south is Craig na Ban (the 'Woman's Hill') called after a certain Kitty Rankin who in bygone days is reputed to have suffered the rude fate of being rolled down this hill in a barrel and burned alive at the foot of it, as a penalty for witchcraft.

The average width of the Dee at this point is some forty or fifty yards. It is still no more than a medium-sized river, but is shortly to be joined by two sizeable tributaries which considerably increase its flow.

The first of these is the Gairn, which runs in from the north-west, five miles below Abergeldie. This small river rises on the southern side of Ben Avon (3843 feet), and has a course of nearly twenty miles through the hills between Deeside and Donside, before it joins the Dee. It provides good spawning ground for salmon, but is of little merit for fishing.

The second tributary is the Muick, which has already been mentioned. This is a sizeable stream originating on the south side of Lochnagar, and its headwaters feed both the Dubh Loch (one mile long) and Loch Muick (three miles long), before it enters the Dee near Ballater. A fair number of salmon and grilse ascend the Muick late in the season; but again this stream, which in all has a course of about twenty miles, is of more significance for spawning than for angling.

Passing Ballater, on its north bank, the Dee soon enters a wider valley past Cambus o' May, Dinnet, and Glen Tana. To the north lies the heather- and pine-clad expanse of the Muir of Dinnet and the high hill of Morven (2900 feet). To the south-west the hills of Glen Tana and Glen Muick dominate the scene, while from Cambus o' May upstream is still viewed the distant bulk of Lochnagar.

The river here has lost none of its impetus, and fine streamy pools succeed each other at frequent intervals.

Fourteen miles below Ballater, on the Dee's north bank, lies the old town of Aboyne. Immediately upstream of this, a third tributary of note, the Tana Water, enters the river on its right bank having its source on the northern slopes of Mount Keen (3077 feet) on the borders of Angus, twelve miles to the south-west.

So now the Dee has reached full maturity in size and volume, there being only one further tributary of any consequence to increase its flow (this being the Feugh at Banchory). At Aboyne the width of the river varies between forty-five and fifty-five yards. To the south in the background lies the Forest of Birse, with heather and pine woods, culminating in Mount Battock (2555 feet), and beyond

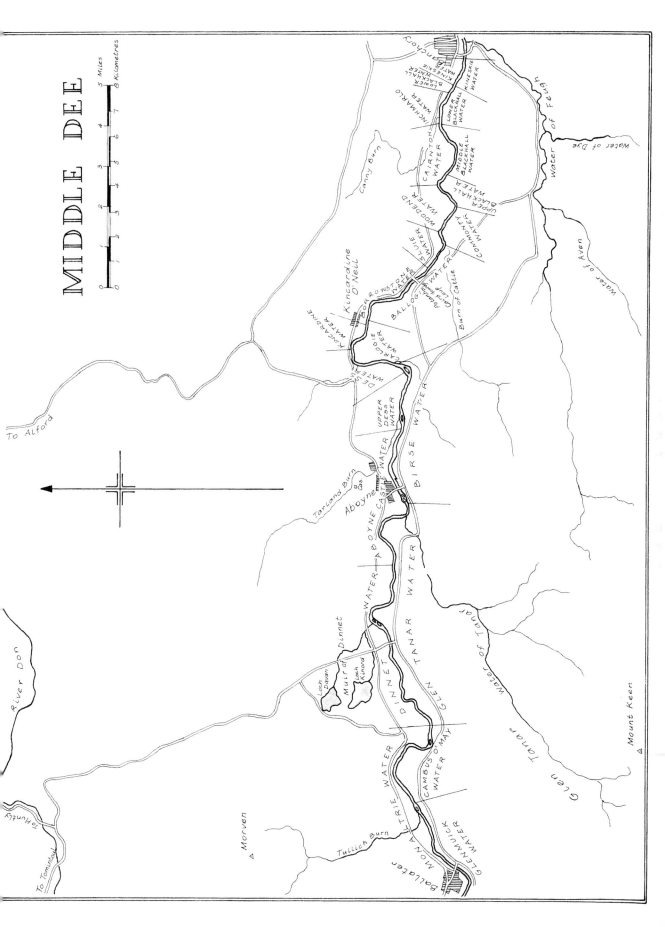

that Glen Esk. Although below Aboyne the river has lost none of its attraction and has still the same fast-running and rocky character, it can fairly be described as now leaving its highland surroundings and entering a softer lowland area, with more cultivation, fewer hills in the background, and these less high and less steep.

Two-and-a-half miles below Aboyne the Dee takes a sharp turn to the north and makes a wide detour past Kincardine o' Neil, before turning south again by Borrowstone House to pursue a rather circuitous course to Banchory, a further ten miles downstream. Five miles before reaching Banchory it is spanned by the handsome three-arched bridge at Potarch, with a fine salmon pool below it. Fifty yards above this bridge, the river in low water narrows to about fifteen feet between rocky outcrops, and it is said that a tinker, by name Caird Young, once jumped from bank to bank here when pursued by the comrades of a tinker chieftain whom he had murdered. These narrows still bear the name 'Caird Young's loup'.

Two miles below Potarch, and close below Woodend, the Dee passes wholly into the county of Kincardine and remains in it for the next eight miles; and a short distance downstream from this point the Canny burn flows into the river from the north side. Here at Invercanny water is abstracted for the Aberdeen city supply. This abstraction dates from a long time back; and, though it started on a small scale, it has now increased to around seventeen million gallons daily. The average winter flow of the Dee at this point is around 850 million gallons daily, and the average summer flow around 170 million gallons daily though in time of drought it can fall much lower. Dee fishery owners are therefore anxious about this abstraction, particularly when the water is low, and hope that in due course it can be lessened through alternative sources being found.

At Banchory, half a mile below the bridge there, is found the mouth of the last and one of the biggest of the Dee's tributaries, the Feugh. This pretty little river rises sixteen miles back to the south-west in the Forest of Birse, and is joined in turn by two subsidiary tributaries, the water of Aven and the water of Dye. These about double its flow, and having started as a pleasant moorland burn, by the time it nears the Dee the Feugh has much increased in size. It is a most attractive stream, as it ambles down between heathery slopes, pine woods and open fields, and not least when it finally passes under the bridge of Feugh, close to Banchory, in a series of tumbling cascades. In low water fish have some difficulty in ascending these falls, but in high water they pass through easily enough.

Below Banchory the Dee pursues a fairly direct course, past Crathes Castle

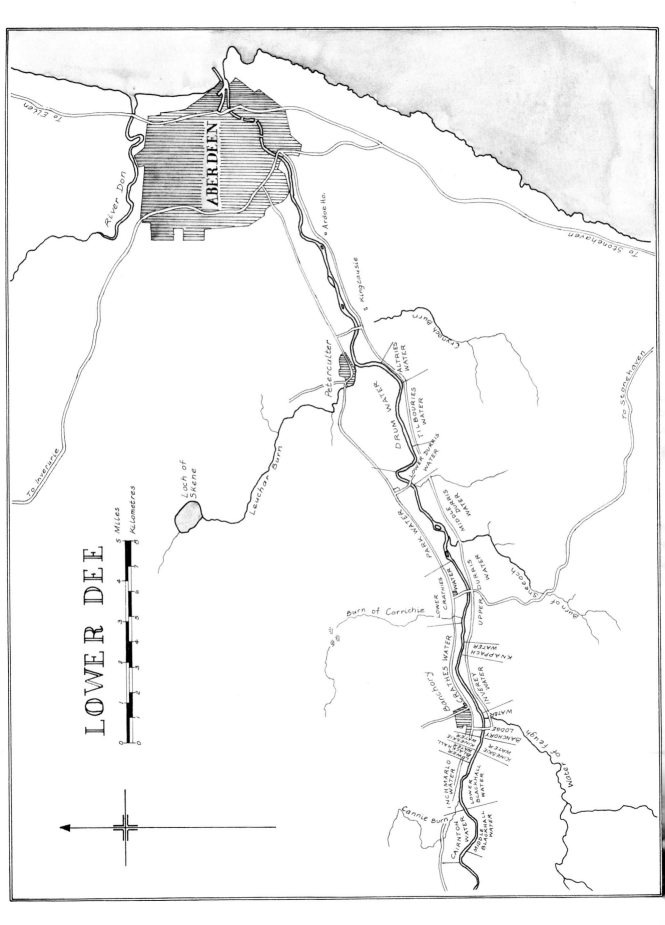

and Park House. Its north bank reverts to Aberdeenshire mid-way between Crathes and Park, so that it forms the county boundary between Aberdeenshire and Kincardine for the rest of its journey to the sea. Although by now it has become a big river by Scottish standards, it still retains its so favourable characteristics of clear water, fast rapids, and a variety of delightful streamy pools. Some of the most attractive pools on the whole river are to be found at Park and Durris.

It is only when it passes Drum, Tilbouries, and Altries, some ten miles from the mouth, that the current of the Dee begins noticeably to slacken. The pools become longer and wider, and boats are sometimes used for fishing. Below Altries the river runs in a direct easterly course, with one or two big bends, past Peterculter, Kingcausie , and Ardoe, to its tidal estuary and mouth between Aberdeen and Girdle Ness. The tidal water leading to the river mouth is not extensive, and only reaches for about two-and-a-half miles upriver.

So much for a brief description of the course of the Dee, and its main characteristics. So far, little mention has been made of the Dee fishing and of its salmon and other fish, and it is now time to turn to this absorbing subject.

CHAPTER 9

Dee fishing and fish—Great extent of good spring fishing
Distribution of fish—Past autumn fishing—Good fly water—The 'fly only' rule
Dee salmon characteristics

There is perhaps a greater length of first-class salmon fishing on the Dee than on any other river in Britain. Calderwood* records that even upstream of the Linn of Dee, not more than eleven miles from the source, H.R.H. Princess Louise (sister of King George V) once had twelve fish in one day. And from this point for another seventy-five miles to around Tilbouries or Drum, the Dee can everywhere be relied upon to produce good fishing at some time or other during the season. Much depends of course on the weather. The Dee is a very early river, on a par with the Tweed in this respect, and fish enter it in numbers sooner than they do the Spey for instance. The Dee fishing season opens on February 1st, and with a cold winter and spring the beats below Banchory benefit, as although there is no obstacle to their passage upstream, fish prefer to rest in this lowest part of the river till such time as the water warms up towards early April. Should the winter weather, however, be warmer and milder, with the river running full, it is true that fresh fish may be found as far upstream as Invercauld on the opening day, and the main spring run may pass upstream of Banchory more quickly. But as a general guide the beats below Banchory have their best fishing between February 1st and mid-April, those between Banchory and Ballater from mid-March to mid-May, and from Ballater upstream from the beginning of May to the end of June.

The Dee is *par excellence* a spring river. Though its spring run may not be as abundant as it was thirty or forty years ago, it is still very good and in fact appears to be nowadays on the increase. Moreover it is safe to say that the Dee at this present moment produces better spring fishing than any other British river, that is as regards numbers. Provided it is not too cold, fish run continuously from the opening till near the end of May. After that the run dwindles, but there are more signs nowadays of a summer run, mainly of grilse, but with a few salmon among them.

---

*Mr W. L. Calderwood was Inspector of Salmon Fisheries for Scotland in the early 1900s.

The fashion in which salmon distribute themselves after entering the Dee is worth further notice. Although odd fish may appear at any point in the river at almost any time, during the fishing season the vast majority of the stock will be found to have settled in one particular area, i.e. lower Dee, middle Dee, or upper Dee, depending on water conditions and time of year. In early spring the main holding area is below Banchory. Later, somewhere about early April, there is a mass movement of fish to the middle Dee between Ballater and Banchory. Fresh fish coming in are then likely to run straight through the lower reaches to join their fellows higher up, while only a limited number of old stagers are left below. Finally, around mid-May, the same type of migration will take place from the middle to the upper reaches above Ballater, and fresh fish will run quickly through to this area – visiting fishermen would be wise to take careful note of this and to appreciate that as a result the good period of fishing on any one beat is likely to be a short one, all the more as the Dee's main run of fish still occurs only during spring. It follows that it is all the more important on the Dee to fish at the right place and at the right time; and to fish even the best of beats either too early or too late, i.e. outside of its good fishing period, is sure to lead to disappointment, even though the river lower down or higher up may be fishing well. This is made more certain by the fact that, unlike the Spey, Tay, or Tweed, the Dee has no appreciable summer or autumn run* to follow the springers. In fact in the lower reaches all the best fishing is now over by the second week of April,† in the middle reaches by the third week in May and in the upper reaches by the end of June. While these dates cannot be fixed arbitrarily and are obviously subject to variation in late or early years, and while fishing continues in most places right to the end of September, fresh fish from June onwards become increasingly rare and are almost non-existent towards the end of the season. Almost all the fish caught towards the back-end are in varying stages of redness, and being near inedible are hardly worth taking out, particularly in view of their value as potential spawners.

*That this was not always the case is clear from abundant evidence in the last century and soon afterwards – e.g. Major J. L. Dickie in *Forty Years of Trout and Salmon Fishing* (1921) describes frequently catching fresh-run Dee salmon in October during the 1880s and after, for instance: 'In October 1889 I had a couple of very good days. The first day, the 23rd I had a clean run autumn fish of 23 pounds, and on the second day, the 29th, I had four of $16\frac{3}{4}$ pounds, $17\frac{1}{2}$ pounds, 19 pounds, and $25\frac{1}{4}$ pounds.'

Another remarkable feat was that of Mr Ernest Crosfield in October 1918, when, at Park, he landed eleven successive fish averaging 23 lbs in weight, biggest 30 lbs. But the rod season now closes on September 30th and if any genuine autumn fish still run they are now no longer in evidence.

The Telegraph Pool, Lower Invercauld

This is a pool on the upper Dee, where the river is comparatively small, but gives lovely fly
fishing in May or June. Opposite bank here belongs to Abergeldie.

It is hard to know what better type of water a keen fly fisherman could ask for. Bait is used, it is true, early in the season when the water is cold; but from mid-April onwards there is general agreement amongst the fishery proprietors that 'fly only' shall be the rule, which seems an admirable arrangement on such a perfect fly river. With very few exceptions this rule is welcomed and observed.

Now a few words as to the nature of the Dee salmon. It should be made clear at once that the Dee is not a 'big fish' river – the average size of spring salmon being small, i.e. 8–9 lb. A twenty-pounder is a big fish for the Dee, though by no means a rarity – thirty-pounders and even forty-pounders are still sometimes caught, though the latter are now very scarce.

Compared to the Tay, Spey, and Tweed (in autumn), the Dee therefore is a poor producer of big fish, though this was not the case in the days of the old autumn run, when fish averaged around 16 lb. However, the Dee salmon nowadays make up in numbers for what they lack in size, and most fishermen, if they could not have both, would opt for the former.

†This is how things stand at present. Before the advent of U.D.N. in 1967, some of the lower beats used to fish well right on to late May.

CHAPTER 10

Fishing beats—Good pools—Mr Wood of Cairnton
Best fishing periods—Single and double bank—Big fish
Big catches—U.D.N.—Grilse—Sea trout—Brown trout

The uppermost beat on the Dee is Mar Lodge, which has both banks to just above Braemar. The river here is small and so are its pools. Fish seldom arrive here till mid-April, and not in numbers till May or June. But from July onwards till the end of the season this water holds a big stock of stale fish, some upstream of the Linn of Dee, but many more below. They are poor takers, and it is rare to get fresh run fish so high up the river even in spring.

Below Mar Lodge comes Invercauld, which has both banks at first, and then all fishing on the left bank of the river as far as Monaltrie, below Ballater. Opposite are Balmoral, Abergeldie, Birkhall, and Glen Muick, in that order. This covers a long stretch of river, over twenty miles, and lovely fishing water all the way – perhaps the best pools are Maclaren's, The Fir Park, Coynach, Duchalls, Polhollick, Newton, and The Red Brae (opposite Ballater golf course). This part of the river is not normally at its best before mid-May, but from then till about the third week in June it provides excellent fishing, in spite of being so far from the sea. Big fish up here are scarcer than lower down; nevertheless there is a forty-two-pounder modelled in the window of George Smith's tackle shop in Ballater, caught on June 18th 1926 by Mr Wood in Newton Pool, Birkhall, on a 'Sir Charles' size 6.

Below Monaltrie and Glen Muick comes the cream of the middle Dee, Cambus o' May, Dinnet,* and Glentana, with such splendid pools as The Long Pool, Tassach, Logie, and Waterside. This is all magnificent fishing with many other good holding pools, as productive as any on the Dee – the only mistake that an angler can make in his choice of this part of the river being to fish it too early or too late in the season. At the right time he is sure of good sport.

Next comes, on the left bank, the Aboyne Castle water and Dess, with the Birse water and Carlogie on the right – all good fishing, though not usually so prolific as the beats immediately above and below.

Below this, on the left bank are Kincardine, Sluie, Upper and Lower

---

*At Dinnet is now to be found the hatchery belonging to the Dee Fishery Owners, which does good work in stocking the headwaters with fry and parr.

Woodend, Cairnton, Inchmarlo, and Kineskie, in that order; and on the right bank Ballogie, Commonty, Upper, Middle, and Lower Blackhall,* and Kineskie. This takes one as far as Banchory bridge. All these beats are first class, perhaps the best now being Lower Woodend and Inchmarlo. There are a number of excellent pools, too many to be listed here; but Moral and in low water the Hut Pool on Lower Woodend, the Grey Mare at Cairnton, The Old and The New Fawn at Inchmarlo, and the Roe's Pot at Lower Blackhall are among the best. This last pool is a big one for the Dee, and a good one too, as parts of it will fish in any height of water. The whole of its right bank belongs to Lower Blackhall, but its left bank is divided, the top half going to Inchmarlo and the bottom half to Lower Blackhall. Banchory golf course is alongside this left bank, which is a high one at that point, and over-ambitious hitters send a large number of golf balls into the pool there, and on to the bank, an unusual hazard for fishermen. The Lower Blackhall ghillie once salvaged sixty golf balls from the bottom of the Roe's Pot in one season.

It would be impossible to mention the Cairnton beat, and the Grey Mare Pool, without reference to Mr Arthur H. Wood, the great fishermen of the earlier years of this century. Mr Wood rented the Cairnton fishing from 1913 to 1934, and he did almost no fishing elsewhere. During this time the Cairnton records show that he caught 3490 fish to his own rod, an average of 159 fish per season, though he missed two springs (1913 and 1919) and did little fishing the last three years owing to ill-health. This is a large number of fish, and there is no doubt that Mr Wood was a skilful and inventive fisherman – but is it such a vast total, considering that Cairnton was reputed to be, in those days, one of the best holding beats on the Dee, and that Mr Wood is said to have reserved the Grey Mare, one of the best pools, entirely for his own use? It was a curious combination, fishing single-handed with a 12-foot rod, and not wading more than knee deep. And have those long-shanked, low-water, single flyhooks, which Mr Wood invented, stood the test of time? How many people use them now?

Also there is a revealing paragraph in Anthony Crossley's interesting book, *The Floating Line for Salmon and Sea Trout* (1939). In the Appendix, referring to Mr Wood's greased line method, Crossley says: 'In April and May 1931 A.H.W. met 336 at Cairnton and killed 179. In March, April and May, I met 323 at Careysville, Cairnton, and Tulchan, and killed 176. In both cases these

---

*Lower Blackhall also has 150 yards of fishing on the left bank, the bottom half of the pool called the Roe's Pot.

were all killed on single hooks. A.H.W.'s average certainly increased between 1931 and until he gave up fishing'... (but Cairnton records show that Wood only killed 76 more fish after 1931, so unfortunately there was not much time for improvement). What are we to make of this? Surely, by modern standards, to kill only 54 per cent of the fish one 'meets' over a long period would be poor going? And was it not largely due to poor hooking and holding by Mr Wood's long-shanked fine wire single hooks? Could not one do better now with modern fly tackle and methods, given an equal opportunity? All these are fascinating questions, and how one wishes Mr Wood was still with us now, so that we could talk it all over with him, and better still see him fish.

But 'de mortuis nil nisi bonum' – Mr Wood was a pioneer in his time; he did a great deal for fly-fishing, and showed how fish could be caught in low clear water by a better method than anyone else had yet devised. He was ahead of his age then, and had he been born two generations later, being a clever and inventive man, he might still have been ahead of all of us now. And it is perhaps unfair to take his theories out of their context and subject them to the harsh light of present-day criticism; when we now have so much advantage through the great improvements in modern tackle, and through subsequent experience of both the merits and weaknesses of the method which he originated.

Below Banchory there are still a number of excellent beats – Inverey on the right bank, and Crathes and Lower Crathes with both banks, then Park on the left bank and Durris on the right (Park owning both sides). The pools here begin to get bigger, but there is still a good stream, and a splendid variety of differently formed pools. As has already been emphasized, however, it is in the early part of the season that this part of the river holds fish. By mid-April most of the fresh fish are usually passing through, and only the old, stale fish are apt to be left here. Fish with sea-lice by that time are often continually being caught in numbers higher up, at Woodend perhaps, or Glentana, or Dinnet – while here it may be difficult to average as much as one fish per rod per day. In contrast, however, the opening day on February 1st can easily see double figures in fish landed on one of these lower beats such as Crathes, provided weather and water conditions are right. This was not always the case – when the spring run was at its most prolific in the 1950s and earlier, these lower beats would fish well till the end of May, and 'fishing well' meant a four-figure catch for the season. One only wishes that the same still applied in the present day.

Below Park and Durris one arrives at Drum on the north bank, and Tilbouries, Altries, and Culter water on the south. Much the same comment applies to these beats – lovely water, and good fishing in early spring, especially with cold water, but of little use after early April when fresh fish are no longer inclined to stop here.

From Banchory down was of course the best of the autumn fishing in the days long past – but now, unfortunately, this is of little more than academic interest.

Nowadays Tilbouries and Drum see the end of the good fishing on the Dee – anything below this becomes very chancy, and is only sometimes good with very cold water in early spring.

As regards the distribution of beats on the whole length of the Dee, if the layout is studied it will be found that there are forty-five recognized separate beats on the river, but that only six of these beats have permanent fishing rights on both banks. This is a drawback, and it is very different from what is to be found at least on the Spey and the Tweed. It is true that on the Dee reciprocal arrangements are often made between opposite banks, to ensure as little mutual interference as possible – always a wise policy. But this is not done everywhere, and since the Dee is not a river of great width, friction between opposite banks can then result. This is always a misfortune, and it would be hard to deny that, in these days of intensive fishing, to have fishing rights on both sides of one's beat is an unmixed blessing. It is one of the justifiable criticisms of Dee fishing that often on this river one is not so fortunate.

When discussing the merits of any river, one is often asked which are the best beats. In the case of the Dee, as of many rivers, it would be very difficult to say. Does 'the best' mean the most prolific, or the pleasantest to fish, or the most attractive in character? None of these descriptions is necessarily synonymous. Many would say that time of year for good fishing also comes into it. Surely fishing on a well-stocked beat in pleasant May sunshine is preferable to a freezing day in February? And if fly-fishing is preferred to bait-fishing, one is more sure of enjoyment on a beat on the middle or upper Dee when the water has become warmer in April or May, rather than on a lower beat earlier in the season.

On the other hand, if numbers of fish are the main consideration, bait-fishing early in the season and on the lower Dee might be the best choice. Amid so many conflicting considerations it is impossible to give an answer that is beyond dispute. But if pressed one might risk saying that Cambus O'May, Dinnet, Glentana, Cairnton, Inchmarlo, and Park in their due season are second to none.

Now a word about the Dee salmon. These fish are small on average, as has already been made clear, but, unlike in the Tweed in spring, there are big fish amongst them, if the fisherman is lucky enough to meet one – forty-pounders in the past have been reasonably numerous, though fifty-pounders scarce – only two of these being on record – i.e. October 1886, 56 lb (or $57\frac{1}{2}$ lb, records vary) killed by Mr J. Gordon, a ghillie on the Ardoe water, which is very low down the river half way between Altries and Aberdeen. This is the record Dee rod-caught fish. The next biggest was caught on October 12th 1918 by Mr M. Ewen, at Park, and weighed 52 lb. Both these fish, it may be noted, were autumn fish of the old days. After these comes a forty-seven-and-a-half-pounder, a spring fish, killed at Durris in the early 1950s by Mr J. A. Carr, and a forty-seven-pounder killed at Kingcausie in 1912.

But without doubt it is in numbers rather than in size of its fish where the Dee comes to the fore. The biggest recorded day's catch for a single rod was at Glentana in May 1886 with twenty-five fish, according to Mr Calderwood, writing in 1909. Unfortunately he does not give the day or the name of the angler. He also records a catch of twenty-one fish on the Aboyne Castle water by Mr Percy Laming who was a noted fisher in the first thirty years of this century, and who landed a total of over 5000 fish on the Dee and Spey, his two favourite rivers. No doubt there have been a number of one-day-catches of this figure, or approaching it, by individual anglers, that have not been disclosed; while ten to fifteen fish for one rod in a day has been commonplace, even in recent years. As to numbers of fish killed during a season, some of the better beats have produced over 1000 on more than one occasion, while the season's catch for the whole river in the 1950s and '60s used to run steadily at between 9000 and 12,000 fish, and it is not greatly less now, but the number of rods has increased. 1964 was the last first-class year in the past for rod-catches, producing over 10,000 salmon and grilse. By 1977 the yearly average had dropped to 6100. In 1978 the rod-catch rose again to over 10,000.

U.D.N. was bad in the spring for six or seven years up to 1976. This caused reduced catches, not only through fish mortality, but it made the fish that survived into poor takers whenever the disease was present and exercised its sickening effect. Fortunately by 1977 this scourge had largely disappeared, and in 1978 it has had little ill-effect, though still present in the background. It is to be hoped that it will soon be completely gone.

The grilse run in the Dee, unlike that of the Spey, has never been of great advantage to rod-fishing. Without doubt there has always been a grilse run in this river, but by the time these fish come in during June and July the Dee is normally at low summer level, and it is rare to get a spate in the midsummer. The result is that a large majority of grilse get caught in the nets, and the survivors, while some go up the Feugh, mostly disappear into the vast expanse of river between Banchory and Mar Lodge, and there is no particular area where they like to congregate. So although they are an additional asset to most beats, their number when dispersed throughout the river is not big enough to make any particular impact. It does seem though that, in the last few years, the grilse run has increased. So perhaps the future for these fish is becoming brighter.

Sea trout also enter the Dee in fair numbers, and the net-catch is considerable. Once in fresh water, however, they also become greatly dispersed, though the bottom half of the river up to around Woodend seems to retain most of them. Many go up the Feugh, but few penetrate to the upper part of the main river. As a whole therefore the Dee cannot be classed as a great sea trout river, and nowhere approaches the Spey or even the Deveron, for example, in this respect.

As to brown trout fishing on the Dee, this is definitely poor, particularly when compared to the excellent results obtained on the Don, Tay, and Tweed, and other east coast rivers. For some reason brown trout on the Dee have always been scarce, and seldom reach any great size, presumably owing to a scarcity of suitable food. Salmon fishermen, however, may well be glad of this, since adult brown trout are rapacious devourers of immature salmon in all stages from the ova to the smolt – also they are, in all stages of growth, competitors for food with the salmon fry and parr.

There are no other fish in the Dee of interest to anglers. Eels of course are there in plenty, as in all Scottish rivers; and an occasional pike (though the current is basically too fast for these), but otherwise nothing. Again the only result is to benefit the salmon stocks.

CHAPTER 11

Net fishing—Past history—Acquisition of nets by the
Dee Salmon Fishing Improvement Association—Illegal drift-netting—Envoi

The history of net-fishing on the Dee affords a conspicuous example of what can be achieved by wise management and control. In 1872 the river was netted as far up as Banchory, and as might be expected the stock of surviving fish was small. In that year however the Dee Salmon Fishing Improvement Association was formed from owners and lessors of rod-fishings, with the object of improving the fishings by leasing net-fishings, working downwards as far as funds would allow. By 1875 all nets as far as Tilbouries and Drum (inclusive) had been leased, and removed. In 1881 this process had been extended as far as Kingcausie, a further two-and-a-half miles down, and by 1896 to Waterside, only two-and-a-half miles short of Aberdeen. Later in 1909 the Association succeeded in taking over two remaining netting stations above the Old Bridge of Dee, on the outskirts of Aberdeen.

Subsequently it has acquired netting rights below this bridge, and since 1968 there has been a still further reduction in netting, the only estuary nets now working being the valuable ones from Victoria bridge down, belonging to the Aberdeen Harbour Commission.

This whole enterprise of reducing the nets, initiated through the foresight and guidance of men who were not afraid to take a risk, has proved an outstanding success. The improved value of the rod-fishings has more than covered the outlay required, and a vastly increased stock of fish has benefited both nets and rods alike, so that everyone is better off in consequence.

Could this not be an example to the proprietors on other heavily netted Scottish rivers?*

As opposed to the legal netting, illegal drift-netting out at sea with long nylon drift nets has been causing much concern during these past three or four years. This has been practised on a considerable scale all up and down the east coast of

---

*Scottish fishery laws, which have always allowed salmon netting above the tidal reaches of any river, in contrast to English, Welsh, and Irish laws, which long ago prohibited it, have never been of help in this direction.

Scotland, and no doubt has taken a large toll of Dee fish as well as of those of other rivers. 1978 however has seen the introduction of stiffer penalties and more energetic measures to curb this menace, which bids fair to ruin the delicately adjusted balance between fish harvest and escapement; and one can only wish the Authorities concerned good success in their vital enforcement of the law against this shameful practice.

Envoi

'The Dee has become the very best angling river in the whole kingdom.' So wrote Sir Herbert Maxwell in 1898, in the light of his wide experience. Agreement in this field can perhaps never be reached. Is it the number or size of the fish, the beauty of the river and its surroundings, the quality and size of the pools, the time of year in which good fishing can be expected, or other considerations, which are the leading factors in any fisherman's assessment of the 'best'?

And what angler in his heart of hearts does not have his favourite river or beat, somewhere or other, that he prefers to all others? As Thomas Tod Stoddart once sang in praise of his beloved Tweed:

> 'Let other anglers chuse their ain,
> An ither waters tak' the lead,
> O'Hielan streams we covet nane,
> But gie to us the bonnie Tweed!'

So opinions are bound to differ, and it is good that this should be so.

Nevertheless in many respects as a salmon river the Dee stands alone, and always has done. And there are not a few fishermen both of past and present who would be happy to re-echo Sir Herbert's conclusive pronouncement of eighty years ago.

PART THREE

The Tay

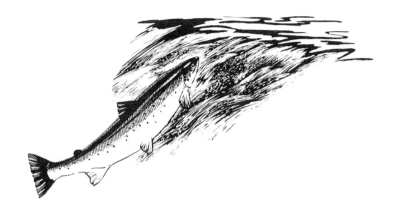

Nicholson

Dunkeld

Silver Grey

Black Dog

Hairy Mary

Benchill

Red Drummond

Popham

Green Highlander

Tim Havers

CHAPTER 12

*General remarks—Size and catchment area—Volume of flow
Source to Loch Tay—Upper Tay to Tummel mouth—Tummel*

That the Tay is the greatest river in Scotland can hardly be disputed, greatest not only in volume of water and width, in length, catchment area and number and size of tributaries, but also in its salmon catch and in the size of its fish.

The Tay's catchment area amounts to approximately 2000 square miles (as compared to that of the Tweed 1500 square miles, and the Spey 1097 square miles). Its length is eighty-six miles from source to the high-tide mark above Perth, or 120 miles to the mouth of the Firth into the open sea. The volume of its flow, like that of any other Scottish river, varies immensely between the extremes of flood and drought; but taking into account the average speed of current, and the width of the river bed (about seventy yards at Dunkeld and 150 at Perth) there is no doubt that the flow of the Tay far exceeds that of its nearest rivals, the Tweed and the Spey.

The true headwaters of the Tay are burns running off the slopes of Ben Lui (3700 feet), on the borders of Perthshire and Argyllshire, which flow northwards to form the Fillan water. This is a moderate-sized stream which runs eastwards past Crianlarich for about five miles to feed Loch Dochart, a narrow sheet of water of about one mile in length and 512 feet above sea-level. Downstream from this loch, the river now known as the Dochart runs first through a second small loch one-and-a-half miles long called Loch Tubhair, and then past Luib for a further twelve miles eastward to enter Loch Tay at Killin. There are some attractive falls on the Dochart, a short distance above Killin, which form an obstacle, though not an impassable one, to the passage of salmon. Fish seldom run them before May, when the water becomes warmer.

Glen Dochart is a wide and bare glen, typical of Perthshire highland scenery, while there are high hills on either side. Ben More on the south side rises to 3843 feet. The winter snowfall on such high ground is substantial, and while it is melting during spring helps to maintain a good flow of water in the main river downstream.

Loch Tay which stretches north-eastwards between Killin and Kenmore is an attractive sheet of water, fourteen-and-a-half miles long with an average

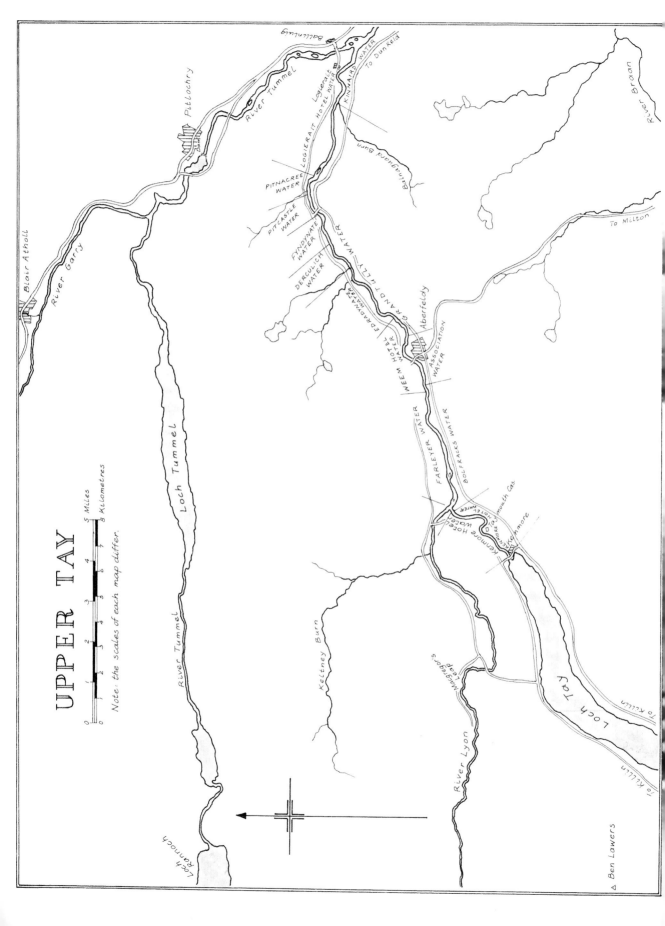

UPPER TAY

0 1 2 3 4 5 Miles
0 1 2 3 4 5 6 7 8 Kilometres

Note: the scales of each map differ.

River Tummel

Loch Tummel

Loch Rannoch

River Lyon

Keltney Burn

MacGregor's

River Garry

Blair Atholl

Pitlochry

Dam

River Tummel

Balnaluig

Logierait

Logierait Hotel Water

Kinnaird Water

To Dunkeld

Pitnacree Water

Binangbuing Burn

Pitcastle Water

Fyndynate Water

Derculich Water

KINNAIRD WATER

EDRADYNATE WATER

GRANDTULLY

Weem Hotel Water

Aberfeldy

Association Water

Farleyer Water

Bolfracks Water

Kenmore Hotel Water

Taymouth Cas.

Kenmore

Loch Tay

To Killin

To Milton

River Braan

River Lyon

△ Ben Lawers

width of one mile. It lies at a height of 350 feet above sea-level and its maximum depth is eighty fathoms (480 feet). It is fed on both sides by a continuous series of burns, including one sizeable stream, the Lochay, which enters it together with the Dochart at Killin. Like the Dochart, the Lochay has falls close to Killin, and for the last twenty years these have been made passable for salmon by the construction of an elaborate ladder.

There are high hills on both sides of Loch Tay, but those on the north side are higher, some of them rising to over 3000 feet and culminating in Ben Lawers (3984 feet).

The Tay proper begins at the outflow from the eastern end of the loch, at Taymouth near Kenmore. Here it is already a river of considerable size, and two miles further eastwards it is joined by one of its bigger tributaries the Lyon, which although now hydro-ed and lacking its natural volume of water does still help further to increase the Tay's flow. Passing the old town of Aberfeldy (pop. 1600), with its picturesque Wade bridge, the Tay continues its course eastwards, until twelve miles below Aberfeldy it reaches the village of Logierait, close to Ballinluig on the Perth–Inverness road and railway. Below Logierait it is joined on its left bank by its biggest tributary, the Tummel, which in itself is a notable river of almost equivalent size. This tributary rises far back to the north-west, close to Loch Ba on the Moor of Rannoch. Flowing through Loch Rannoch (twelve miles long), and Loch Tummel (now enlarged by the Hydro and seven miles long), and the artificial Loch Faskally formed by the Hydro Dam at Pitlochry, the Tummel has a course of no less than fifty-eight miles before it joins the Tay. This is as long as the course of the Tay itself, together with its headwaters, up to this junction. Nevertheless there is no doubt which river has the greater flow and produces the better fishing, especially now that the Tummel has the disadvantage of being hydro-ed.

CHAPTER 13

Middle Tay from Tummel mouth to Islamouth—Isla Ericht

In the neighbourhood of Logierait, and downstream of the Tummel mouth, the Tay makes a wide bend towards the south, and runs in that direction for the next nine miles of its course, to Dunkeld. Thanks to the influx of the Tummel it has now nearly doubled in size and is a big river. Below Dunkeld it soon leaves the hills and emerges into the wide valley of Strathmore. Up to this point its course has lain amongst typically highland surroundings, high hills in the background, with heather-covered lower slopes or rough fields descending to the well-wooded banks of river or loch side. But below Dunkeld, where it turns eastward again, towards Caputh and Delvine, the Tay enters a flatter lowland country of rich rolling farmland, interspersed with fine woods. This type of countryside continues along all the rest of the river as far as Perth, and is reminiscent in many ways of the surroundings of the lower Tweed below St Boswells. But although the hills have now receded into the background and its fall is less steep, the Tay maintains a good rate of flow in this area, in fact some of the strongest streams in its whole course are to be found in the neighbourhood of Islamouth and Stanley, neither of them far above Perth. Five miles below Dunkeld the Tay reaches the village of Caputh and passes under a road bridge, while a further three-and-a-half miles downstream, below Delvine, it makes a sharp right-handed bend towards Meikleour, and for the rest of its fifteen-mile course runs almost due southwards to Perth. Just below Meikleour, with its famous 120-foot beech hedge and picturesque bridge at Kinclaven,* the Tay is joined from the east by its second largest tributary, the Isla. This also is a sizeable river in its own right, forty-seven miles long, and rising far back in the hills to the north-east, where the counties of Perthshire, Aberdeenshire, and Angus meet. Near Alyth, in mid-course, the Isla runs through a gorge 100 feet deep and descends a series of high falls, which effectively bar the passage of fish. Further downstream from Meigle to Islamouth, where it joins the Tay, a distance of twelve miles by river, the Isla is markedly sluggish and meandering, without any rapids or well-

*In very low water it is possible to wade across the Tay from bank to bank immediately above this bridge.

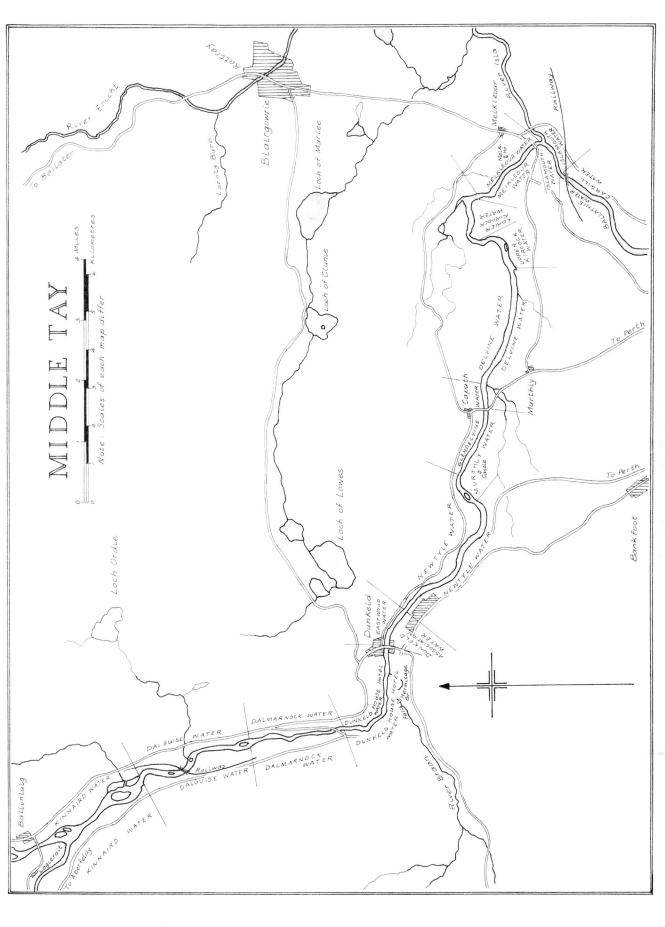

defined pools, a most unusual type of flow in Scotland, even for a lowland river, and is of little use for spawning fish. A smaller tributary, the Ericht, joins the Isla downstream from Blairgowrie. This also comes from the hills further north, one branch of its headwaters, the Blackwater from near Glenshee, and another, the Ardle, near Kirkmichael. There is no obstacle to the passage of salmon up the Ericht, apart from some now surmountable weirs at Blairgowrie, and a considerable number of small salmon and grilse run far up this small but attractive river, which is rocky, fast-flowing, and much of it in a deep and narrow gorge; in fact fish seem to prefer the Ericht to the main Isla.

About this latter there is little more to be said. It continues on its sluggish, winding course, without quickening, until it passes under Isla bridge and merges with the Tay at Islamouth.

In spite of being an uninspiring river, the Isla does at times have a considerable effect on the flow of the lower Tay. The fact that its extensive catchment area lies towards the east coast means that with an east wind bringing rain off the North Sea, as it frequently does, particularly from Lammas time onwards, the Isla rises and causes the Tay below Islamouth to follow suit. By contrast, all the other sizeable tributaries of the Tay, as well as the main river itself, rise far to the west or north-west. So it is rain from the west, off the Atlantic rather than the North Sea, which chiefly affects these. The consequences can be disconcerting for Tay fishermen below Islamouth. Here the main Tay can rise in dirty flood, thanks to the Isla in spate with rain from the east, while above Islamouth it remains steady and clear. Equally, of course, with rain coming from the west the Tay can rise, but the Isla remain steady. That the Isla

Kindaven Bridge

becomes dirty when in flood is only to be expected, running as it does through low-lying agricultural land for much of its course. But in contrast the main Tay is usually remarkably clear, clearer than the Spey or the Tweed and almost rivalling the Dee in this respect; such is the advantage derived from the filtering effect of the many lochs higher up on both the main river and the Tummel. Sizeable lochs on its course are an undoubted advantage for any salmon river,* both as a 'settling tank' for peat or other discolouring matter, as well as some sort of sanctuary for fish, and as a reservoir of storage water that helps to maintain the flow of the river downstream.

*Compare Loch Ness, Loch Oich, and Loch Garry on the Ness river system; also Loch Lochy, Loch Arkaig, and Loch Laggan on the Lochy; and Loch Shiel and Loch Awe on their respective rivers. There are many other examples, e.g. on the Naver, Helmsdale, and Laxford.

CHAPTER 14

Lower Tay from Islamouth down—Size and strength of river
Linn of Campsie—The 'Dam Dyke'—Tidal water at Perth
Perth Angling Association—Absence of pollution
Gravel displacement

Below Islamouth, for the first mile or so, the Tay runs noticeably faster, and rapid and pool follow each other in quick succession, so that the river is reminiscent of a double-sized Spey. Once past the railway bridge at Ballathie, however, the current steadies, and the pools become longer and deeper until three miles downstream the Linn of Campsie is reached. Here, in the words of Scrope, an 'awful barrier of rocks' exists, 'which rise right up athwart the stream extending from bank to bank. The waters, having worn their way in some places through this barrier,* tumble madly through the rocky gorges; down they go, thundering with stunning sound, into the enormous cauldron below.' This is a vivid and realistic description of an unexpected natural obstruction on the lower reaches of a large river; nevertheless, although this is the most formidable obstacle that salmon have to face before they reach Loch Tay, the Linn of Campsie, even in the very cold water of early spring, has never been a serious obstruction to the passage of fish. Far worse, until six or seven years ago, was the artificial dyke or weir from bank to bank across the river known as the 'Dam Dyke' or more formally as 'Stanley Weir', half a mile further downstream. Fish were definitely unwilling to run this dyke early in the season while the water temperature was still in the 30's F, until the pass was recently improved and the passage made much easier.† Now, like the Linn of Campsie, it forms little obstacle to their upstream path.

The Tay now skirts the village of Stanley on its right bank, and at this point it is interesting to see that its current, instead of becoming slacker as might be expected so low down the river, actually increases in speed. In fact over a mile or so one is forcibly reminded of a Norwegian river, so strong is the stream. Soon,

---

*There are in fact two main apertures and one smaller one.

†With the advent of the Hydro, Stanley Mill adopted electricity as its source of power rather than water, so that the dyke became redundant. Seven years ago four breaches were made in it to facilitate the passage of fish.

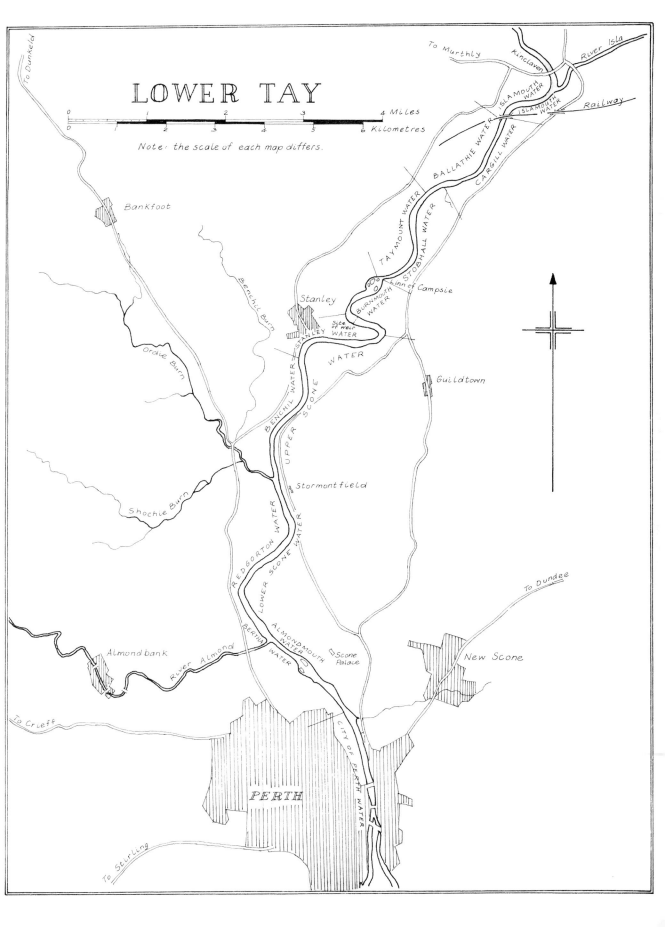

however, this last burst of speed dies away and from Redgorton downwards the flow steadies. One more tributary, the Almond, runs in from the west, joining the Tay two miles upstream of Perth, and shortly below Almondmouth the river begins to be affected by high spring tides. It is not always realized that at Perth itself there is a considerable rise and fall in river level, dependent on the state of the tide. This, of course, does not imply that the water here is salt or even brackish; it is simply that the rise and fall of the tide in the Firth below acts as a piston in backing up the river water at high tide.

Below Perth the river enters the estuary proper, and soon takes a sharp bend towards the east and the North Sea. It is perhaps surprising that the river bed does not widen to more than half a mile at high tide, until below the mouth of the Earn, five miles below Perth. All this part of the Tay is intensively net-fished, and is of little interest from the angling point of view, except that the Perth Angling Association fishes the water in the immediate neighbourhood of Perth itself.

The Earn, a river of considerable size, forty-six miles long and draining Loch Earn to the west, enters the Firth so far down the tidal water that it seems hardly reasonable to call it a Tay tributary. So although it is a salmon river of some note, no further mention will be made of it here.

This completes a brief description of the Tay and its course from source to mouth. To recapitulate, the main features of interest, apart from the exceptional size and strength of the river, are the variation in surroundings from the wildest highland country near the source to the rich lowland farmland of the lower reaches. Also the Tay has a catchment area both to east and west, and can be affected by weather coming from either direction. Its waters are unusually clear, and pollution is negligible. In this respect it compares favourably with the Tweed or the Spey. There are few distilleries on its course, and few towns of any size upstream of Perth. Those that there are seem to have their sewage disposal and other possible sources of pollution well under control.

One further feature has not so far been mentioned, and that is the immense downward displacement of gravel in the Tay which takes place with every big spate. Almost all Scottish rivers shift gravel seawards in varying quantities, but the Tay does this on a greater scale than any of the others. Presumably this is only to be expected in view of its greater size and strength.

CHAPTER 15

Fishing and fish—Past history—Harling—Trolling in Loch Tay
Wading—Casting from boat and bank—Both banks—Junction pools

There is a great deal to be said on the enthralling and extensive subject of Tay fishing and fish, and to start with it might be well to have a look at what happened in the past. It appears that up to and including the early years of this century, the established method of fishing in the Tay was by 'harling'. Fishing was confined to spring and autumn; and casting from a boat was sometimes practised, though not often. Wading was seldom attempted; it was thought to be ineffective and in most places too dangerous. 'Harling' was a system of boat-fishing, whereby there were normally two boatmen each with a pair of oars, and either one or two fishermen, in a large and strongly-built rowboat. There would be two or three stout rods placed in the stern of the boat, trailing flies or baits of appropriate size in the current on varying lengths of line. The boat would then be rowed to and fro across a pool, dropping a few yards downstream on each crossing or 'harl'. It is easy to see that if the boat was well managed, this was a very efficient method of covering large and wide pools in a big river, and if a sizeable stone was placed on the slack line between reel and butt-ring on the seat or floorboards of the boat, fish could usually be relied upon to hook themselves when they took. There would be boats stationed at suitable intervals on the river, ready for use; and at the end of the day they would have to be pulled upstream by the boatmen or else transported back on a farm wagon, so as to be in position again for the start of the next day's fishing.

From the fish-killing point of view this was an efficient and easy method. It was not difficult for two boatmen to keep the boat under control, however strong the stream, and to land the fisherman to play his fish off the bank when the right moment arrived. The skill in covering the pool satisfactorily lay mainly with the boatmen, and the fisherman's task, apart from playing the fish, was only to see that the flies or baits fished properly, i.e. that they did not get tangled up with each other, or with weed or leaves, or with the bottom, and that they fished at the right depth.

Such was the general procedure of 'harling', and in a river of the width and volume of the Tay it was thought to be the only process by which the pools could be efficiently covered.

Nowadays also, anyone who knows the Tay in early spring running high with melted snow, or in autumn after heavy rain, might well be pardoned for taking a similar view about harling, at least in the middle and lower reaches of the river. In fact it is still practised on some beats and at certain periods of the season. The recent introduction of powerful outboard motors, taking the place of oars, has made the whole process far easier; the crew strength can now be reduced to a single boatman per boat, and the boat can be propelled under motor power quickly and upstream against all rapids, when wanted, which saves much time and labour.

But is harling a sporting method? Many fishermen would say not, and would prefer not to fish than to practise it. To others, on the other hand, particularly the elderly, the physically handicapped, and the inexperienced, it obviously

holds a strong appeal; so there is still no lack of Tay harlers (at least in the spring).

'Trolling', as practised in Loch Tay for over a hundred years past, is a similar method to harling, apart from one essential difference that it is used in still water instead of stream, which demands different tactics on the part of the boatman. Success depends on keeping the boat moving at the right speed, and in the right area where fish are likely to be found; experience alone can teach the boatman this. Salmon in a loch have their favourite lies, just as they do in a river. In spring, with cold water, they prefer a depth of twelve to eighteen feet with a hard rocky bottom; though in summer, with warmer water, they will sometimes lie in as little as four or five feet. When a strong wind is blowing they are inclined to move towards the downwind shore, and such a wind is always favourable for fishing, with the surface of the loch broken by rough waves.

There are a number of boats which fish the loch, based on Killin, Kenmore, and intermediate stations; about 200–250 salmon are caught most years by trolling, but most of them between the opening of the season on January 15th and the end of April. One wonders why fly-fishing later in the season is not more successful in this loch, as it is for instance in Loch Lomond or Loch Naver or many other lochs. Is it because it is not tried often enough? Or is it because fresh fish, once the water warms up, do not reach Loch Tay in sufficient numbers as it is so far from the sea? (Loch Lomond by comparison is a mere six miles from the Firth of Clyde, via the river Leven.)

Reverting to the River Tay, harling, even with the assistance of outboard motors, has nowadays much decreased; and more and more fishing is done by casting from an anchored boat, or by wading, or from the bank. Fish are caught both on fly and bait, more on bait in the spring, and more on fly from May onwards, particularly in August and September.

Wading is also much more frequently practised, in spite of the fact that it is usually difficult and in some places dangerous. It is often necessary for the fisherman to wade in deep, right up to the top of his long waders, if he is to obtain the maximum advantage. The Tay is no river for the inexperienced or careless wader, and fatalities through drowning are not altogether rare. In some places there is a shifting, loose, gravelly bottom, which if it suddenly drops into deep water is the most dangerous wading hazard of all, especially if it is coupled with a strong stream. The danger is all the worse for not being obvious, and may not be appreciated before it is too late. Some stretches, particularly in the lower Tay, are in any case impossible to wade. The water near the bank is too deep and the current too strong.

Where wading is possible, however, and particularly when the water is low, the sport so achieved is superb. The width of the river and the strength of the stream enable hooked fish, especially the bigger ones, to run out an immense length of line, with all its consequent dangers – more so than in any other British river. It takes much more skill for a wading angler, fishing alone and without the assistance of a boatman (let alone a boat) to cope with this.

The usual alternative to wading is to cast from an anchored boat, controlled by a boatman, or more fun still when the fisherman is running the boat single-handed with a long rope and anchor in the Spey fashion. This can lead to the most exciting dramas, though undoubtedly the assistance of a boatman, and the ability thus to follow a hooked fish in the boat when necessary rather than on the bank, makes things much easier. Running a boat single-handed on the other hand is far from easy, and for the inexperienced to attempt it is a prelude to certain disaster, of one sort or another.

There are also some pools which can be fished reasonably well off the bank without wading, but they are few and far between.

The whole of the main Tay, from Loch Tay as far as Perth, provides good fishing at the appropriate times; and there are a large number of different beats, too many to attempt here a description of each one in detail. But before anything further is said about various beats, the reader's attention should be drawn to the great advantage which Tay fishermen generally enjoy of having fishing rights from both banks of the river. Sometimes a proprietor is lucky enough to own both banks outright, or failing this to have a lease of the opposite side. But even where this is not the case, reciprocal arrangements have almost everywhere been made between opposite banks to organize the fishing in such a way as to ensure the least possible mutual interference. One may not always fully appreciate what a blessing such arrangements are, until one is unlucky enough to be on a river, fishing from one bank only, where no agreement exists or can be made to exist with the opposite side. It will then soon be realized that where all is left to chance, vexation, to put it mildly, is sure to follow.

Junction pools, where a fair-sized tributary joins the main river, have everywhere a reputation of being good holding places, and the Tay confirms this theory, in that two of the best beats on the river are at Kinnaird and Islamouth, immediately below the influx of the two biggest tributaries, the Tummel and Isla. No doubt the tributary fish are apt to stock up in such stretches, before they part from the main river. Possibly also the main river fish are apt to halt there, before moving upstream on a diminished flow.

CHAPTER 16

*Fishing in Upper Tay—In middle Tay—In lower Tay—Best fishing
periods—Spring fishing—Summer fishing—Net-fishing—Autumn fishing
Past records—Big bags—Big fish*

Above the mouth of the Tummel, where the Tay is smaller, there are many
well-known beats such as Logierait, Grandtully, Findynate, Farleyer, and
Taymouth amongst others. Such beats expect to produce 150–200 fish apiece
for the season, and have many good pools. For numbers of fish this may not
compare with the lower Tay, and the autumn fishing so high up the river may
not be so good. But the character of the river here is different. It is narrower, and
has more variety.* Though boats are sometimes used, particularly in spring and
autumn, there is generally little boating and more wading, and more fishing off
convenient croys and rocky points. All fishing takes place amid delightful
highland surroundings. The sum of these attractions, when added together, is
adequate compensation, some might say, for a somewhat smaller catch.

Lower down, below Kinnaird, past Dunkeld, Murthly, and Delvine, there is
good fishing most of the way, especially at Kinnaird, Dalguise, Murthly, and
Glendelvine, both in spring and autumn. The river below Tummel mouth is
bigger and wider and more boat-fishing becomes necessary. There is also more
interval between rapids, and pools become deeper and longer; in fact the
character of the river definitely changes. In this part of the river, also, one begins
to find stretches of slack deep water here and there, which cannot be classed as
'pools' or even 'flats', and which although they hold an odd fish are hardly worth
fishing owing to their slow flow and general lack of incident. There is no doubt
that salmon prefer reasonably streamy water, and a broken bottom to give them
plenty of shelter. That there is nearly as good a chance of a really big fish in this
part of the river as there is lower down is obvious. Was not Miss Ballantine's
sixty-four-pounder caught at Glendelvine? (see page 98) and in 1977 the biggest
Tay fish for the season, $43\frac{1}{2}$ lb, was caught at Dalguise, just below Kinnaird.

---

*In some places, it is true, the water is inclined to be dull and flat, but in others, particularly for
instance at Grandtully, there are fine streamy stretches, rocky and tumbling. Of recent years,
however, these upper reaches of the Tay have definitely not held the quantity of fish that might
be expected.

While at Kinnaird itself several forty-pounders and two fifty-pounders have been killed.

Below Delvine comes Meikleour, and from there down is at present the cream of the Tay fishing. More fish are being killed in that area than anywhere else, Islamouth (the best of all), and other good beats such as Ballathie, Cargill, Taymount, Stobhall, Stanley, Scone, Benchill, Redgorton, and Almondmouth are to be found here, and are household words in any Tay fisherman's vocabulary. Though none is good all the time (what fishing is?) all are definitely good for some of the time, and that in most of these cases is a substantial understatement. It is down here that the majority of the Tay leviathans have been caught, also where the largest catches have been made, both for a day and for the season.

As on most east coast rivers, spring and autumn are the two main fishing periods everywhere on the Tay, the rod season opening on January 15th and closing on October 15th. The best spring month is usually April, and by the third week in May the best of the fishing is over until the autumn. In former days the Tay had a splendid run of big spring fish, they used to average 16–17 lb – and could be found in numbers early on in the lower reaches. Some would even be as far up as Loch Tay on the opening day.

Nowadays, alas, this spring run is reduced, as in most other rivers. What is the cause? U.D.N., Greenland nets, over-fishing off our own coasts and in estuaries, or natural change in the habits of the fish? Who can tell for sure? Most likely it is a combination of all these factors and of others as well. At any rate the numbers of Tay spring fish for some years now have tended to get less (although 1975 was a better year). What is equally significant is the drop in average weight. This has now shrunk to 11 lb, which means the majority of spring fish have spent only two winters in the sea instead of three. Bigger fish in the thirty- and forty-pound class are also much scarcer than formerly, although they do still appear from time to time.

Nevertheless, Tay spring fishing is still well worthwhile, and better than in most other rivers; while at the moment of writing (February 1978) the auguries for this coming spring appear more favourable than for many years.*

Certainly the upper reaches above the Tummel entry have always fished best in spring, in April and May for choice; though lower down the river for these past twenty years the autumn fishing has so greatly improved that it has produced a far larger number of fish.

*This optimistic view has later been borne out. 1978 has produced the best spring fishing for many years.

The Tay at Dunkeld
The great width of the river is clearly shown in this picture of the middle Tay. Further downstream below Islamouth the Tay becomes even larger, but many of its pools can still be fished by wading when the water is low.

From mid-May onwards and during June and July the run of salmon
invariably decreases. Most beats take their boats off by the third week in May,
and only replace them in the second half of August. A good number of grilse
enter the river during summer, but there are few places where they like to
congregate, and they are difficult to catch.

How far this reduced run in summer is due to the intensive netting in tidal
waters, coupled with the normal low water which keeps fish back, is difficult to
discover. Only the netsmen can form an accurate estimate of the number of fish
that attempt to ascend the river then, and their lips are sealed. Netting is carried
on all the way down the Tay estuary by the Tay Salmon Fisheries Company, as
far as the mouth of the Earn and beyond into the Firth. That their catch is heavy
is undoubted, particularly during the summer months, but it is never disclosed.
The end of the netting season is on August 20th each year. The uppermost
netting station is now at Almondmouth, and two nets are still worked above
Perth.*

The history of net-fishing on the Tay is interesting. Calderwood, the then
Inspector of Salmon Fisheries in Scotland, in his *Salmon Rivers of Scotland*
(1909) refers to the years between 1830 and 1846 and talks of 34 netted fisheries
'all the way up the Tay to well above Dunkeld', producing an average of 70000
salmon yearly. By 1909, however, he said that all net-fishing above the Linn of
Campsie had ceased, and that between the Linn and Perth netting was carried
on only till May 31st each year, which he regarded as a great improvement. He
did not say how many netting stations were fished above Perth in those days, but
no doubt it was more than now. So present-day Tay rod fishermen may perhaps
be thankful that, as regards legal netting, things are no worse than they are, and
the last net above Stanley ceased to operate about six years ago.

On the other hand, what does now worry both rod fishermen and authorized
netsmen alike is the recent escalation of illegal drift-netting at sea outside the
coastal limit. It is greatly hoped that measures will soon be taken to stop this
menace.

Legal drift-netting off the Northumberland coast is also causing concern, this
type of netting being at present legal in England though illegal in Scotland.
Recently a salmon caught in the Ericht near Blairgowrie was found to have been
tagged off that coast. It has long been supposed that nearly all the many fish
caught by drift-netting there have been making their way northwards to

*On rare occasions a net is still also liable to be worked above the 'Dam Dyke' at Stanley.

Scottish rivers, and this episode has added fuel to the fire of Scottish indignation, both amongst nets and rods.*

To return to Tay fishing, after August 20th when the nets are lifted, the autumn run, or perhaps the late summer run would be a truer designation, has increased beyond all recognition during the past twenty years. At any time from mid-August onwards the lower river starts to stock up with fish, and some of them push on by degrees, helped by any spates that may occur, into the middle and upper river. By September their number runs into thousands, and this increase continues up to the end of the season.

Many of these fish, both salmon and grilse, are by then in varying stages of redness; but bright silver fish are plentiful in August and the first half of September, and an odd one, though not many, can still be found in October. Rod-fishing ends after October 15th, none too soon, as most of the fish appear to be near spawning by then, and the Tay seems to lack a true autumn run of fresh fish in October and November, like that of the Tweed.

But the rod-fishing in late August, September, and early October, anyhow as far as the lower and middle reaches are concerned, is now first class; and there is as yet no sign of it deteriorating. At this time of year too there is always a chance of hooking a really big fish. Twenty-pounders are common, thirty-pounders not infrequent, and a forty-pounder or (dare one breathe it?) even a fifty-pounder is not out of the question.

A comparison of present-day fishing with what we know of the past is interesting. No doubt our grandfathers' generation had excellent fishing, as can be seen from their records. But their tackle was more primitive than ours, and they certainly did not fish so intensively or for such long hours as we do now. Also they seem to have relied largely on harling, and to have fished in the spring and autumn only. One would infer from this that there were more fish in the river than now, to produce the bags which they achieved.

A particularly fascinating piece of evidence in support of this assumption is in the possession of the present Marquess of Lansdowne. It is a rough notebook

---

*In 1977 there were 670 salmon tagged, under the arrangements made by the Ministry of Agriculture and Fisheries in four areas off the Northumberland coast, i.e. Seahouses, Amble, Blyth, and Sunderland. Of these fish 158 have been recaptured, all of them in Scottish waters. The majority of these were caught in the estuaries of the Tweed and Forth, but a significant number also in the Tay estuary and in the coastal nets further north. All these fish, except three, were recaptured by net; and all four tagging areas produced recaptured fish. Only three fish were recaptured by anglers, one in the Lyon, one in the Tay above Perth, and one in the Tweed at Coldstream.

kept by J. Cockburn, the head boatman at Meikleour in the 1870–80 period. This shows a total of 926 salmon averaging 18 lb, and sixty grilse averaging 6 lb, killed on the Home Beat at Meikleour during the years 1869–76. The numbers of these fish are perhaps not so outstanding, but it must be remembered that in those days fishing was not nearly so industrious as it is now; it was probably only done when the river was in first-class order. On the other hand the *average* weight of 18 lb is surely remarkable, with thirty-pounders being killed most weeks; and the more fortunate rods seem frequently to have killed double figures in the day. Some of these fish were killed in spring, but most in autumn, and most if not all on fly, no doubt great 4/o, 6/o, and 8/os. Whether they were caught by harling or casting however is not made clear, which is a pity.

Many other wonderful rod-catches have also been made in the Tay, both at that time and in more recent years. For instance Major Baker Carr on March 9th 1922, fishing at Lower Stanley caught seventeen fish to his own rod, weighing altogether 276 lb, i.e. an average of 16 lb with the biggest fish 30 lb. Another even greater catch was that of Mr Charles A. Murray, who fishing the Taymount water (just upstream of Stanley) caught twenty fish in a day, in autumn, weighing 365 lb, an average of $18\frac{1}{2}$ lb, and all on fly.

Nowadays fishermen for various reasons have become more reticent about their catches than they used to be, and no doubt many outstanding bags in the past twenty-five years or so have been made, though in autumn rather than spring. Double figures to one rod in a day has been commonplace, but detailed information is hard to obtain. One thing however is obvious, that is that whatever may be their numbers the average weight of fish caught, in spring as well as autumn, has dropped by nearly half, and grilse are probably more plentiful in mid-summer than they used to be. In spite of this drop in weight, however, there is no doubt that as a 'big fish' river no other river in Britain approaches the Tay. There is much talk, not unexpectedly, of the Wye,* the Awe,† and (in the past) the Shannon in this capacity; but a study of records shows clearly that for numbers of big fish caught by both rod- and net-fishing, the Tay stands on a pinnacle alone. In the table overleaf is a list of recorded rod-caught Tay fifty-pounders (which is probably not complete):

*J. A. Hutton in his *Wye Salmon and Other Fish* (1949) records eleven fish of 50 lb or over killed on rod in the Wye between 1910 and 1946. Wholesale netting on the Wye only ceased in 1903.

†Nine fifty-pounders are recorded from the Awe, a remarkable number from a river only three-and-a-half miles long (but now, alas, hydro-ed).

Weight in lb	Date	Caught by	Where caught	Fly or bait	Recorded by
64	Oct. 7th 1922	Miss G. Ballantine	Glendelvine	Spinning 'Dace'	P. D. Malloch and others
61½	Oct. 1907	Mr T. Stewart	Perth Association Water	Worm	P. D. Malloch and others P. D. M. gives the weight of this fish as 63½lb
61	March 1870	Mr J. Haggart	Stanley	Minnow	P. D. Malloch and *Where to Fish*
55½	Sept. 26th 1898	Capt. A. G. Goodwin	Scone Palace Water (just below Woody Isle)	Minnow	P. D. Malloch and *Where to Fish*
55½	Oct. 1903	Mr P. M. Coats	Stobhall	Fly 'Wilkinson'	P. D. Malloch
55	Oct. 1883	Marquis of Zetland	Stanley 'Mill Stream'	Fly 'Claret Major'	P. D. Malloch
54	1969	Mr V. Ianetta	Ballathie		
54	1884	Lord Ruthven	Taymount 'Findford Stream'		P. D. Malloch and *Where to Fish*
54	Oct. 1942	Mr J. T. Ness	Almondmouth		*Where to Fish*
53	Oct. 15th 1923	Sir Stuart Coats Bart.	Cargill	Fly 'Jock Scott'	*Where to Fish*
53	Oct. 1898	Lord Blythswood	Stobhall 'Sandy Ford'	Fly 'Black Dog'	P. D. Malloch and *Where to Fish*
53	1915	Mr Dow	Perth Association Water		*Where to Fish*
53	Oct. 19th 1924	Mr P. M. Pritchard	Lower Scone	Fly	*Where to Fish*
52	1917	Mr A. MacBeth	Kinnaird		*Where to Fish*
51½	July 1875	Mr J. Gellatly	Ballathie	Sea trout fly	P. D. Malloch and *Where to Fish*
51	Oct. 1903	Mr Fletcher	Perth Association Water	Minnow	*Where to Fish*
51	1905	Mr E. Fieldhouse			*Where to Fish*
51	Oct. 7th 1913	Sir Stuart Coats Bart.	Upper Ballathie		*Where to Fish*
50	July 1928	Major F. Pullar	Stobhall		*Where to Fish*
50	Oct. 1928	Miss Lettice Ward	Kinnaird	Fly	*Where to Fish*
50	1874		Loch Tay	Bait	A. E. Gathorne Hardy *The Salmon*
50	1880		Loch Tay	Bait	*The Salmon*
50	Sept. 23rd 1883	Cdr. H. Clarke-Jerwoise	Taymount 'Findford Head'	Fly 'Jock Scott 2/o'	P. D. Malloch

N.B. It is noticeable that only one of the above fifty-pounders was a spring fish, with the presumable inclusion of the two from Loch Tay.

As to forty-pounders, the number caught is far too numerous to list; it runs well into three figures. But two of them are worth noting, as they were both caught on the same day, September 12th 1924, by Mrs Radclyffe on the lower Scone water, and weighed 42 lb and 41 lb.

It may also be noted from the above list that Sir Stuart Coats caught two fifty-pounders, though not on the same day. This is a rare achievement in Britain, though it was equalled on the Awe by Mr H.T. Thornton with fish of 56 lb and 51 lb and by Major Huntington with 57 lb and 51 lb.

CHAPTER 17

Miss Ballantine's sixty-four-pounder—The 'Bishop Browne story'

If size is the criterion, no description of Tay fishing would be complete without the story of the capture of the record British rod-caught fish, by Miss Georgina Ballantine, on October 7th 1922, on the Glendelvine water. An excellent account of this feat was published long ago in *The Field* and here it is:

Saturday, 7th October 1922 started well for Miss Ballantine. In the morning she took three respectable salmon, weighing 17 lb, 21 lb, and 25 lb. At dusk on the same day, her father, James Ballantine, who was then fisherman for the Laird of Glendelvine, Sir Alexander Lyle, took her out in the boat for an hour's harling, that curious form of fishing indigenous to the Tay and scarcely practised elsewhere. The boatman, in this case James Ballantine, rows back and forth across the current – the Tay is roughly 60 yards wide – skilfully covering salmon lies that have been known and studied for hundreds of years. Sometimes even three rods are set up to trail fly or lure over the stern.

On this evening there were two rods; a split-cane with a Wilkinson fly, and a great heavy greenheart attached to a now obsolete revolving lure of a mottled brown colour called a 'dace'. The weather, Miss B. recalls, was quiet and balmy, as fine an autumn evening as one could wish for.

At 6.15 the dace was taken suddenly and violently. The shock nearly pulled the rod from her hands, but she regained control, keeping the line tight and clear of the other rod. Her father held the boat steady; somehow they managed to get the other rod in and clear the scene for action. At that point she knew 'there was something very, very heavy on'. The unseen monster led them back and forth across the river in sweeping 50-yard rushes. At one point it slipped behind a rock into a deep lie. Terrified she might lose it, Miss B. kept a tight but delicate control of her line while her father swiftly manoeuvred the boat downstream of the rock to keep the line from rubbing and fraying. Suddenly the fish shot clear, Miss B. kept a tight line and the fish was still hers.

Slowly they were towed down river to a point opposite their cottage. They saw Mrs Ballantine on the river-bank, lantern in hand, peering into what was now a pitch-black night. They shouted to her what was happening and followed the fish hoping for even a glimpse of it. But not once did it surface; there was nothing but the great silent weight and the line slicing through the black water.

A hundred yards below the cottage is Caputh bridge. The bridge has two pilings, and as the boat hugged the left bank of the river their quarry made a determined rush for the far shore. Inevitably the line would be broken. With waning strength Miss B. applied as great a strain as she dared and slowly the fish turned, slipping between the pilings where James Ballantine rowing frantically, could just follow. She was ready to drop from exhaustion, but her father refused to touch the rod. This was a challenge only she could answer.

It was nearly two hours since the salmon had been hooked in the Boat pool. Now they were half a mile down the stream. Once more, keeping a tight line, Miss B. reeled in, and felt with aching arms that the creature she had not yet seen was almost ready to be taken. It was moving slowly, in short bursts. Gently she urged it closer to the boat until they could see that the line entered the water almost vertically; somewhere, three or four or five feet down was her fish. Certainly it was ready to be gaffed, but gaffing even a normal-sized fish in the dark is not easy. How were they to manage this leviathan?

James inched his way aft, set the gaff against the line and slowly moved it down until he felt the knot of the leader. Had he not made it himself? Did he not know precisely how many blood knots he had made in the expensive silk-worm gut? He ran the head of the gaff down into the water, counting each time he felt a tiny protuberance. Three, four, five ... the fish must be just below. He pushed forward gently then turned the gaff and drew it up quickly. There was no mistake; with his great strong hands he brought his daughter's catch to the surface and, with one big heave, he dragged it over the gunwale.*

The fish, even after more than two hours, was by no means exhausted, and leaped and flapped in the bottom of the boat. 'Father thought it was going to jump back into the river and threw himself on top of it.' Miss B. sipped her tea, her eyes sparkling. 'My whole arm felt paralysed, and I was so utterly exhausted I could have lain down beside the fish and slept.

*I have since learnt from Col. A. M. Lyle that according to the Glendelvine records this account of the gaffing is not strictly accurate. In fact, at his first attempt, James let the gaff slip out of his hand and the fish went off with it. Only when he had procured a second gaff was the monster successfully landed.

'Well, two men were hailed to carry it slung on a pole to the farm, where it was weighed and witnessed by 16 people.' Many times before the morning she woke with nightmares, and found herself clutching the brass railing of her bedstead as she had clung to the rod that afternoon. Her arms remained swollen for two weeks.

Her name was famous when she woke. Papers throughout Britain carried news of her achievement and every detail of the fish. Weight 64 lb; length 54 in; girth 28½ in.

Miss B. said; 'Next day, Sunday, the news went round like wildfire and people came from far and near to see the monster. Our laird, Sir Alexander, gifted it to the Perth Royal Infirmary where it went over with both patients and staff. The fun began on Monday when it was taken to Malloch's the tackle shop in Perth. I happened to go round by Scott Street in the afternoon and there was a big crowd around Malloch's window. I thought there had been an accident; instead the fish was displayed in the window with a placard stating its weight and that it had been caught by Miss Ballantine.

'I went round to the back and stood for a moment beside two old chaps with white side-whiskers. One said to the other "A woman? Nae woman ever took a fish like that oot of the water, mon, I would need a horse, a block and tackle, tae tak a fish like that oot. A woman – that's a lee anyway!" I had a quiet chuckle up my sleeve and ran to catch the bus'.

What a struggle that must have been! One can imagine only too vividly the thrill of the moment when Mr Ballantine edged his gaff shaft knot by knot down the gut trace, in the dark, until he estimated the right depth had been reached. Then came the well-judged lift of the gaff-point into the unseen monster, and the heave that brought over a half hundredweight of salmon, alive and kicking into the boat.

One other classic Tay 'big fish' story cannot be omitted, the 'Bishop Browne' story, even though it may already be well known to many readers. The best account is perhaps that given in A.E. Gathorne-Hardy's *The Salmon* (1898) – the hero of this drama being Dr Browne, Bishop of Bristol in 1868: this account runs as follows:

'The scene of the adventure is that part of the Tay where the Earn joins its waters with the larger stream, and the estuary proper commences. The rise and fall of the tide amounts to twelve to fourteen feet, and as the stretch of the water is three-quarters of a mile across at high tide, harling is the usual and only reasonable method of fishing adopted. The fly was practically abandoned, not rising more than one to six as compared with the minnow, and that one never more than a sea trout.

'The "Night with a Salmon" was the last night but one of the rod season of 1868, and the fish was hooked at about half-past twelve in the morning, high tide having been about ten. The monster took the minnow on the lightest of the three lines, a mere makeshift, composed of two trout lines seventy and fifty yards long, the splice of which had not been tried. He first went nearly out to sea, playing the boat rather than the boat playing him, and having the full advantage of both tide and current. Many dangers had to be surmounted; first the sparling nets with their high poles and ropes, and then the channel of the South Deep, where Mugdrum Island divides the Tay into two streams and the bottom is "gey foul", and the tide runs like a mill race. At half past three the boat approached Newburgh, with its wild expanse of estuary beyond, and for the first and last time touched the shore for a second, but not long enough for either passenger to land. The writer gives a vivid account of the sorrows of the unfortunate third man, not an enthusiastic angler, wet, cold, and hungry, and longing to get ashore – at one time even threatening to jump overboard and swim. The change of the tide made the fish frantic, but he decided on going up with it, and did so at a great pace, and shortly afterwards showed himself at last, springing two feet out of the water – a monster as large as a well-grown boy – and proving that he was not foul hooked, as had been surmised from his behaviour, for the line led fair from his snout. Soon afterwards a strand of the line parted within twenty yards of the end, through the constant friction of the wet line running through the rings for so many hours; and the problem became complicated by the necessity of keeping the flaw as far as feasible on the reel. The necessity of keeping close on the fish led the boatman such a life as he will never forget. At last night came on in earnest; it was half-past six and all but dark before the pier was reached from which the boat had started seven hours before.

'Here, after one churlish refusal, a boat was induced to come alongside, and the unfortunate passenger was transhipped at about eight o'clock with injunctions to send off food and a light. It was an hour before the boat returned with an excellent lantern, a candle and a half, a bottle of whisky, and cakes and cheese enough for a week. Dr Browne now put in force what, in a letter to me, he states that he "regards as the most brilliant idea that ever came into his mind". A spare rod, short and stiff, was laid across the seats of the boat, with the reel all clear and a good salmon line on, with five or six yards drawn through the rings.

They waited until the fish was quiet a minute or two under the boat, and gently taking hold of the line he was on, passed a loop of it through that at the end of the salmon line. After two or three failures the loop was got through, a good knot tied, and the old line snapped above the knot. The danger surmounted might then be properly estimated from the fact that the flaw when examined turned out to be seven inches long, and half of one of the remaining strands was frayed through. The only thing now to be avoided was coming into close contact with the fish, as the loop, of course, would not run through the rings. This was rendered more difficult, as the manoeuvre of transferring the fish from one rod to another was facilitated by his being attracted by the light and keeping close to the boat. For a few moments it was proposed to hang the light over the stern and gaff him when he came up to it, but this method was rejected as unworthy of so noble a foe. I quote the conclusion of the article:

"Time passes away as we drift slowly up the river towards Elcho. Ten o'clock strikes, and we determine to wait till dawn, and then land and try conclusions with the monster that has had us fast for ten hours. The tide begins to turn and Jimmy utters gloomy forebodings of our voyage down to the sea in the dark. The fish feels the change of tide, and becomes more demoniacal than ever. For half an hour he is in one incessant fury, and at last, for the first time, except the single occasion when he jumped and showed himself, he rises to the surface, and through the dark night we can see and hear the huge splashes he makes as he rolls and beats the water. He must be near done, Jimmy thinks. As he is speaking the line comes slack. He's bolting towards the boat, and we reel up with the utmost rapidity. We reel on; but no sign of resistance. Up comes the minnow minus the hooks! Jimmy rows home without a word; and neither he nor the fisherman will ever get over it!'"

What comment is to be made on this? Presumably Bishop Browne had hold of one of those huge Tay fish, so freely described by P. D. Malloch, and we will never know its size. It could have been a mere sixty-pounder – or could it have rivalled Wullie Walker's eighty-four-pounder taken in the sparling net? One can only say that it was a disaster that the Bishop's tackle was not sounder, even though it did hold out for ten hours! By contrast, Miss Ballantine killed her sixty-four-pounder in just over two hours, and Mr Craven his 53-lb Spey fish in fifteen minutes.

One can only guess that Bishop Browne may have been nervous about the strength of his tackle, alarmed at the size of the beast he had hooked, and so did not, or perhaps could not, put on enough strain. It does sound like the classic case of 'the fish playing the fisherman', rather than the other way round, particularly as it was certain the fish was not foul-hooked.

The story could be left at that, except that A. Courtney Williams in his *Angling Diversions* (1945) gives an interesting sequel. He writes:

Another exceptionally fine fish, which nearly made history, was a 71-pounder which was on view at Messrs Grove's shop (then in Westminster) in the year 1871. This specimen was 52 inches long, with a girth of 31 inches. It might well have been the record British rod-caught salmon, as it was hooked at noon one day in the Tay by the Bishop of Bristol (Bishop Browne), who played it for 10½ hours when the trace broke. Two days later it was taken in the nets, with the Bishop's small Phantom still in its jaws.

The observant reader will see at once that this account does not tally with A. E. Gathorne-Hardy's, which in describing the final break with the fish says, 'Up comes the minnow minus the hooks,' i.e. leaving no doubt that the minnow was not left in the fish's mouth. Also the year in which this event took place differs in each account. Gathorne-Hardy gives it as 1868, saying that the account was first printed in the *Cornhill Magazine* for 1869 and that he has the authority of its author for saying that all the details are exact in every particular. Courtney Williams on the other hand gives the date as 1871. So there is some discrepancy here, and the exact truth may never be certain, except that it is too much to believe that Bishop Browne hooked more than one such monster!

CHAPTER 18

*Net-fishing—P. D. Malloch's observations—Sea trout
Brown trout, and other fish*

As to net-caught Tay fish, there is not as much information as one would like. 'Jock Scott' gives the biggest fish as one of 84 lb caught in a sparling* net in 1869 by one Wullie Walker. This fish is mentioned by several other reliable authorities, and no doubt it was authentic.

P. D. Malloch, in his excellent *Life History and Habits of the Salmon* (1908), referring to the Tay nets, has some interesting remarks. He says: 'The average weight of the heaviest salmon taken each year on the Tay for 14 years is 60 lb. The largest fish taken this year was $63\frac{1}{2}$ lb.' He further says: 'Fish between 50 and 60 lb in weight are often caught in the nets on the Tay, while a few between 60 and 65 lb are sometimes captured, but beyond this weight fish are rare. I have noted as many as 40 fish over 40 lb in weight, all caught in one day in the nets.'

Malloch gives the average size of spring fish, in his day, as 20 lb (nowadays 10–11 lb).

What more is there to be said on the subject of Tay net-caught fish? From the angler's point of view, perhaps the less the better! No doubt the monsters of modern times are few by comparison, but no doubt some are still taken. And certainly the extent of the water legally netted has decreased. It may be well to leave it at that.

Other fish in the Tay, besides salmon, are many. Sea trout take first place, and the net-catch of these is large. But curiously enough neither the Tay nor its tributaries have ever been rated as first-class sea trout waters for rod-fishing – in no way comparable for instance to the Spey. Whether it is that salmon fishing so dominates the scene, or whether the Tay is so large that sea trout get 'lost' in it, and fail to congregate anywhere, or whether too many get caught in the nets leaving too few for the rods, is difficult to say – or there may be some other unfavourable factor. But, whatever the reason, individual rod-catches of sea trout in the Tay are not high, compared with those of many other rivers, even though big fish of 6–8 lb are sometimes caught.

*Sparkling is a species of small fish, also described as a 'smelt'. It was said that Wullie Walker could talk of little else than this 84 lb fish for the rest of hs lifetime.

June and July, as usual in most rivers, are the two best months for sea trout in the Tay.

Brown trout on the other hand are numerous, all up and down the river. To stand on any vantage point such as Kinclaven or Caputh bridge, and watch a big rise taking place, is quite an experience. The whole river seems full of rising fish. Of course there are sea trout or finnock and well-grown parr all rising at the same time, but no doubt brown trout predominate.

Big fish up to 4–6 lb are occasionally caught, and fishing for trout is very popular amongst local fishermen, even on Sundays. It is surprising what strong gut and large flies or baits are often thought necessary for their capture!

Other fish which are to be found in the Tay and its tributaries are pike, grayling, perch, and, in Loch Tay, char. But most of these fish prefer slack waters like those of the Isla and none is of much interest to fishermen.

Also, there are, of course, as in all Scottish rivers, a vast number of eels. It is surprising that no one appears to have taken the trouble to fish for these commercially, neither on the Tay nor any other Scottish river, as is done in Ireland. They fetch a high price at Billingsgate.

CHAPTER 19

Fishing in tributaries: Garry, Tilt, Tummel, Lyon, Fillan,
Dochart, Lochay, Ericht, Almond—Conclusions—Envoi

A brief description has already been given of the course of the Tummel and the
Isla, but there is more to be said about their fishing capacity as well as that of
many other smaller tributaries. Unfortunately, two of the best of these, the
Garry and the Lyon, have been hydro-ed, in addition to the Tummel. Anyone
who motors from Blair Atholl on the main road towards Newtonmore cannot
fail to notice the dry bed of the Garry on the left-hand side. This is a sad sight as
the Garry was formerly a small and pretty salmon river of considerable merit,
both for fishing and as a spawning ground. Now it is virtually dry, except after
exceptionally heavy rain or a big snow-melt, and all its water has been diverted
through a tunnel into the Tummel. Only the Tilt, joining it at Blair Atholl, still
continues to bring a permanent flow into the lower part of the Garry bed; and
this sizeable headwater, rising some fifteen miles back in the hills towards the
north, still attracts a number of small salmon and grilse, and provides some
small river fishing during the latter part of the season.

Turning to the Tummel, this river reinforced by the Garry water still holds
salmon, but it is dammed back in two places by large Hydro weirs, one near
Tummel bridge five miles downstream from Kinloch Rannoch, and the other at
Faskally close to Pitlochry. As a result, artificial lochs are created immediately
upstream of both these weirs; the lower one, known as Loch Faskally, is two-
and-a-half miles long, and salmon are caught in it both by trolling with boats
and by fly-fishing from its banks. These Hydro weirs have salmon ladders in
them, and fish late in the season penetrate as far upstream as Kinloch Rannoch,
but only in small numbers. Loch Tummel, as well as Loch Faskally, holds
salmon together with brown trout, pike, and perch; and it seems that, once they
have ascended the weir at Faskally, fish as a rule prefer to stay in one or other of
these lochs until late in the season, before making their way further towards
their spawning grounds.

Every salmon and grilse which passes through the ladder in the Hydro weir at
Faskally is counted. The Hydro have spared no pains or expense in building an
efficient ladder with an underground electrically lit window, where every fish

can be observed both ascending and descending. To watch through the window is fascinating, as the fish take no notice of spectators, and about 5000 salmon and grilse ascend every year. In 1977 5500 were recorded, the biggest being estimated (by length) at 47 lb, a very big fish nowadays for the Tummel. The Hydro have also done their best to compensate for the loss of spawning ground in the Garry by stocking with large numbers of artificially reared salmon fry and parr.

But as a fishing river the Tummel has been badly hit by the Hydro. The best parts of it at Faskally, below the former Falls of Tummel, are now submerged under forty feet of water, and in bygone days, when spring fish averaged 16 lb, this was a magnificent stretch of fishing. Now the Tummel above Loch Faskally is but a shadow of what it used to be; a fair number of salmon are still caught in the lower Tummel below Pitlochry, but the operation of the Hydro is apt to cause a substantial rise and fall in the water-level every day, which does not help fishing. Incidentally, this rise and fall is sometimes carried down into the main Tay, even as far as tidal water. Its effect on fish is quite interesting. It obviously does not move them in the same way as a natural spate, presumably because the extra flow consists of stored stagnant water from Loch Faskally, which is lacking in oxygen and probably of a higher temperature compared to freshly fallen rainwater running in off the hill. Nevertheless a continual and artificial rise and fall of this sort does do a certain amount of harm, in putting fish off the take and making many of them change their lies at frequent intervals.

Another famous tributary which has been sadly affected by Hydro schemes is the Lyon. This most attractive river flows out of Loch Lyon, which lies back towards the high hills bordering the south side of the Moor of Rannoch. The Lyon runs eastwards past Meggernie and Fortingall, through what is reputed to be the longest glen in Scotland, to join the main Tay near Comrie, two miles below Kenmore. It has altogether a course of thirty-two miles and formerly was a first-rate medium-sized salmon river of delightful character with a splendid variety of pools. The big spring Tay salmon, some of them thirty-pounders, used to run up here. But what can be found now since the Hydro took over? Sad to say a permanently diminished stream, always at low summer level during the fishing season, except that once a week a so-called 'freshet' of about eighteen inches artificial rise in water is allowed down for twenty-four hours. Where are the big melted snow spates, the three- or four-footers of former years? or the Lammas and autumn floods which used to draw up so many fish? 'Gone as long as the Hydro lasts' must be the depressing answer, probably beyond the life-time of most of us. In fact the main flow of the Lyon is now diverted through a pipe through the hillside to the bottom reaches of the Lochay, close to Killin. Although the weekly 'freshet' is better than nothing and one must be thankful for it, it is never enough to give the river a proper scour out, so that the bottom during the fishing season remains fouled.

Nevertheless, although the Lyon can never now be again what it was, a certain number of salmon and grilse still ascend it. And for anyone who is satisfied to fish in lovely surroundings with the prospect of catching a limited number of fish from April onwards, this river still has its attractions.* And it must still hold considerable value as a spawning ground.

The Fillan and the Dochart have already been described. They are not in fact tributaries, but the headwaters of the main Tay itself. Owing to the falls of Dochart, fish do not normally enter these before May and by that time they are apt to be stale, having been in fresh water anything from one to three months. During the rest of the season, some fish may certainly be caught in both Fillan and Dochart, which are pretty but small waters; but such fish are apt to be red and of no great size.

The Lochay, which runs into Loch Tay jointly with the Dochart, has what formerly were impassable falls two miles upstream from its mouth. Now salmon and grilse can use the new ladder to bypass these falls, but the Lochay's main function is that of a spawning stream.

The Bran which rises near Amulree, and runs into the Tay at Dunkeld, also unfortunately has impassable falls within a mile of its mouth. And another tributary which has falls on its upper course, as has already been mentioned, is the Isla. One wonders whether, if fish passes were constructed on all such falls, the increase in both fishing and spawning ground might not justify the expense?

An extra thirty miles or so of river might be made accessible on the Isla and Bran but the Isla falls might present too much of a problem, there being two separate falls of sixty feet near Alyth, as well as two smaller falls below.

The Ericht, together with its two component headwaters, the Blackwater and the Ardle, is a tributary of the Isla and has already been described. It is a most attractive small river and has considerable fishing potentialities, running for some miles in a steep and winding valley, with alternate rapids and pools of all varieties. It is further blessed with good spawning grounds in its headwaters, and given the chance, plenty of fish run up it. If properly looked after there is little doubt that the Ericht would provide first-class 'small river' fishing, but it

*In 1978 for instance the Lyon fished surprisingly well.

has two substantial drawbacks – the first is that there are artificial obstructions, i.e. weirs, low down its course near Blairgowrie. Though these are provided with ladders, fish find them difficult to run in low water. The second is that the river has for a long time been subjected to flagrant and persistent poaching by every sort of means. This is a long-standing practice, now almost traditional, and it would need a bold team of bailiffs to stop it.

There is only one other Tay tributary of any consequence and that is the Almond, which runs in on the west bank, two miles upstream of Perth. It rises twenty-five miles in the hills to the west, not far to the south of Loch Tay. Unfortunately, this river is of little value for angling. Salmon seldom ascend it before the first autumn spate, and there are several weirs in it, which formerly tended to check the passage of fish, but which are now provided with adequate passes. Except in spate, the flow is attenuated by water abstraction for Perth. In high water, however, a number of salmon run the Almond, and some are caught in it by rod fishing. Fish can now run up to and spawn in its headwaters, if they want to. It is perhaps a pity that such fish do not run further up the Tay to spawn.

Conclusion

Enough has now been said, it is hoped, to give to the reader a fair idea of the wonderful character of the Tay river system, and of its fishings both past and present. There is no other river where he would have a better chance of catching a forty-pounder or making, in autumn at least, a double figure day's catch. The older generation of Tay fishermen may well have their complaints that, while the number of rods increases, the spring run of salmon has diminished and the average weight of fish is down by nearly half; the fishing on several of the tributaries has been largely spoilt; and poaching by 'trout fishers' as well as illegal netting with nylon drift nets at sea, has greatly increased. Also the general cost of fishing has escalated beyond all belief. Sad to say, this is all true enough.

Nevertheless there is another side to the picture. The rod-catch on the Tay and its tributaries is still likely to exceed 10,000 salmon and grilse each year. Twenty- and thirty-pounders are still common, forty-pounders are not out of the question, and there is still a chance, remote though it may be, of a fifty-pounder. The autumn run has increased out of all recognition, there is still a sizeable spring run including some big fish, and in summer there are grilse with some salmon amongst them.

Can any other British river present a better record than this in these hard times?

Envoi

'River Tay of the salmon
That comes from the sea of rough waves,
Which is belly spotted, small speckled,
And supplied with tough strong fins;
Leaping at every false fly
Seizing flies on the tops of the waves;
They are numerous in every pool,
Spawning in the water bottom of the land.'

(From the Gaelic 'Song of Breadalbane')

PART FOUR

The Tweed

Silver Wilkinson

The Lady of Mertoun

Garry Dog

Thunder and Lightning

Durham Ranger

Blue Doctor

Jock Scott

Toppy

Silver Doctor

Tim Havers

CHAPTER 20

General remarks—A Border river—Tweed Commissioners—Various drawbacks
Prolific salmon run—Good spawning grounds—Spring fish—Autumn fish

The Tweed is the second largest river in Scotland, after the Tay. It may fairly be classed as a Scottish river, seeing that three-quarters of its course and catchment area lie entirely in Scotland. But at the same time it should not be forgotten that for the bottom nineteen miles of its course it forms the boundary between Scotland and England, until it reaches Gainslaw, some four-and-a-half miles above its mouth at Berwick, when it passes altogether into England.

Fulfilling thus the role of a Border river, the Tweed has a background which in many ways is unique. It was the witness in earlier history of incessant Border warfare between Scots and English, which only finally ceased with the accession of King James VI of Scotland to the English throne in 1603. But Scots and English mutual hostility left a legacy of potential trouble so far as salmon fishing was concerned, in that, although the Tweed spawning grounds, also the main part of its course, lie wholly in Scotland, the mouth and one side of the lowest part of the river (i.e. that part which has always been net-fished) are in England. This peculiar situation resulted in the Tweed being rated, in modern parlance, as a 'Special Case', independent of other rivers on either side of the Border. Its first special legislation dated back to 1771, and in 1859 an independent body of local Tweed Commissioners was set up, to control the fishery management, both for nets and rods, on the whole of the Tweed and its tributaries. This was obviously a wise move towards obviating any likelihood of Anglo-Scots disagreement over fishery matters, and it catered exclusively for the Tweed's particular needs.

Other noteworthy characteristics of the Tweed should not be overlooked – for instance could any other river system, it might well be asked, be so burdened with intensive net-fishing for thirteen miles upstream from the river mouth, and with liability to pollution from so many towns, such as Galashiels, Melrose, Peebles, Hawick, and Jedburgh with their many tweed mills,* not to mention

---

*It is not for nothing that the River Tweed has given its name to the familiar material which we all so often wear, dyed in endless different shades and patterns.

Kelso and Coldstream, and still produce such an impressive head of salmon? And there are other handicaps, one for instance is the ever-increasing water abstraction from the headwaters for the benefit of the urban areas around Edinburgh. This is now being carried out at a number of different points on the upper river, and its extent is causing concern. It would do little harm if the water so extracted was returned (unpolluted) to the Tweed catchment area; but in fact it is lost. How far can this process be extended, it may well be asked, without irretrievable damage being done to the fisheries?

On the Tweed and its tributaries there is also the long-standing practice of local poaching and fishing by foul means, chiefly though not entirely in the upper reaches. And now there is a comparatively recent menace, the great increase in large scale drift-netting with nylon nets along the Northumberland coast, which is legal in England though not in Scotland. There is no doubt that this netting accounts for a great number of Scottish fish making their way northwards both to the Tweed and to other east coast Scottish rivers. In addition there is at present much illegal drift-netting further north off the Scottish coast, and outside the coastal limit. But it is an amazing tribute to its fecundity that the Tweed still overcomes these drawbacks in producing such a fine run of salmon throughout the season, even though the large majority of them, during the netting season between February 15th and September 15th, are caught in the nets. This abundance of salmon, it cannot be too clearly emphasized, is primarily due to the magnificent and widespread spawning grounds to be found in the headwaters of the main river and its many tributaries. Some of these latter are sizeable rivers on their own account, for instance the Teviot and Jed, the Ettrick and Yarrow, and the Till; and many salmon find their spawning grounds in them as well as in the whole network of minor tributaries – many also spawn in the main Tweed itself.

So this river is indeed fortunate to possess such wonderful breeding grounds and it is doubtful whether any other Scottish river system is so well endowed. What is more, apart from its spring and summer run, the Tweed is almost the only river in Scotland which still has the genuine autumn run, so much renowned in our grandfathers' days. Fresh silver fish enter this river in numbers during October and November, after all netting has ceased. This autumn run is a priceless asset for fly fishermen (fishing after September 14th being limited to 'fly only'), especially as some of these fish run large, occasionally up to 40 lb or over. Moreover the autumn fish, approaching extinction as they were in the 1940s, have been steadily increasing in numbers over the past twenty years. Not only is this run now large, but it appears still to be on the increase. To assert however that the Tweed is the most prolific salmon river in Scotland, as has often been done, is arguable. This is to put it in rivalry with the Tay and the Dee, and in present times both the net- and spring rod-catch in the Tweed has considerably fallen off, owing to the reduction of the spring run, while that of the Tay and Dee remains large. But this is an argument about imponderables, because without exact figures of the net-catch in all these rivers, which are unobtainable, no definite conclusion is possible. One can only say that although, as in other rivers, the former very prolific spring run of the Tweed has sadly diminished,* the autumn run has now become excellent.

*Since the above was written, the 1978 spring season proved a first-class one for most east coast rivers, with the notable exception of the Tweed.

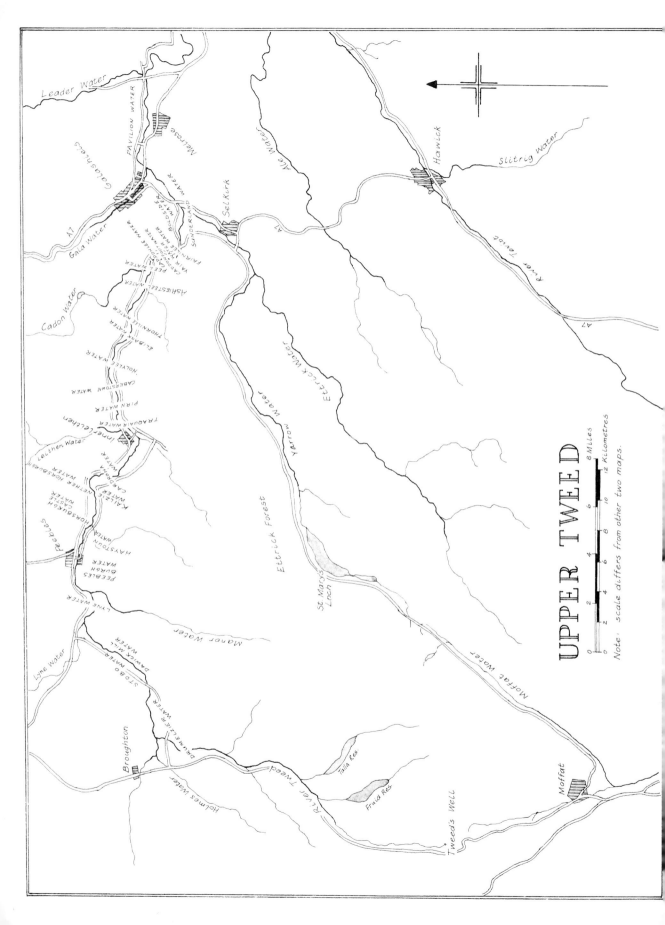

UPPER TWEED

Note: scale differs from other two maps.

CHAPTER 21

Catchment area—Upper Tweed—Source to Ettrick mouth—Ettrick and Yarrow
General surroundings

The Tweed has a catchment area of approximately 1500 square miles, of which some 300 are in England and the remainder in Scotland. For descriptive purposes it is convenient to divide the river into three sections. From the source to Ettrick mouth may be regarded as the uppermost of these. The Tweed rises at 1500 feet above sea level at Tweed's Wells on Tweedsmuir. Its source is on the county boundaries of Dumfries-shire and Lanarkshire, about six miles north of Moffat and close to the headwaters of both Clyde and Annan. Its length before falling into the North Sea at Berwick is just over 100 miles. Unfortunately the hill ground, which gives it birth, is not high enough to provide a reservoir of snow, frozen hard enough to feed it through April and into May. The Spey and the Dee alone among Scottish rivers have this valuable asset. But from the point of view of a good return from spawning it is perhaps just as well that the Tweed's headwaters do not start at too high and cold an altitude.

For the first six miles of its course the Tweed runs northwards and is but a hill burn, until at Tweedsmuir Kirk it is joined by its first tributary of any note, the Talla. This is another hill stream, rising at 2500 feet towards the south-east, which after a precipitous course of six miles joins the infant Tweed and used nearly to double its size until for some years past most of its flow has been abstracted for the Edinburgh water supply.

Continuing northwards for a further six miles, the Tweed passes close to the village of Broughton, where the Biggar water runs in from the west. This again is a tributary of only modest size, but it considerably increases the flow of the Tweed. All these headwaters, as has already been pointed out, provide useful spawning grounds for salmon.

At Broughton the Tweed turns eastwards, and except for minor vagaries runs in this general direction for the rest of its long course to Berwick. At Broughton too, although still more than 600 feet above sea level, it enters a wider valley, better cultivated, and here it assumes the character of a sizeable river rather than a mere upland stream. More tributaries soon join it – the Lyne water from the north and Manor water from the south are the main ones. At the mouth of

Eddlestone Water lies the county town of Peebles (pop. 6000) – a royal burgh since mediaeval times. That the burgh arms represent three salmon, one swimming to the right and two to the left, is indicative of one main local occupation; but on the other hand the Pebbles tweed mills have given anxiety on the score of pollution for many years past. There is a fine five-arch bridge across the Tweed at Peebles, which dates from 1467. It carries modern traffic, but has twice been widened and adapted to do so. Also the first cauld or weir across the river is at Peebles.

Below Peebles the Tweed runs quickly past Innerleithen on its north bank, where the little Leithen, much obstructed by mill weirs, joins it from the Moorfoot hills to the north, while half a mile upstream the Quair water, rising upon Dun Hill (2433 feet), runs in from the south – Traquair House, close by the mouth of the Quair, is said to be the oldest inhabited house in Scotland, dating back to the early middle ages. Then, some eight miles below Peebles, the Tweed passes by the village of Walkerburn, where it flows over another cauld. Below this it soon passes out of the county of Peebles into that of Selkirk, and another six miles downstream it is joined by one of its three most important tributaries, the Ettrick. This in itself is a considerable river, almost as big as the main Tweed upstream of this point. It rises back in Ettrick Forest, to the south-west, and has a course of twenty-seven miles, being reinforced midway by its tributary the Yarrow, which fed by Megget Water and St Mary's Loch is also sizeable and has an independent course of twenty miles. Where Ettrick and Yarrow merge is the field of Philiphaugh, the scene of Montrose's disastrous defeat by Leslie in 1645, and a mile and a half downstream is the town of Selkirk (pop. 5650) dating back to the twelfth century. This unfortunately for the salmon is another town which has thrived on the tweed industry, and in the past has been a constant source of pollution. It also used to have a cauld across the Ettrick, a former scene of much poaching activity; but this cauld is now demolished. Below Selkirk the Ettrick runs for only another two miles before it joins the Tweed.

Before considering the further course of the main river below this point, mention should be made of the natural beauty of the surrounding countryside, both in the valley of Ettrick and of Yarrow, as well as in that of the upper Tweed itself. This landscape is delightful, as anyone who knows the road between Galashiels and Moffat, via Peebles, or between Selkirk and Moffat, via St Mary's Loch, will agree.

Apart from the constant sight of fast-running river and burns, or a quick view of St Mary's Loch and the Loch of the Lowes as one drives past them, one is always aware of the surrounding presence of woodland and steep hillside, the latter sometimes grass and sometimes heather covered, rising at intervals to 2000 feet or over, much of it obviously unchanged for the last thousand years. It is not spectacular scenery, such as one meets in the Alps or Norway, or even on the west coast of Sutherland or Ross-shire, but it has a charm and character all of its own, peaceful and unspoilt, the home of the sheep, the grouse, the salmon, and the brown trout, one of the most attractive regions to be found in all Scotland.

CHAPTER 22

Middle Tweed—The Eildons—Local legends—Gala water—Leader
Melrose—St Boswells—Dryburgh—Mertoun—Makerstoun
Floors—Teviot—Kelso

From Ettrick mouth to Teviot mouth may fairly be classed as the middle Tweed, which now at once owing to the influx of the Ettrick almost doubles in size; and it is in this part of it, as will be shown later, that the best of the salmon fishing is at present to be found.

Two miles below Ettrick mouth on the right bank of the Tweed stands Abbotsford, the house built and much loved by Sir Walter Scott. The site is lovely, but this house has been described architecturally as a 'hotchpotch of Victorian fantasy', though the relics inside are full of interest.

The hills here, although still present, start to recede into the distance, with the notable exception of the triple peak of the Eildons, the legendary burial place of King Arthur. These dominate the scene on the south bank, and form a familiar and well-loved landmark for the whole neighbourhood. As long ago as Roman times the 'triple peak' was recorded as being a welcome sight to the marching legionary, as he neared the great fortress of Newstead at its foot. Later, in mediaeval times, the Eildons formed a spell-binding background for the many local legends and ballads about the 'gude neighbours' (i.e. the fairies) of the neighbourhood. Perhaps the most delightful of these ballads is that which concerns 'Thomas the Rhymer', a local prophet who is supposed to have lived from 1219 to 1299, and tells how the Queen of Elfland carried him off to her mysterious realms beneath the Eildons, where he was forced to serve her for seven years. At the end of that period he was released to wend his way home to Ercildoune on Tweedside, though bound to return to Elfland when he was summoned. This summons was finally served by a hart and a hind standing in the middle of the village street, which was considered a great 'ferlie' or marvel. Thomas recognized and obeyed the call, and followed the animals into the forest. He has never been seen again, but we are told to await his coming when the Queen of Elfland sees fit to release him. If anyone in these modern days of jet planes and motorways sees fit to laugh at such superstitions and fairy stories, he should realize what a firm hold they had on the imaginations of people in the past. For instance in 1586, or four hundred years ago, a very short span in the existence of the human race, a wretched woman called Alison Pearson, a native of Tweedside, was convicted, sentenced, and legally burned to death at the stake, on the charge of witchcraft – the principal accusation against her being that of 'hanting and repairing with the "gude neighbours" and Queene of Elfland, this divers years past, as she had confest'. No laughing matter for Alison Pearson! Such was only one episode of this type out of many during the sixteenth and seventeenth centuries.* And even in the days of William Scrope the Eildons were still the subject of strong local superstitions, as is clearly shown by the pusillanimous behaviour and narratives of 'Wattie', Scrope's fisherman at Melrose. In fact the whole countryside is saturated with legends, ballads, and fairy tales of all sorts.

Below Ettrick mouth two well-known tributary streams soon flow in from the north – the first is the Gala Water, which rises in the Moorfoot hills, and has a course of twenty miles before passing through Galashiels (pop. 13,000) and falling into the Tweed one mile further downstream. Once again in this town there has been in the past the usual trouble of serious pollution from tweed mills and other sources, but it is to be hoped that this evil has now been remedied. At Gala foot the Tweed passes out of the county of Selkirk into Roxburghshire, and skirts the extensive industrial estate of Tweedbank, recently built, which sad to say does not add to the beauty of the countryside.

The second tributary, the Leader or 'Lauder' is of about the same size as the Gala, but rises further to the east in the Lammermuir Hills, and has a course of eighteen miles before it merges with the main river. It is not polluted, but is apt to run very dirty after rain and to colour the whole of the Tweed downstream, to the discomfort of the many fishermen in that area.

Between Gala mouth and Leaderfoot, on the south bank of the river, lies the town of Melrose (pop. 2170) another very ancient foundation, with its magnificent ruined abbey where the heart of King Robert the Bruce was buried before the high altar – and three miles below Leaderfoot is St Boswells (pop. 1400), and Dryburgh Abbey. The latter is an ancient but beautiful ruin which like the abbeys of Kelso, Jedburgh, Selkirk, and Melrose, suffered at the hands of the English in the savage border wars of the sixteenth century. It is now surrounded by a fringe of handsome trees, yew, elm, and beech, a fitting site for the burial place of Sir Walter Scott, and of Field-Marshal Earl Haig.

*The many Acts against witchcraft were only repealed as lately as 1736.

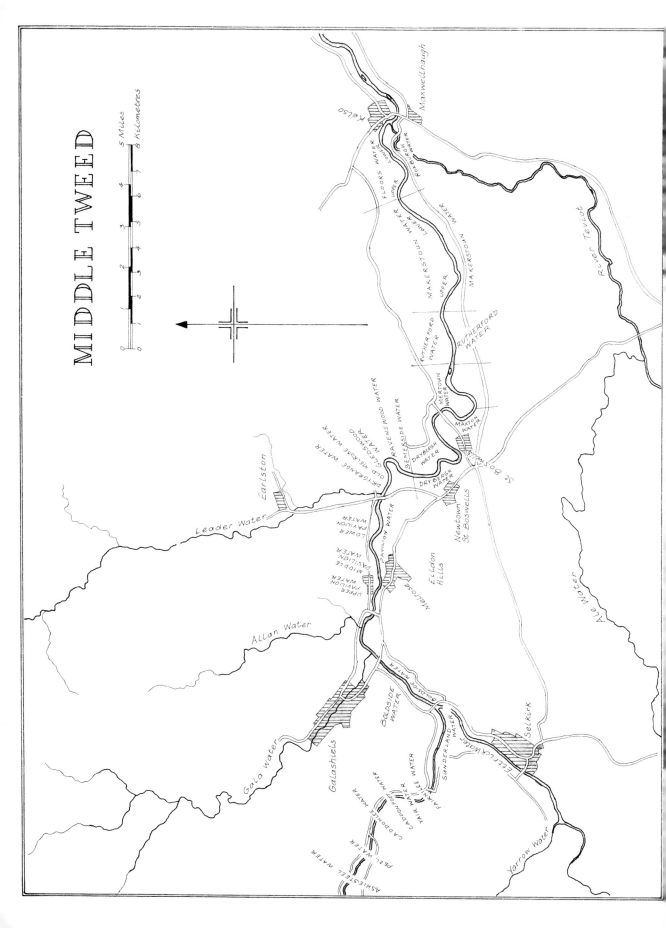

MIDDLE TWEED

5 Miles
8 Kilometres

Shortly below Leaderfoot the Tweed has taken a sharp right-handed bend southwards. It runs here in a deep valley, in places almost a gorge, and its banks are often heavily wooded. It is all most attractive, except that the big leaf-fall into the river in autumn is another bugbear for fishermen. In the neighbourhood of St Boswells and Mertoun, three miles further down, it winds in a most unruly fashion before resuming its normal eastward trend.

At St Boswells the Tweed emerges from the hill country, and for the rest of its course of forty miles to Berwick it has a fall of only 200 feet. Now the higher hills recede into the distance, and the countryside, though still rolling, becomes gradually flatter and more intensely cultivated. Rich farmlands of Roxburghshire, Berwickshire, and Northumberland line the river's bank, right to the tidal estuary.

In spite of its more gradual fall, however, the Tweed still has a strong flow in this part of its course, at least as far as Kelso, a further seven miles downstream from Mertoun. There are some lovely streamy pools here, and several massive rocky outcrops such as at Craigover, near Mertoun, and in two places near Makerstoun, where the river again flows through a narrow wooded gorge for nearly half a mile. In fact the whole river in this area presents a continuous variety of pool, rapid, and flat, with a flow now broken and streamy, now deep and winding, which cannot fail to delight the eye of any viewer, whether he be fisherman or otherwise. In some respects one is here reminded of the lower Dee below Banchory, though really the Tweed has a unique character and charm all of its own.

Below Mertoun, where Scrope as a guest wrote much of his *Days and Nights of Salmon Fishing*, the river runs rapidly past Rutherford, Makerstoun, and Floors, all famous names in the fishing hierarchy – and at Kelso, below Kelso cauld, it is joined by the biggest of its three main tributaries, the Teviot, which is in itself a salmon river of note. This tributary rises thirty-seven miles back in the hills towards the south-west, where the shires of Dumfries and Roxburgh meet. Its actual source is five miles upstream of Teviothead, on the road between Hawick and Langholm. Together with its two main tributaries the Slitrig Water and the Jed, the Teviot drains the northern slopes of the Border hills in that area. Flowing through Hawick (pop. 16,500), a Border town of considerable size and great antiquity but another centre of the local woollen and tweed industry, its course lies directly north-east, past its junction with the Jed at Jedfoot, some two-and-a-half miles below Jedburgh (pop. 3800), to cover a further nine miles before joining the Tweed at Kelso. The Teviot in itself is a river of pleasant character and lovely surroundings, streamy and rocky, and similar to the upper part of the main river. Besides providing both spring and autumn fishing in its lower reaches, it is a valuable subsidiary to the Tweed in providing good spawning grounds and a useful increase of flow.

Goosander

CHAPTER 23

Lower Tweed—Slower flow—Entry into England—Till
Tidal reaches—Whiteadder—River mouth—Discolouration—Pollution
Spates—Past history—Castles and Peel-towers—Caulds

From Teviot mouth to Berwick is the lowest section of the river. Reinforced by the Teviot, the Tweed turns more towards the north-east, and has a fairly direct course first to Coldstream (thirteen miles down), and then to Berwick, another sixteen miles. Besides being bigger and wider, the river here has a slower current, longer intervals between pools, and fewer rapids. As far as Tillmouth, two-and-a-half miles below Coldstream, it still maintains a reasonable rate of flow, sufficient to produce good fishing water, though at summer level the stream is sadly shrunken. At Carham, seven miles below Kelso, the south bank passes into England where it remains as far as the mouth at Berwick, while at Tillmouth it is joined by the third and last of its main tributaries, the Till.* The thirty-mile course of this latter river lies wholly in Northumberland, and together with its tributaries drains the northern and eastern slopes of the Cheviot Hills and the low-lying country around Wooler. Throughout its length the Till has a peculiarly meandering course, passing near Ford and Etal in its lower reaches, and close to the battlefield of Flodden. Many sea trout and a fair number of salmon and grilse ascend it, and at times the fishing in its lower reaches can be quite good, helped as it is by a cauld near Tillmouth. There are also other obstructions further upstream.

To return to the main river, the Tweed below Tillmouth and for the remainder of its eleven-mile channel to Berwick takes on the character of a

---

*No description of the Till, however brief, would be complete without inclusion of the age-old saw, which puts its warning so pungently:

> 'Says Tweed to Till
> "What gars ye rin sae still?"
> Says Till to Tweed
> "Although ye rin wi'speed,
> And I rin slaw,
> for ae man that ye droon
> I droon twa!"'

typical big lowland waterway, winding and slow-running. Gradually the clear cut distinction between pool and rapid dies away; and, in the stretches where they operate, the net fishermen have removed all rocks and other obstructions on the bed of the river, which could interfere with their activities.

Horncliffe, five miles above Berwick, is generally considered the highest point upstream to be affected by spring tides, though when exceptionally high these on occasion have been known to back the water up as far as Norham, a further two miles upstream.

Below Horncliffe there are only left the tidal reaches, which have both banks in England, the County of Berwick on Tweed lying on the north side and Northumberland on the south. Two miles above Berwick the tidal Tweed receives the influx, on its north bank, of the last of its tributaries, the Whiteadder. This rises some thirty miles to the north-west, in the Lammermuir hills in Haddingtonshire. It pursues a tortuous course, and is joined in its lower reaches at Allanton by a main tributary of similar size, the Blackadder. This in turn also runs off the Lammermuirs, and rises near Greenlaw. Both these rivers hold sea trout and brown trout in numbers, while the lower reaches of the Whiteadder also attract a fair number of small salmon and grilse.

Finally the main Tweed runs directly into the North Sea, with the ancient town of Berwick (pop. 11,760) and its fine bridges lying at its mouth.

The course of the Tweed has now been traced from the high and remote uplands of its birth, through its middle reaches where fed by hill tributaries from both north and south it becomes enlarged to a full-sized river with mills and towns and rich farmlands set upon its banks, and lastly to its lower reaches, separating the two kingdoms with its wider and more restrained flow.

That its water has not the same clarity, in anywhere but its headwaters, as some other more fortunate rivers has already been indicated. There is too much agricultural land along its banks and those of its tributaries, and too many towns that are apt to bring in fouling matter of one sort or another. Even light rain is apt to cause some discolouration, while a downpour normally means a dirty flood. It is seldom that the Tweed runs fully clear, after the manner of the Dee or even of the Tay, and then only in low water. In addition, reference has already been made to the former pollution from the many mills and towns on both main river and tributaries. At one time this was a running sore, widely deplored, and epitomized in his day by Andrew Lang (1844–1912) in his *Ballade of the Tweed*:

> De'il take the dirty, trading loon
> Wad gar the water ca' his wheel,
> And drift his dyes and poisons doun
> By fair Tweedside at Ashiesteel!

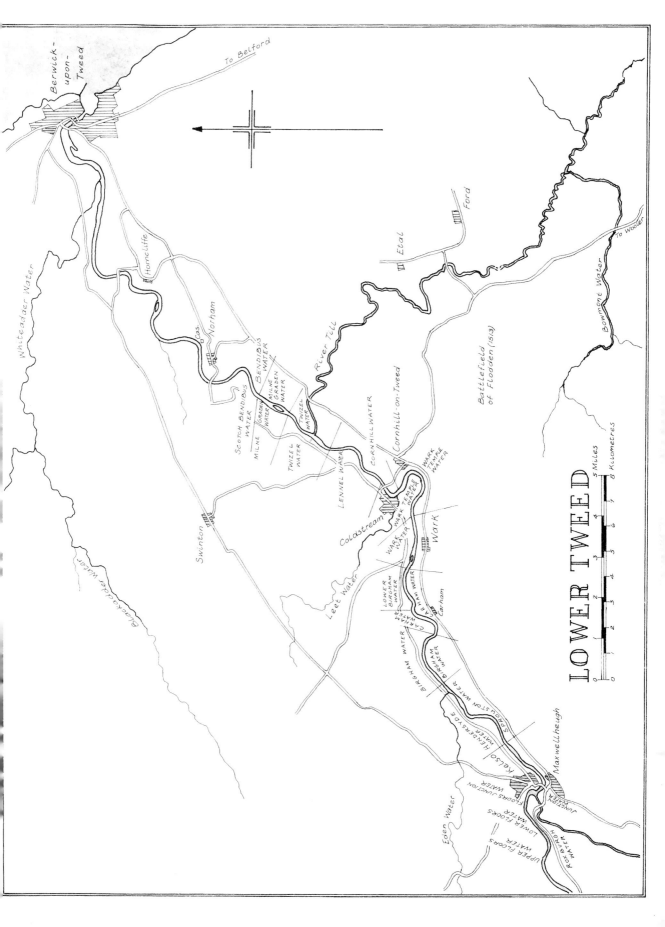

LOWER TWEED

Berwick-upon-Tweed

To Belford

Whiteadder Water

Horncliffe

Norham

Ladys

Blackadder Water

Scotch Bendibus Water

Bendibus Water

Milne

Graden Water

Milne Graden Water

Twizel Water

Twizel Water

River Till

Etal

Ford

To Wooler

Bowmont Water

Battlefield of Flodden (1513)

Swinton

Lennel Water

Cornhill Water

Cornhill-on-Tweed

Coldstream

Wark Temple Water

Wark

Wark Temple Water

Wark

Work

Leet Water

Lower Birgham Water

Carham Water

Carham

Birgham Water

Birgham Water

Eden Water

Kelso Hendersyde Water

Sprouston Water

Maxwellheugh

Floors Junction Water

Junction

Lower Floors Water

Upper Floors Water

Rox Burn Water

5 Miles

8 Kilometres

0 1 2 3 4 5 6 7 8
0   1   2   3   4   5

In modern times however, thanks to the activities of the Tweed Commissioners and their officers, and to the co-operation of the various authorities concerned, pollution, if not wholly eradicated, has been curtailed to a point where its harm is negligible. Let all Tweed fishermen be grateful. Much good work has been accomplished in this field, where it has been so much needed.

There are big floods from time to time which help to keep the bed of the river clean. The three biggest of comparatively recent times were on February 9th 1831, August 13th 1948, and in early November 1977 when on each occasion the water rose between twenty and twenty-five feet at Kelso. High-water marks can be seen engraved on the wall of the mill at Teviot mouth. But although they are apt to shift a vast amount of gravel, Tweed floods are less impressive, have less impetus, and do less damage than their counterparts on faster rivers, particularly the Spey, which runs at nearly twice the speed. As with other rivers, the level of the Tweed rises much faster nowadays than it used to, owing to improved drainage; equally it falls faster which can be a disadvantage for fishing.

As to the general history of the Tweed and Tweedside, this is so involved, as might be expected on a Border river, and going back as it does to Roman times, that there is hardly the opportunity or space to go into it in any detail in a book primarily concerned with salmon fishing. For those who are interested, however, the great Roman camp at Newstead by Melrose, and lesser camps at Chesters and Lyne, and the Roman altar with its Latin inscription built into the staircase of the Abbey at Jedburgh, all bear silent witness of the past. So for that matter does the endless chain of ruined castles and peel-towers from Berwick up to Neidpath, one-and-a-half miles upstream from Peebles, and Stobo a further five miles upstream. Up to the middle of the sixteenth century the Scots and English were almost continuously at war with one another, with frequent forays on either side of the Border, and during the rare periods of peace between the kingdoms the Scots themselves were often engaged in internecine feuds. So there was every need for such strongholds, of which the most noteworthy surviving ones with walls still standing are Norham, the Northumberland fortress three miles downstream from Tillmouth, Bemersyde Peel-tower close to St Boswells, Elibank Castle half way between Galashiels and Innerleithen, Neidpath Castle above Peebles, and Newark Castle on the Yarrow. And there are numberless other ruined fortresses, both smaller and larger than these, many of which such as Roxburgh Castle have disintegrated, with only their foundations, or fragments of wall still visible. Also can be seen the lovely ruins of the abbey churches at Kelso, Melrose, Dryburgh, and Jedburgh, all destroyed by the

The Coach Wynd, Lower Floors
A good pool on the Tweed one mile upstream of Kelso. This pool is typical of the larger pools on the middle and lower Tweed. It fishes well in spring and autumn, and in any height of water, except high flood. A boat is needed if the whole pool is to be properly covered; but the neck can be fished by wading.

English in the savagery of Border warfare in the sixteenth century, while anyone who fishes at Lower Floors may be shown the holly bush on the north side of the river, planted to mark the spot where King James II of Scotland in 1460 killed himself through the explosion of an overcharged cannon, 'Long Tom', which he had fired at the walls of Roxburgh Castle, held by the English at that time.

But a legacy from the past of closer interest to Tweed fishermen is the existence of many weirs or 'caulds', as they are locally termed, built from bank to bank across the main river and its tributaries. These were all built of stone for the same purpose, to give a head of water providing water-power for mills. In Victorian times and earlier, water-power when available was a cheap, abundant, and reliable source of energy, and from time immemorial it had been widely used. These caulds, even with fish passes built into them, tended to check the passage of salmon, particularly in spring or late autumn when the water was cold; usually a long deep pool, known as a 'dub' was formed above them, and a fast stream, probably deepening into a good holding pool, below. From a fishing point of view they were therefore a mixed blessing; they provided good fishing in their immediate neighbourhood both upstream and downstream, while simultaneously they tended to hold fish back from the reaches above, and to give an opportunity for the illegal extraction of ascending fish by poachers.

It must be many years since the last cauld was built, and if not properly maintained and repaired after spates it seems that they do not take long to disintegrate. In fact, the only caulds still maintained and in full working order on the main Tweed are now at Coldstream and Kelso. Elsewhere there are still caulds in a fair state of repair at Sprouston, Rutherford, Upper Mertoun, Melrose, Walkerburn, and Peebles – but all these now have apertures through them which facilitate the passage of fish, and it may be that unless kept in repair they will not stand up to many more spates. Many other caulds have already completely disintegrated.

There were also, formerly, many caulds on the tributaries, some of which as at Selkirk have been demolished or allowed to crumble. But some still remain, for instance at Hawick, Jedburgh, Galashiels, and on the Till, all of which have fish passes in them.

As already noted, opinions have been divided about the merits or otherwise of caulds so far as fishing is concerned, but two things are certain – they profoundly influence the flow and depth of the river both upstream and downstream of their site, and they help considerably to oxygenate the water through the turbulence of the sudden fall in the water level which they cause. Perhaps something approaching the best of both worlds can be achieved by keeping them in good repair, with a reasonably-sized breach through them, to allow an easy passage for fish that want to ascend.

CHAPTER 24

Fishing and fish—Different runs of fish—Early spring run—Effect of netting
Length of netting season—'Westerners'—Drift-netting—Summer run
Autumn run

There is no other river where the great sporting traditions of salmon fishing go back further than they do on the Tweed. Anyone who is interested in the background of Tweed fishing should not fail to read that masterpiece already mentioned, William Scrope's *Days and Nights of Salmon Fishing in the Tweed and Other Rivers*. This was first published as long ago as 1843, with the result that some of Scrope's ideas on the life-story and habits of the salmon are somewhat awry, and too much time should not be devoted to studying these. But his accounts of early nineteenth-century angling and 'leistering'* on the Tweed (the latter still legal in those days) make fascinating reading. Scrope's fishing career covered roughly the period 1820–45. He was a first-class raconteur of both fact and fable, and often wrote with his tongue in his cheek in the most entertaining fashion. His salmon fishing experiences date from that day on the Ettrick when Sandy, who he met by chance, admits to the dumbfounded young tyro (Scrope) that he has 'ta'en twa saumon, ane wi' Nancy† and the ither wi' a Toppy†, baith in the Faldon-side Burnfut'. And Scrope's account of his subsequent adventures, his devotion to the sport thus aroused, grip the attention of the reader and give a vivid picture of contemporary life on Tweedside and elsewhere, together with fishing anecdotes mainly based on Tweedside, but also on the Tay, Shiel, Spey, and other rivers.

Altogether this is one of the best fishing books ever written; it has been followed by a multitude of others, but surpassed by none.

In Scrope's time fish appeared to ascend the Tweed indiscriminately throughout the season, and judging by his figures of the net-catch there were a

---

*The 'leister' was a five-pronged and barbed salmon spear, usually wielded from a boat and by torchlight.

†Two old Tweed flies, the first called after Nancy Dawson, who was born on the Tweed near Little Dean Tower, and the second, one of Scrope's favourites, with a wing of black turkey tail tipped with white, a black hair body, red cock's hackle and red head.

large number of grilse as well as salmon. But as it was then legal to fish for and kill kelts* his spring records are misleading.

All through the nineteenth-century, and in the early twentieth, it seems that the rod-fishing was best in autumn, i.e. in October and November when the netting had ceased after September 14th.

But turning to more modern times, to gain a general picture of Tweed rod-fishing it should be realized that there are, and apparently always have been three separate runs of Salmon in spring, summer, and autumn.

The spring fish are small, averaging 7–8 lb. A fifteen-pounder is a big one and a twenty-pounder a rarity (it is worth noting however that on April 23rd 1920 a forty-three-pounder was caught at Rutherford, a veritable Goliath amongst his kindred, or was this a late-run autumn fish? We shall never be sure now).

Tweed springers, provided the river runs fairly full and not too cold during the winter months, start entering fresh water very early, odd ones even in November or December.† By the opening day for rod-fishing, February 1st, they may be found in numbers as far up river as Kelso cauld, with sometimes a few still further upstream. From then on, given normal weather and water conditions, the spring run continues to build up till the water falls to near summer level in late April or May. Thereafter the nets seem to get an almost 100 per cent kill, operating as they do nearly up to Coldstream, some thirteen miles upriver. That this is too far above the high-tide mark to be justifiable has long been the plaint of Tweed rod-fishery owners and anglers – and indeed the Tweed is netted further upstream than any other river in Scotland. Nowadays with the spring run in any case diminished the only hope of getting a good head of spring fish into the river is either that there should be spates throughout February, March, and April, at frequent intervals; or better still that the river should run consistently high from January onwards, so that fish enter it in numbers before the nets start operating on February 15th, and continue to get past them afterwards. Nets also fish later on the Tweed than in any other Scottish river, being lifted only on September 15th.

As to summer salmon, these run slightly larger than spring fish, and grilse come with them; but without summer spates, which are rare, these fish are of little benefit to rod-fishermen, as the nets take a prohibitive toll. Rod-fishing

*Until the Salmon Fisheries Act of 1862.

†Such spring fish will therefore inevitably overlap with late-run autumn fish, that come in during December and January – the essential difference being that the latter are ready to spawn almost at once, while the former will delay spawning for ten months or so.

between late May and mid-September therefore, except on very rare occasions, is a waste of time. Even the weekend 'slap' is of little help in summer, because fish hardly have time to clear the thirteen miles of netted area before the nets start operations again early on Monday morning, and low summer water makes this situation worse.

One curious theory held by some of the netsmen is that many of the spring fish enter the river purely for purposes of investigation, and that they drop back to the sea without waiting to spawn. They say that they catch these fish between April and June and call them 'Westerners'. That such fish have obviously been in the river for some time can be deduced from their condition and colour. It would be ill-work to argue with anyone as experienced as a Tweed netsman about the habits of Tweed salmon. But is this theory wholly credible? It is an interesting one, and perhaps worth closer scrutiny.

That some salmon in a river drop downstream at times, particularly during a big flood, is certain. In time of spate they can be seen at times falling back over a weir, and Spey netsmen for instance have no hesitation in disclosing that after a big summer flood they catch plenty of red fish that have obviously dropped back from the river into the estuary or the sea, and are coming up for a second time.* So fish do not always behave according to the accepted rules.

But if a spring salmon does drop downstream, and gets caught in river nets, especially when such nets are worked as far upriver as those on the Tweed, does it necessarily mean that it is not going to spawn, if left to its own devices, in another five or six months time? Surely there is plenty of time for it to run upriver again?

A further hazard now menaces the Tweed spring and summer salmon as well as those of other east coast Scottish rivers, and that is the growth in legal drift-netting with modern nylon nets off the Northumberland coast, such netting being illegal off the Scottish coast. In addition there is the illegal drift-netting now carried out on a large scale outside the coastal limit off the Scottish coast, and which the Authorities concerned have so far failed to suppress.

That the Tweed rod-fishing season remains open until November 30th is another danger to the spring fish, by autumn in the upper river or headwaters, and spawning or about to spawn. At this stage they fall an easy prey either to legitimate fishing methods, or to other means less reputable, just when they most need protection.

*Other curious things can happen; kelts, for instance, sometimes move upstream in company with fresh salmon, or drop back to the sea and at once re-enter the river again, carrying sea-lice.

All things considered, it seems that the Tweed spring and summer runs are now at great risk; they are already sadly diminished, and if additional protection for them is not speedily forthcoming, it seems possible that they will shrink to a point of no return for the present generation of fishermen.

Once the nets come off in mid-September, however, and the equinoctial rains start to raise the water level, the picture changes. Now the autumn fish start to enter in ever increasing numbers, and there are now no nets to take a toll of them. This Tweed autumn run is impressive. It starts at any time after mid-September with the first substantial rise in water, it appears to be still increasing every year, and it produces the best fishing of the season. Most of the fish come out of the sea bright silver in colour, the only difference between them and the earlier fish being that their spawn or milt is more developed. Such fish come in right to the end of November, and later; and this is obviously an example of the old-fashioned autumn run, that we read so much about in our grandfathers' day, but which seems to have died out everywhere except on the Tweed. These autumn fish are inclined to run quickly upriver, given a fair height of water, quicker than the spring fish. No doubt they are in a greater hurry to reach the spawning beds, and unlike the springers they are not going to remain in the river for eight months or more before spawning.

Only if the river stays very low do they remain in numbers low down the river, where fishing under such conditions during September can be good. But nowadays autumn fish seem to be passing through the lower reaches more and more quickly, and the best autumn fishing is normally above Kelso.

Autumn fish are good eating, boiled or grilled, almost as good as spring fish, provided they are fresh run, preferably with sea-lice – otherwise they make excellent smokers.

In weight they used to average 16–18 lb, but now, unfortunately, there are many small fish of 7–9 lb, which has brought the average weight down to around 11 lb. There is a theory that these fish are grilse of large size, being late run, and thus having benefited from some extra months sea feeding. This seems quite probable and examination of their scales would show. All the same, fish in the 20-lb class are still common, thirty-pounders are killed every year, and forty-pounders are not too rare.

Two factors have sometimes in the past brought discredit to autumn fishing. First, that, when the spring fishing was at its height in the 1920s and '30s, autumn fish became very scarce and by the 1940s were a rarity, so the spring fishing got all the kudos. And, second, that not every fish caught in the river as a whole during the autumn is a fresh one, far from it. A moment's reflection will show that inevitably this cannot be the case. If the fishing season is to remain open till as late as November 30th in order to cater for the main autumn run, it means that particularly in the upper reaches of both main river and tributaries a large number of stale spring and summer fish, ripe for spawning and all but inedible, are bound to be caught. Such fish would be far better left in the river.* The middle and lower reaches are mostly free of them, since such old residents have nearly all passed higher upstream so late in the year. But if the whole river is to remain open for fishing, this class of fish is bound to be encountered somewhere, and no one has yet found a satisfactory answer as to how they should be protected. Possibly the season might well be closed a fortnight earlier for the whole river, or some dividing line might well be drawn at a suitable midway point, above which no fishing would be allowed after the end of October, or some other curtailment be devised on these lines. But one can see that the argument from the upper reaches around Peebles would then be that overfishing by net and rod in the lower reaches allows too few spring and summer fish to reach them; and many of the spring fish in any case go up the Ettrick. It is thus only the autumn fishing which is any good to them and it would be unfair to take away a period of this, while the whole of the lower river still continued fishing. That there is something to be said for this argument must be admitted, but it is unpleasant to see numbers of fish on the point of spawning being removed often by none too sportsmanlike methods,† while only an occasional fresh fish gives justification for fishing with legal lures being continued.

Lower down the river things are different. There, stale spring fish are a rarity; and fishermen who are expecting fresh silver fish with sea-lice usually return to the river any red or black old-stagers which fall to their fly.

---

†e.g. The use of such 'lures' as the 'Walkerburn Angel', a horrid contraption of weighted hooks used for illegally foul-hooking fish, is both deplorable and despicable.

*This is nothing new – Sir Herbert Maxwell writing in 1908 says: 'It remains true at the present time, as Stoddart wrote 70 years ago, that, except in unusually wet seasons, the salmon fishing above Ashiesteel' (immediately above Ettrick mouth) 'is hardly worth attention. Plenty of fish are taken above that point, but, as he truly said they are in execrable condition'.

CHAPTER 25

Rod-fishing methods—Boating—Wading both banks—Limited good fishing heights

Rod-fishing on the Tweed starts on February 1st and continues till November 30th. Net-fishing starts on February 15th and ends after September 14th. During the period when rods may fish but nets may not, i.e. February 1st to February 14th and September 15th to November 30th, 'fly only' is the rule for the rods. In former days big single-hooked flies up to 6/o or even 8/o were used, but now they have been largely ousted by treble-hooked flies. At all other times rods may use any sort of legal bait, as an alternative to fly. There is no Sunday fishing allowed on the Tweed, not even on the English bank.*

It can be a cold business fishing in February and March; often there is 'grue' or floating ice in the water, and rod rings may get full of ice. When the water is very cold, below 40°F, there is no doubt that salmon are reluctant to run Kelso cauld. This is not a difficult ascent, there is an adequate fish pass, and the cauld itself is not high; it is simply that in very cold water fish are unwilling to attempt the passage of any sort of obstacle, natural or artificial. But as soon as the water becomes warmer, fish pass up this cauld at will, and the reaches above soon become stocked. Sprouston cauld, two-and-a-half miles below Kelso, and the cauld at Coldstream do not check fish to the same extent. Their passage must be easier, and they also have efficient ladders.

It is a pity that fly-fishing is not more generally practised on the Tweed, which provides so much good streamy fly water over all its course. Only when the river is well coloured or high and very cold does bait hold a decided advantage. Floating line and small fly is deadly in April or May, anywhere where a stock of fish has gathered; and even in the cold water of October and November, autumn fish will take a big fly readily, as spring fish will in February or March if the river is not too coloured.

In the lower reaches from Kelso downstream fishing is mainly done from boats. Below Teviot.mouth the river is normally so wide that it is difficult to

*Salmon rod-fishing on Sundays being legal everywhere else in England, though nowhere in Scotland

cover the water properly by wading; and though odd pools, such as Hempseed-ford below Kelso, and a few streams lower down can be adequately waded or even occasionally fished off the bank, they are few and far between. As a general rule a boat is a great advantage. Above Kelso, where the river is smaller, boats are still useful in many pools; but there is much more wading. Above Ettrick mouth, where both Tweed and Ettrick are half the size, boats are discarded, and wading- or bank-fishing comes into its own.

To regard the Tweed pre-eminently as a boating river, as is sometimes done, is therefore to hold a false picture. It is only in the lower reaches that boats take the leading place, and in the middle and upper reaches there is a great deal of wading. Another factor is that no one finds it pleasant to wade in early spring or late autumn, when both weather and water are unduly chilly – also for the elderly and physically handicapped there is no doubt that a boat, with a comfortable fishing seat and a companionable boatman, are invaluable assets. So resort is often had to boats when, strictly speaking, it may not be necessary. Tweed boats are light and very manoeuvrable – drawing little water. The boatmen prefer to manage them by rowing continuously, which appears hard work, but in fact is not so, unless there is a strong downstream wind or a fast current. Occasionally, where practicable, they let the boat down, ottering it on a long rope from the shore; but the method of letting the boat drop down from an anchor while held on a long rope, i.e. in the Spey fashion, has never been practised here. No doubt rowing gives easier and quicker control. Fishing is always done by casting from the boat, whether with a fly or bait, and never by harling, as on the Tay. And most Tweed beats have both banks, either through outright ownership or through mutual arrangement, which here as everywhere else makes fishing more peaceful and pleasant. One noticeable feature of the Tweed is that, compared to most other large rivers, it has a limited variation in effective fishing height. Many pools in the Tay, Spey, and Dee for example can provide good fishing between summer level and four to five feet above it. But the Tweed's variation in effective heights tends to be narrower, seldom beyond three feet. Perhaps this is partly due to Tweed spates now bringing down so much colour in the water, but it is not only that. In the Dee, Tay, and Spey, with a high river, fish in many places like to shelter close to the bank, and can be caught very close inshore. But for some reason this seldom seems to happen on the Tweed. Perhaps the bottom is smoother, and there are fewer big stones or rocks near the bank to give shelter. But for whatever reason it may be, the water does not have to rise very far to put the lower and middle Tweed out of order for fishing, while only in the smaller upper river can sport still be expected.

CHAPTER 26

Rod-fishing beats—On the middle Tweed—On the lower Tweed
On the upper Tweed—On tributaries

As to the principal fishings on the Tweed, the best section of the river (except in early spring) is undoubtedly that which lies between Ettrick mouth and Teviot mouth. This includes such good beats as Boldside, The Pavilion, Tweedswood, Bemersyde, Dryburgh, Mertoun, Rutherford, Makerstoun, Upper Floors, Lower Floors, and Floors Junction.* These are all first-class fishings both in autumn and in spring. They comprise some of the loveliest parts of the river, with a splendid variety of pools, suitable both for wading and boating. The Junction Pool at Kelso, where the Teviot enters, certainly used to be the most prolific pool on the whole river, both in spring and autumn; though for some reason (probably gravelling) it has fallen away considerably during these last two or three years. Generally speaking, however, good fishing could confidently be expected on any of the above beats, provided the fisherman is there at the right time of year and the river is in good fishing order. If a choice of the best beat had to be made it might well be either Upper Floors or Mertoun, but how difficult a decision where all are good!

Below Kelso there are other such famous beats as Hendersyde, Sprouston, Birgham, Carham, North Wark and South Wark, the Lees, and Lennel. Tillmouth too can produce fish in a low-water autumn, though in spring its rods have to compete with the net-fishing. In the past these beats have all produced outstanding catches on occasion, both in spring and autumn; it was down here for instance that the very big spring catches of the 1920s and 1930s were usually made, and the relevant beats have since been held in just renown. But during these last five or six years, sad to say, this part of the Tweed has greatly fallen off throughout the season. The only stretch that can be relied upon is the Sprouston–Hendersyde beat, which is no doubt helped by its cauld. Otherwise the fish nowadays seem mostly inclined at all times to run straight through to Floors Junction or beyond (though 1977 was a better autumn down below, which is perhaps a good augury for the future).

*Partly, the Teviot runs in on this beat, but there are good pools lower down.

Looking back upstream to the Tweed above Ettrick mouth, here we find a smaller river (though a very pretty one), and definitely less prolific. The drawback here in spring is that, while the water is still cold, fish tend to move upstream very deliberately. Many are caught lower down, and many undoubtedly go up the Ettrick. So by the time spring fish reach the Innerleithen–Peebles area, their ranks are well thinned and they are apt to have been long in the river.

In autumn, however, it may be a different matter. If the river runs high and full for any length of time, fresh fish may well be found here; and fishing may be good up here when lower down in the normally more productive areas the water may still be too high and too coloured. But the drawback, so far up the river, is the one already mentioned, that stale spring and summer fish, that have already spent long months in the river, are certain to be caught here. These are of little use from a sporting or culinary point of view, and would be far better left untouched as valuable potential spawners.

Of the Tweed tributaries, from the fishing point of view, without doubt the Ettrick and Teviot are best. Both have a sizeable run of spring and autumn fish; and both provide rewarding fishing, given one important condition, that they have a fair height of water. In dry weather they both shrink to small river status, fish cease to enter them, and the resident stock becomes virtually uncatchable. Any fisherman who applies himself to these rivers should therefore offer a prayer for rain and high water, without which he is likely to have to kill time by other means than fishing.

Another Tweed tributary that can produce some salmon and grilse, in its lower reaches, is the Till. A fair number of fish are caught there, but higher up, the river as a rule is winding and sluggish and of little attraction for fishing. There are several caulds on it, which check the upstream passage of fish, and it holds a large head of brown trout, grayling, and such coarse fish as pike, perch, dace, and eels, none of them welcome denizens of a small salmon river. Sea trout ascend the Till in fair numbers; but so far as salmon are concerned it is fair to say that, except in the lowest reaches near Tillmouth, the Till is of little account.

Some small salmon and grilse are also caught both by net and rod up the Whiteadder, but this river and its tributary the Blackadder are chiefly renowned for their sea trout, or 'whitling' (i.e. herling), as they are locally designated.

Other tributaries of the Tweed have little significance from the salmon fishing angle, but nevertheless provide excellent and widespread spawning grounds, as has already been emphasized.

CHAPTER 27

Big Tweed fish—Big catches

Of big fish the Tweed in the past has had its full share. Admittedly it cannot compete with the Tay as a 'big fish' river, and probably not with the Wye, but it is ahead of all other British rivers in this field. Usually in the big and steady-running pools of the middle and lower Tweed, there would be plenty of elbow-room to play a big fish. Nor are there many obstacles on the banks or obstructions in the river, the upshot being that it would most probably be a far easier proposition to land a fifty-pounder here than it would be for instance in the faster and rockier Spey. Autumn is the time for big fish in the Tweed, they have almost invariably been caught then, and the following is a list of outstanding examples:

Date	Weight	Caught by	Fly	Where caught	Remarks
1743	$69\frac{3}{4}$ lb	Lord Home	—	—	That this fish really existed and was accurately weighed has been confirmed from written records, by the present Lord Home. The only doubt is how many ounces were reckoned to go to the pound at that long ago date. For this reason this great fish is not accepted as the record British rod-caught salmon.
Later in the 18th century	61 lb	William, Earl of Home	—	—	True weight uncertain (for the same reason as above).

Date	Weight	Caught by	Fly	Where caught	Remarks
Oct. 27 1886	$57\frac{1}{2}$ lb	Mr Pryor	Silver Wilkinson 4/0	Upper Floors	This is the record Tweed fish of modern times – Mr Pryor caught 15 fish altogether that day. The fish diary simply states: 'Biggest $57\frac{1}{2}$ lb' – This fish was weighed in the evening in front of the Duke and Duchess of Roxburgh and was thought to be over 60 lb but next morning a local tradesman made it $57\frac{1}{2}$ lb. It may therefore have lost a little weight overnight.
1889	55 lb	Mr Brereton	A 'small' Wilkinson	Mertoun	Recorded by A. E. Gathorne-Hardy in *The Salmon*.
Nov. 1913	55 lb	Mr W. A. Kidson	—	—	He had another of 49 lb recorded in *Where to Fish*.
1873	$53\frac{1}{2}$ lb	—	—	—	Recorded by A. E. Gathorne-Hardy in *The Salmon*, as above – no details.
Oct. 1922	$51\frac{1}{2}$ lb	Dr Fison	—	Norham	Recorded in *Where to Fish*.
1902	$51\frac{1}{2}$ lb	Gen Home	Jock Scott	Birgham Dub	Recorded in *Where to Fish*.
1921	51 lb	Mr Howard St George	Jock Scott	—	Recorded in *Where to Fish*.
Nov. 9 1925	$50\frac{1}{2}$ lb	Mr Rudd	—	Birgham Dub	Recorded by 'Jock Scott' in *Game Fish Records*.

N.B. Forty-pounders are far too numerous to list here. The last one of 43 lb was caught at Tillmouth three years ago. All these big autumn fish were caught on fly.

Sadly the tally of such leviathans is now much thinner than it used to be, fifty-pounders seem to have disappeared and forty-pounders, once frequent, are now captures of great note; and even thirty-pounders are not common. For whatever reason it may be, the Tweed, sad to say, is going the same way in this respect as the other 'big fish' rivers.

Big one-day catches in the Tweed are too many to list in any detail. The two best spring catches were by Col. Taylor and Lady Joan Joicey (see below), but double figure spring catches have been so numerous as to be of no particular note.

Autumn catches have been even more impressive, and it must be remembered that these in the past have consisted of fish averaging between 16–20 lb, instead of 7–9 lb, in spring, and all on fly, instead of (usually) bait in the spring.

As an outstanding instance, Mr G. McCulloch's great catch on Lower Floors on November 20th 1903 should be quoted. He caught nineteen salmon that day, averaging $20\frac{1}{2}$ lb. All these fish were on fly, and the largest weighed 39 lb. On another day in 1903 he caught eighteen fish of similar size, while in 1901 he had also caught eighteen fish in a day.

Another occasion of an even greater day's sport was when the Duke of Roxburgh in the 1880s caught twenty-seven fish in one day in Maxwheel, the pool below Kelso bridge. These too presumably averaged not less than 18 lb. This is probably the most outstanding catch of all, and though well authenticated is hard to credit in these present days.

Another fine achievement was that of the Rev. Robert Liddell, who in the autumn of 1887 at the advanced age of seventy-nine, and in the last year of his life, caught eighteen fish in one day in Birgham Dub, two of them over 30 lb. In fact, during those halcyon autumn days around the turn of the century, double-figure catches for a single rod in a day were so common that, unless they neared the twenty mark, they did not arouse undue interest. What wonderful fishing this must have been, especially considering the average weight of the fish, and compared too with nowadays, when five or six autumn fish of much smaller size make a fair day's bag for one rod.

To take a step forward into the 1920s, autumn fishing on the Tweed during those years, as on other rivers, went sharply downhill. In contrast, this was the time when spring fishing came prominently to the fore. It was in the 1920s and '30s that the massive runs of small spring fish, averaging around 8 lb, reached their height. On February 15th 1935 Lady Joan Joicey caught twenty-six salmon in the day averaging that weight, while in March 1937 Col. Taylor fishing at Hendersyde caught thirty fish in one day, averaging the same.

These fish in early spring were all caught on bait, and there were other double figure catches without number, both before and after the 1939–45 war. Later in the season, during April and May, there were also outstanding bags made on fly, especially above Kelso.

Meanwhile by 1945 the autumn fish had almost died out, only the odd one being caught. It was a depressing situation. Gradually, however, during the last twenty years the wheel has turned a full circle in an astonishing way. By degrees autumn fish have once more come into their own, and there is no doubt nowadays about which way the wind is blowing. The autumn run seems to increase every year, in numbers at least, though the average weight does not compare with that of the past. Admittedly it is not yet easy for a single rod in autumn to reach double figures in a day, but is it too optimistic to hope that in due course this autumn fishing, improving all the time as it is, will once again achieve its former excellence, at least in numbers if not in weights?

CHAPTER 28

Other fish—The future—Envoi

So much for salmon and salmon fishing. But the Tweed holds myriads of other fish, 'bull trout' and sea trout (now identified as the same species), brown trout, grayling, pike, dace, and other coarse fish: 'Bull trout' were long thought to be a separate species, but icthyologists now say not. They do not make good eating, are poor takers, and are usually caught by salmon fishermen on salmon tackle. So they are not granted much respect, even though at times they reach an outstanding size, toward the 20-pound mark or over. Brown trout in both the Tweed and its tributaries have always taken a prominent place both for numbers and size, particularly in the upper reaches. This is a good argument up one's sleeve to put to those who maintain that salmon and brown trout cannot co-exist and thrive. The Tweed river system bears resounding witness to the contrary. The upper reaches where salmon spawn, and indeed the whole river, has always earned an outstanding repute for brown trout fishing with both wet and dry fly, though unfortunately the hatch of natural fly is now nothing to what it used to be. For this we presumably have to thank the various pollutions of the past, as well as any chemicals or insecticides which may be sprayed on adjoining fields. Grayling also abound in the lower and middle Tweed and its tributaries – and provide some sport for local fishermen. It is doubtful however whether their presence is an asset in a river where salmon parr, and brown and sea trout take pride of place. They were thought to have been originally introduced in the Middle Ages by the monks of Jedburgh to their stewponds, and to have escaped from these into the Jed, and thence into the Teviot and Tweed.

And what of the future? He would be a bold man who would forecast. So far as salmon are concerned, it seems that a reduction in netting, both in sea and river, is urgently called for. Is not netting nine miles above the high-tide mark and thirteen miles above the river mouth too far upstream to be justifiable? And would not rods be willing to reciprocate for a curtailment of netting by cutting down their own season? And can the illegal drift-netting not be suppressed? And is it fair that drift-netting should be allowed along the Northumberland coast, when it is banned in Scotland? These are some of the thorny present-day problems which need solution. U.D.N. in the past ten years has affected the Tweed, as it has other rivers. But its effects seem now to be dying out, for which one must be thankful.

And do spring fish breed spring fish? (the experts know, but they differ). If they do, spring fishing by rod in the Tweed for at least the next decade will be poor unless netting is curtailed. But autumn fishing may become very good; in fact it is so already, given the right weather and water conditions. It has been said that no one river has been able to provide both good spring fishing and good autumn fishing simultaneously for any length of time. This principle appears to be basically accurate, whether by accident or through the process of natural evolution. But let us all hope that, in the case of our beloved Tweed, it may yet prove to be ill-founded, and that in both their spring and autumn fishing Tweed fishermen may yet be fortunate enough to enjoy the best of both worlds!

Envoi

'Let ither anglers chuse their ain,
    An ither waters tak the lead;
O'Hielan' streams we covet nane,
    But gie to us the bonnie Tweed!
And gie to us the cheerfu' burn
    That steels into its valley fair –
The streamlets that at ilka turn,
    Sae softly meet and mingle there –

The lonesome Talla and the Lyne,
    And Manor wi' its mountain rills,
An' Etterick whose waters twine
    Wi' Yarrow frae the forest hills;
An' Gala, too, an' Teviot bright,
    An' many a stream o' playfu' speed;
Their kindred valleys a' unite
    Among the braes o' bonnie Tweed.

Oh the Tweed! the bonnie Tweed!
    O' rivers it's the best;
Angle here or angle there,
    Troots are soomin' ilka where,
Angle east or west.'

(Thomas Tod Stoddart)

PART FIVE

Fishing the Rivers

CHAPTER 29

General considerations in big river fishing

My publisher has made the kind suggestion that further remarks on the actual process of fishing the Spey, Dee, Tay, and Tweed would not come amiss, together with various topics of interest concerning this. The following chapters provide some suggestions, but I would like to make it clear that these are primarily meant for those whose experience of these four rivers is limited, or who intend to fish any one of them for the first time. They may also make sense in the case of other sizeable rivers in Scotland – or even of the smaller ones – I leave it to my readers to judge this.

As to the experts who are long experienced, I don't pretend to be able to teach them anything, but if they dip into my remarks and find anything of interest, I shall be pleased and grateful. As previously said, it is fatal to lay down the law about what to do in fishing, and I certainly don't intend to do it here. What suits one person does not always suit another. One can but suggest and generalize, even if one does it by a candid statement of what one thinks. There is always more to be learnt about fishing, and one never gets to the end of it. To be too dogmatic about it is therefore a great mistake.

Thanks to the kindness of many friends, I have been lucky and have fished on all these four rivers a great deal. I am only too pleased to pass on any useful information which I have gathered over the last forty-eight years (I caught my first salmon at Abergeldie on the Dee in 1931). This fishing has all been one long delight, and I am envious of the younger generation of fishermen who still have much more than myself in front of them.

Though the Spey, Dee, Tay, and Tweed differ in many respects, they still have much in common. For instance by British standards, except in their headwaters, they are all big rivers. It is no use going to fish them with the same tackle and tactics that you would use on smaller rivers, such for instance as the Findhorn, Helmsdale, or Naver, or in England the Dart, or the Tamar. This particularly applies when they are running at a high or medium level, which is usually a good fishing height. Your methods and ideas must be different.*

*This naturally applies to the main waters only of these rivers. Tributaries and headwaters come under the 'small river' category (except for the Tummel).

'In what way?' comes the immediate response. Well, I suppose that one of the first essentials in a big river, whether you are fishing either fly or bait, is the ability to throw a really long line. With a bait this is relatively easy, thanks to the efficacy of modern casting reels, but with a fly much more difficult; and I mean here that twenty-five yards is a short line, thirty yards reasonable, and thirty-five yards or over better still. In addition to the line being long, it must fall reasonably straight right through to the fly at the end of the leader. It is noticeable that many small river fishermen, when they first come to a big river are quite unable to throw such a line. Not only is their tackle unsuitable, but they simply lack the ability and have not previously appreciated the need. In Jock Scott's excellent book *Fine and Far Off* one reads how Alexander Grant, a leading fisherman of his age, in 1895 cast the staggering distance of sixty-five yards without shooting any line – not that such feats are necessary for ordinary fishing purposes, but they do give food for thought.*

Why is a long line an advantage in a big river? For the obvious reason, to begin with, that it covers more fish – perhaps many more, and perhaps sometimes the only fish in the pool. If the percentage of likely takers amongst a stock of fish is a small one, how much more important it is that as many of them as possible should be covered, and properly covered. This applies particularly in a hard-fished water, where the fish lying within easy casting range are covered by all casters, bad as well as good; and, if not caught, quickly become 'educated'. If a fisherman, on the other hand, can cast well enough to reach the far-out fish as well, beyond the reach of the average caster, his chances will be better. 'Properly' covered too is a significant point. This means landing the fly or bait well beyond the fish and not over his head, so that by the time it reaches him it is fishing well. This is all the more necessary at times when the water is cold, and the fish's reactions consequently slower. In a big river, where fish are lying far out, a long cast and the ability to put out still an extra bit of line when needed are important aids towards this end.

In cold water, whether in spring or autumn, with a long line the fly fishes slower and deeper, which is what is wanted. At any time of year, too, fish can often be picked up from slacker water at the far side of a strong stream, if the line thrown is long enough and downstream enough for the fly or bait to fish at a reasonable speed. The movement of a line with a moderate amount of drag

*The author is not suggesting that beginners should attempt casts even as long as 25 yards, let alone 30 yards or over. These long distances are quoted only as targets *eventually* to be aimed at.

through comparatively slack water seems to exercise a particular attraction for salmon. If any reader knows the Boat Pool on the Easter Elchies water of the Spey, or Creichie from the Aikenway bank, these are good examples of pools where this applies. But this tactic is seldom of any use with anything but a long line, otherwise the fly or bait is pulled away too quickly by the current and fish are reluctant to chase it into a strong stream.

Being able to cast a good distance into a strong adverse wind is a further advantage. And how often in spring or autumn on east coast rivers one seems to have to struggle with such winds! Time and again fishermen with fly-rods of thirteen feet or twelve feet or shorter (American anglers are particularly addicted to single-handed rods) are simply blown off the water by winds which are nothing more than an inconvenience to strong rods of fifteen or sixteen feet and a heavy line.

On a small river by contrast the important thing is accuracy, and length of line hardly comes into it. A short cast of twenty yards or so, easily achieved, is usually enough; but it may be desirable to land the lure within an inch of the far bank. This is quite different to the problem on big rivers. Consider an angler wading in the Spey or Tay. His job is to get out and keep out a long line with the minimum of effort against all obstacles in the shape of winds, and rocks or trees behind; unless he wants to cover some specific lie beyond his usual casting range, accuracy is of little importance and general direction is enough. But how splendid it is to see a really competent exhibition of long-distance casting, and how few fishermen can do this well! If any of my readers who are interested in this happen to find themselves near Inverness and can spare time to watch some of the experts on the Association water there, on the river Ness, they will see what I mean. They could find no better casting performance anywhere.

Apart from the fisherman's manual and physical ability, appropriate tackle is essential for long casting. The fly-rod length should seldom be less than fourteen feet; indeed in spring and autumn, with their high winds and high water, a 15-foot or 16-foot carbon graphite or fibre glass rod is a suitable implement.* Only in very low-water summer conditions is there any call for rods of thirteen or twelve feet. For my own part I would never, even in summer, go below a 14-foot carbon rod, or a 13-foot glass or split cane, the carbon for choice. Not only is the long rod a help in casting, but it is also of great value in controlling the passage and speed of the fly through the water and over the fish.

*Carbon rods of up to 20 ft in length are now obtainable. 18 ft is by no means an unreasonable length. Such a rod weighs less than a 14 ft split-cane.

Inability to do this adequately is one of the main arguments against a short rod, and the shorter the rod the less the control. The long rod is also a help after a fish has been hooked in keeping the thick part of the dressed line clear of the water, and thus avoiding it being 'drowned'. (I will write about this later. It is one of the main hazards of playing fish in a big river.)

The great objection to a long rod until recently has been its weight. Mention of any length over fourteen feet was apt to start fishermen talking about 'weaver's beams' and 'telegraph poles'. Now this is completely a thing of the past, with the advent of fibre glass and, better still, carbon graphite as a rod material. Out of interest I have checked the weight of some of my rods, with the following results:

Rod length*	Greenheart	Split cane (spliced)	Fibre glass	Carbon graphite
16 ft			30 oz	14 oz
15 ft	35 oz	28 oz	25 oz	$13\frac{1}{2}$ oz
14 ft	30 oz	23 oz	21 oz	$11\frac{1}{2}$ oz
13 ft	$24\frac{1}{2}$ oz	$18\frac{1}{2}$ oz	17 oz	10 oz
12 ft	19 oz	$14\frac{1}{2}$ oz	13 oz	9 oz

I have thus found that my very powerful 16-foot fibre glass rod weighs the same as my 14-foot Grant Vibration Greenheart, my powerful 15-foot fibre glass weighs only two ounces more than my 14-foot split cane, my powerful 15-foot carbon graphite weighs less than my 12-foot split cane, and my lighter 14-foot carbon graphite weighs much the same as an 11-foot split cane. Where is now the objection to long rods in fibre glass and carbon graphite on the grounds of weight? In addition, good patterns of rods in these materials cast superbly, so the best of both worlds is now obtainable. Incidentally, on looking through a catalogue the other day, I saw that a 20-foot carbon graphite rod is now on the market. The interesting thing about it was not so much its length, nor its price (£300), but the fact that it weighs only as much as a 14-foot split cane.

Holding a rod at the point of balance, while the cast is being fished round, with the butt away behind instead of in one's stomach, is another labour saving trick; the longer the rod the greater is the relief.

Turning to fly lines, there are many modern plastic-coated types, most of

*Additional rod weights are as follows:
Carbon 20 ft $20\frac{1}{2}$ oz
Carbon 17 ft   18 oz
The author used rods of these lengths on occasion on big rivers and found them admirable.

which are good and help to make fishing easy – floating and semi-floating lines, floating lines with a sinking tip, and slow- or fast-sinking lines. All have their uses. Two words of advice, however. First, if you use the sinking-tipped floater, see that this tip is not too long. Tackle makers often put seven or eight feet of tip at the end, and this has the effect of converting the line into a modified sinker. (This idea of the sinking tip is simply to stop the fly 'skating' on smooth water. Two feet of sinking tip is enough for this. You may find it best to splice your own short piece of sinker to the end of your floating line.)

Second, if you are fishing with a sunk line in cold water, don't imagine that you have got to scrape the bottom. Three or four feet down is normally quite deep enough to catch fish. Only if the water is near freezing point, and the pool deep, is it better to fish nearer the bottom. Even then it is better to fish slower rather than deeper, at a time when fish's reactions are so retarded.

As to the colour of a fly line, this makes little difference. Floating lines are often coloured white, an advantage as it makes it easier to see them on the water, and so to judge the position and speed of the fly, and so perhaps to spot the inconspicuous rise of a timid fish, which does not take first time but may do so later. If anyone tells you that the conspicuous white of these lines will frighten fish, just ask him why a fish's belly is white.* For sinking lines a dull colour such as dark green is as good as anything.

The weight of a fly line is important. Tackle dealers often recommend too light a line for fear of the rod being overstrained. It is a mistake to use such a line, which fails to make the rod work properly. The best rule for fishing a big river is to use the heaviest tapered line which the rod will comfortably carry. This helps both long casting and competing with a wind, and you should try out various sizes of line until you hit upon the right one.

So much for the long line and the tackle that helps towards it. If however, in spite of all the aids, you still find yourself unable to throw more than a moderate distance, there remain more remedies. The first is to find a good casting tutor, either amateur or professional, who will help you further; the second, to attempt whenever possible to wade in that extra bit further than normal, which will increase your fishing range; and the third, to fall back on the use of a boat.

Boat-fishing is a common practice on the Spey, Tay, and Tweed, and is occasionally done in the lowest reaches of the Dee. Casting from a boat is a perfectly sportsmanlike way of fishing, and as boats can if wanted be brought

---

*Criticisms have been levelled at white lines, that their conspicuous colour puts fish off. The author accounted for over 3000 salmon using white lines and did not complain about them.

close to the lie of the fish, it makes it far easier for fishermen to cover large pools efficiently. It also makes the use of a long line less needful, although it is still an advantage. At times, in certain pools and with the water at certain heights, the use of boats may well be essential if fish are to be covered, and the wider the river the more this applies. Boats also make fishing easier and less tiring, and they are a welcome relief from wading in early spring or late autumn, when weather and water can be bitterly cold, not to mention at other times.

Boats normally entail boatmen, so that fishing becomes something in the nature of a partnership, and it is perhaps not always appreciated how greatly a day's successful outcome may be due to the skill and knowledge of a good boatman, in willing co-operation with his 'rod'. The majority of boatmen or 'fishermen', as they are sometimes termed, are splendid men whose company contributes greatly to the enjoyment of the day. Never neglect an experienced boatman's opinion or advice. It is odds on that he knows the water and the lie of the fish far better than you do, and his freely given help can make all the difference to your day's sport. At the same time, if salmon are unresponsive or scarce, are there not topics of local or outside interest with which you and he can enliven an otherwise dull day?

Incidentally, if you can learn to work a boat single-handed and with safety, using a long rope and anchor in the Spey fashion, and fish out of it on your own when no boatman is available, you will find this adds tremendously to the scope of your fishing and it is great fun. But it is no easy game for the inexperienced, and when afloat one can find things going wrong remarkably quickly – so if you try it, watch out!

'Oh no, we don't use boats, they frighten the fish.' Time and again one has heard this sort of remark. How true is it? Boats don't cause panic amongst fish, as would seals or otters, but if taken too close they undoubtedly cause fish to move out of their lies, to which they will not return as long as the boat or its anchor rope remains close by. What is too close? This again may vary according to the speed and depth of the water, and whether the surface is ruffled or calm. In fast ruffled water and deep water a boat can be brought much closer to a fish without shifting him than in calm and shallow water. When fishing is at a standstill it is amusing to try experiments, taking a boat down a pool and watching to see how close you can get to fish without frightening them. There is a good deal to be learnt in this way. As a rough guide eight yards is near enough; if one approaches closer the fish will soon sheer off, and if one is standing up in the boat and casting it makes it worse.

The remedy is obvious, keep the boat at a respectable distance from the lie of the fish, at least until you have finished fishing it. In this way no harm will be done. But if you or your boatman are incapable of doing it, even in a high wind, you shouldn't be boating. And by the way, can you both swim? If not, the same applies. Every big river has its drowning victims each year, whether fishermen or otherwise. Don't risk adding to the number.

If you don't boat, you must wade. There are a few pools in these four rivers, it is true, which can be fished off the bank in any height of water, such as Broom at Delfur, the Piles Pool at Arndilly, the Long Pool at Knockando to name three on the Spey, much of the Cairnton and Inchmarlo water on the Dee, and the March Pool at Meikleour on the Tay. There are also many others which can be bank-fished occasionally, whenever the water is high. At such places thigh waders or gumboots (preferable to ordinary shoes) are all that is wanted. It is better to wear something in which you can walk into the water dryshod, if necessary.

At all normal times and places, however, if you don't boat you must be prepared to wade at least above the knee and most probably waist deep. So make sure you are equipped with a good pair of long trouser waders, with the best type of non-slip sole, felt or cleated, whichever you prefer. If you are happy without a wading staff, well and good; but if you don't know the water well, you will probably be better off with one. It will give you added confidence and may save you a ducking. You should be fully aware that except in some of the lower reaches of these rivers which are too deep, too wide, and too strong, wading is both a normal and essential part of the process of fishing. The more competent the wader, prepared to go in deep in a strong stream when necessary, and to step on freely between casts, the greater will be his success. In big pools, and in these rivers the majority of them are big, you should normally fish quickly, especially when fish are scarce. On no account pause to do two or three casts in the same place (this is an almost endemic fault in nervous waders). This leads to a deplorable waste of time. Keep moving on steadily at a rate of two or three yards between each cast and so get the water covered. Only if you locate a spot where likely takers are lying, or if you rise fish that do not take hold, should you slow up. It is much better to fish a big pool twice, fairly fast, in a given period of time than once, slowly.

Do therefore try to become a competent and sure-footed wader, who can move freely in all types of current and on all types of bottom. By doing this you will both catch more fish, and have far more fun.

CHAPTER 30

Further general considerations

Another factor common to these four rivers (except to the Tweed in spring) is that there is the chance in any of them of hooking a really big fish, say of 35lbs or over.* The possibility of such a fish should always be borne in mind. Don't fish too fine therefore, especially when there are big fish about; it you do feel the urge to use fine low-water tackle in summer, take great care and do it as a calculated risk.

Another reminder, don't forget a gaff,† preferably one with a long handle that can also be used in a dual role as a wading staff. Even if you land almost all your fish by beaching or with a landing-net, when the great day comes and you hook your fish of a lifetime (let alone a mere thirty-pounder), you will surely be glad to have your gaff with you. It may put you near to what Bromley Davenport so aptly describes in that superb book *Sport* as 'the topmost pinnacle of angling fame, the practical possession of the largest salmon ever taken with a rod', and save you from disaster 'deeper than ever plummet sounded in the depths of dejection'. The fact is that using a strong gaff is by far the best way of landing big salmon, unless you are lucky enough to have a good boatman or ghillie with you, armed with a large enough landing-net.

Before leaving the subject of tackle, it cannot be emphasized too strongly that it pays every time to use the best tackle that can possibly be obtained. Don't spare cash or trouble in getting it, and seek the advice of some experienced friend if necessary. Have nothing second-rate, nothing slipshod or unsound, and remember that the most expensive is not necessarily the best. By doing this you will always score by increasing both your fun and your catch. Take care too that your tackle is 'balanced', e.g. don't use a big fly on a fine monofilament leader suitable for a No. 8, don't use too light a rod with a heavy sinking line or

---

*There are now unfortunately few other British rivers where this chance still exists; in the Wye no doubt, and possibly in the Hampshire Avon; but where else?

†Except on the Tweed in spring or autumn where gaffs are not allowed.

vice versa, don't use a big heavy reel with a light rod – there are many such examples. Keep everything in proper proportion from your rod-butt down to your hook-point. This may mean possessing a wide variety of rods, reels, lines and other items to suit all different conditions in different places. There is no way round this if your fishing is to be extensive, but what fun it is acquiring and maintaining a treasure trove of this sort!

To return to the Spey, Dee, Tay, and Tweed, one sees other ways in which they are akin – for instance they are all east coast rivers, which have a substantial spring run, very different to what happens on the west coast. Their effective season is therefore a long one, as (except the Dee) they all produce good fishing in late summer or autumn, as well as in spring. The Spey for instance, can produce good fishing in one or other part of its length throughout its seven-and-a-half months legal season, and there is at least one beat on the Tay, Islamonth, that will fish well throughout eight months.*

These rivers also have the common feature of a fast-running streamy current, more so the Spey if less so the Tweed, together with normally clear water, all combining to produce excellent fly water, better than the more sluggish rivers further south. The waters of the Dee and Tay are the clearest. The Spey after rain suffers from peat water and the Tweed from the drainage off agricultural land; but even then their fish take the fly well enough if the colour is not too bad.

At this point readers may well have remarked that the author is biased in favour of fly-fishing. This is true, and I make no apology for it; and I never enter into argument about the merits or demerits of bait-fishing. For at least twenty years I was as keen a bait-fisher as a fly-fisher, and the number of fish I have killed on different types of bait runs a long way into four figures. But gradually I used bait less and less, and finally about fifteen years ago gave it up altogether. Why? Simply because I was tired of it, and I enjoyed fly-fishing so much more. I think it is much more difficult to catch fish consistently on a fly in all types of weather and water, but that with modern tackle and methods one can still catch all the fish one needs for good sport. Not easy perhaps, and it may take long to learn how; but was anything easy ever really worthwhile? Herein lies a large part of the fascination of fly-fishing. I say no more, and merely offer this as the

*It should be realized that the legal fishing season on most British rivers is different from the 'effective' season, i.e. that period when there is a reasonable chance of catching any number of fish. On most rivers the legal season extends over at least eight months, but nearly all their fish are caught during the best three or four months within that time. For a beat or a river to fish well during seven or eight months continuously is quite exceptional.

experience of one individual. Others may think differently, and good luck to them if they do.

If one can tie one's own flies, it adds a wealth of interest to fishing. Do learn to do this if you possibly can. Learning from an already skilled tyer is without doubt the best and quickest way. Half a dozen preliminary lessons should be enough; after that you can carry on well enough from a book. Learning entirely from a book is possible, but much longer and more laborious. Once you can tie reasonably well, an entirely new field of invention and experiment in your fishing lies open before you. You are a big loser throughout your fishing career if you miss out on this.

Another suggestion – do learn to Spey cast (both single and double Spey) if ever you get the chance. On all rivers, and particularly on large ones, this method of casting is of the greatest value. It is particularly useful for throwing a long line with less effort, for competing with most winds, and for eliminating difficulties from obstacles behind. There is only one way of learning how to do it, i.e. by having repeated lessons from an already skilled performer, and by constant practice. You may find such a tutor on the Spey, or on the Ness, but you will be lucky to find him elsewhere. Full achievement again is difficult, and slow, and necessary both right- and left-handed according to which side of a river you are fishing from. But, once gained, how great is the reward!

There is one hazard, which occurs frequently in playing fish in big rivers, and which is therefore worth mentioning – that is the danger of the line being 'drowned'. This applies to both bait and fly lines, but far more to the latter which are heavily dressed for thirty or forty yards. When there is a fast current in midriver, a strong and active hooked fish, if he is able to run out a long line through the midstream into the slack water beyond, can get the line 'buried' in the central current. He may then run further and further upstream in the slacker water on the far side while the main part of the line is held fast by the current in an ever-increasing belly. If he cannot get the line clear of the water, the fisherman can thus lose all direct touch with his fish, and be run further and further on to his backing, until the fish may be eighty or more yards upstream of the place where the backing disappears into the river. This 'drowning' is an unnerving thing to happen to anyone. The classic description of it is in Scrope's *Days and Nights of Salmon Fishing*, Chapter V, where the author gets not only 'drowned', but ignominiously 'cut' as well, i.e. broken round a rock. In the end the fish will either give way to the weight of line which he is towing against the current, and drop back fast downstream, in which case the fisherman will have to reel in at top speed to keep in touch with him and prevent him getting round snags; or else he may jump and thrash wildly, which is a severe strain on tackle and hook hold, as the fisherman with his line 'buried' can do little to relieve the pressure. Whatever happens, being 'drowned' constitutes something of a crisis which is much better avoided if at all possible. How to do this? To start with, using a long rod helps. It makes it much easier to keep the main part of the dressed line clear of the water when a fish is being played. Secondly, do not necessarily come out of the pool as soon as a fish is hooked. Most fishing books say that the first thing to do when you hook a fish is to get to the bank. In many pools in big rivers no advice could be worse. You should stay well out in the water and move downstream or even upstream with your fish as needed, keeping your rod vertically upright and lifted high if necessary. It is odds on that you will thus be able to prevent your line being 'buried', until such time as you have got your fish more securely under control; and only then should you venture back towards the shore. Or else, if there is a high bank behind you it may pay you when you hook a fish to come ashore at once, as the books tell you, and play the fish off a high vantage point – anything to keep the belly of the line clear of a strong central current. Also it is far more difficult for a fish to 'drown' your line if you keep well upstream of him instead of vice versa. You may in any case have to decide and move quickly; and any decision, even if the wrong one, is likely to be better than none at all when the fish will probably have the laugh of you.

If you are boat-fishing, avoiding being 'drowned', though this can still happen, becomes easier. The remedy is to take the boat out into the river, if you have a willing and able boatman, and follow the fish as closely as may be necessary, even to the far side of the stream. What is more, intelligent anticipation of the 'drowning' risk can do much to help. Certain pools, owing to their conformation, are notorious for line-drowning. Anyone who has fished the Spey pool known as 'Creichie' from the Rothes side will know what I mean. In the many years when we fished it this small pool was a first-class taking place, but a horrible one for being 'drowned'. To come ashore as soon as a fish was hooked led to almost certain disaster. But if one stayed well out and waded upstream, keeping level with or above one's fish, one could usually keep the line clear, and all would go well. Knowing beforehand what a hooked fish was likely to do was a great help there, as in many other similar places.

Lastly, if in spite of all your efforts to avoid it you are badly 'drowned' (it happens to all of us not infrequently), don't despair. Keep calm and don't pull hard. If your tackle is sound you should be all right. Watch out for the moment when the fish turns downstream, you will feel the pull on the line suddenly ease, then reel in your fastest, walking downstream at the same time – this is in the effort to keep in as close contact with the fish as possible, and so avoid getting snagged. You may not succeed in keeping the line taut, it is very difficult to do so once the fish has got a start on you, but the nearer you can get to doing it the better. He will be much tired by his recent efforts, and you will probably be lucky and land him in spite of all.

If you want to add an extra element of excitement to your fishing in a big river, once you get down to using a floating line and small flies, and to give yourself the chance of more fish, you can try using a dropper. Now these are a double-edged weapon, and should be treated with caution. They certainly give added fun, together with scope for experiment in the simultaneous use of different patterns and sizes of fly. One dropper is enough, but if tied in about four feet up the leader from the tail fly, this pair of flies fished together ought to cover the water more thoroughly and allow the angler to fish more quickly. In theory at any rate droppers should increase the bag. If around 30 per cent of the fish landed are hooked on the dropper (a normal proportion), is not this an indication that the two flies have caught a bigger total than one fly only would have? This question could no doubt lead to a good deal of dispute; perhaps someone will put it to a computer? Although you will surely have disasters using a dropper, which would probably have been avoided with one fly only, you may think that a lot of extra interest, and perhaps fish, makes up for these, and so decide to try one? The choice is yours.

If you do decide in favour, you may care to bear some of the following points in mind. The main drawback of droppers is their horrible likelihood to cause tangles, together with much time lost, because tangles *must* be undone at once. In big rivers, as already made clear, a long line is needed, and dropper tangles occur more easily with this than with a short one. Therefore extra care is necessary in casting. Some fishermen use two droppers, making three flies in all. This may be all right on a short line in small rivers, or in lochs; but in big rivers with a long line the resulting tangles are too formidable. One dropper is enough. It is also as well to use a single-hooked fly as a dropper, whatever you use on the tail, again for the avoidance of time-wasting tangles. A snecked round bend is probably the best type of single hook.

Great care must also be taken about the use of a sound knot for the attachment of the short dropper leader to the main cast. There are several good knots for this,* so do learn one thoroughly, otherwise you will be sorry; and don't on any account use the spare end of a blood knot! Though it looks good,

---

The Angler's Knots in Gut and Nylon by Stanley Barnes is a good reference book.

for salmon it is just not strong enough.

The main danger in the use of droppers is that the disengaged fly becomes snagged in some solid obstruction while a fish is being played. You will be very lucky to land your fish if this happens. Therefore don't use a dropper anywhere where there are numerous snags, such as rocks, sunken branches, weeds, and so on. A less obvious hazard with droppers is fish lying thick in a pool. There is a real danger that the disengaged fly can be taken by a second fish or more likely may foul-hook him. In either case you can say good-bye, probably to both fish and your flies as well.* Even a sea trout intruder can cause a break. So forego your dropper when there is a big stock of fish. Also, while on the subject of foul-hooking, it has already been mentioned that a four-foot interval is about the right distance between the two flies. Much closer than this, and there is a fair risk that a fish which rises at the dropper, but turns away at the last moment without taking it, will be foul-hooked by the tail fly. You will then probably lose the best part of a good morning's fishing in playing him. Too wide apart, and there is an increased risk of the tail fly fouling something when a fish is hooked on the dropper. So keep the interval between flies at somewhere close to four feet.

One last precaution with droppers: when you have either landed or lost a fish, be sure to examine *both* flies for damage to hook or dressing, not just the fly on which the fish was hooked – a small point but an important one, as both flies have been at risk while the fish was being played.

A question of a different sort has been put to me from time to time, and that is how to obtain fishing on the Spey, Dee, Tay, or Tweed, or on other rivers for that matter, in these days when it is so much sought after. I am afraid there is no short answer to this, assuming that you are not lucky enough to be an owner or a long-term tenant of fishing. If you are a relation or friend of an owner it goes without saying that welcome invitations may come your way. If they do, you will hardly need advice to be meticulous in your observation of any directions or 'orders of the day' given you by your host. They should be cheerfully obeyed to the last iota, whether you like them or not. Initiative does not always make a good dog, and obedience is a better one.

If no welcome invitations come your way, you will have to rent fishing. This may consist of a beat for several rods, either for the whole season, which you are

*It is true that two fish have more than once been recorded before now as being landed, together; but only grilse or small salmon, and only on small rivers or lochs.

unlikely to get nowadays, or else for a shorter period such as a fortnight or a week. You can then have friends to fish it with you, who either pay their share of rent and expenses, or else come as your guests and pay nothing. It is up to you and them to make some suitable arrangement. Alternatively you can sometimes rent a single rod on a beat, in which case you will no doubt have to share it with other unknown fishermen, or perhaps two or more rods in which case you can be sure of having at least one or two friends with you. Rent should be paid well in advance, which is only fair, and you may reasonably expect to get a first refusal again in a following season. In any case when renting a fishing you should make sure that you know exactly what you are in for; for instance, is your beat on the right part of the river for the time of year? (A list of previous catches for the period you are renting should make this clear, or else enquiries from well-informed friends.) Has your beat got both banks? and if not what are the arrangements with the opposite bank? Have you got sole fishing rights? or is anyone else entitled to fish, either for salmon or trout? What about ghillies or boatmen, and who pays their wages? How many rods are you entitled to fish? (it usually pays to fish one less rod than the number quoted). Do the fish you catch belong to you? (they usually do, but not invariably). Is the fishing 'fly only'? and if so, does the opposite bank observe this rule? and how many rods do they fish? Are there any time limits to your fishing? or a limit on the number of fish you may kill? All these are the sort of queries which you are entitled to put, and you would be wise to know the answers before you rent a fishing having agreed to the lease, and to give them full consideration.

If you can rent a beat direct from the owner or through his factor, this is much the most satisfactory method. Failing this you will have to apply to one of the main sporting agencies in London, Edinburgh, or elsewhere, who specialize in such leases. Such an agency, however well-intentioned, will be unlikely to give you as close attention as would a private factor, owing to the simple fact that it probably handles scores of different leases all over the country, also it is in less close touch with what is actually taking place on the river.

All good leased fishings are nowadays very tightly held from year to year, and you may have to be content with being on a waiting list for several seasons, or with fishing a beat outside of its best time, pending a vacancy at a better period. You may have to be very patient; it is anything but easy in present times to get good fishing, the demand far exceeds the supply. Once you are the tenant of a good beat, you would consequently be unwise to give it up in a hurry after a bad season, or even two or three of them, unless you have a better alternative already up you sleeve. Remember that even the best fishings have bad patches from time to time; make sure therefore that something permanent has gone really wrong before you throw in your hand.

As a last resort, if you can get nothing better, you can fall back on hotel or association water, but even then you may have to be on a waiting list. Most hotel waters are grossly over-rodded, which is unpleasant for their own fishermen and worse for an opposite bank.

As to rents, in present days these seem to escalate alarmingly, but how can it be expected otherwise, with the value of money now falling every year? Unlike in pre-war times, most fishermen now are forced to sell much of their catch, and salmon also appreciate in value, so this helps to some extent towards rent and expenses. What is remarkable is that high rents are now paid for most indifferent fishings as well as for good ones. It seems that the demand for fishing is so great that someone is always unwise enough to pay first and complain later. There is really no excuse for this, as records of previous catches should always be available for prospective tenants who ask for them. Such records, if covering a period of several years past, should reveal all likely prospects; and if none are available, or if the water is said to have been 'very lightly fished', or something of that sort, with consequent low bags, you should beware.

In this modern age it is safe to say that all the good fishings in Scotland are well known, and when leased are bound to command a high rent. You will not, sad to say, discover any unknown anglers' paradise in this country, undeveloped, full of fish, and let at a low rent. So be prepared to put your hand in your pocket for a good and reliable if well-known beat. As has often been said it is the best fishing which in the end is the least expensive, and produces the best value for money. This dictum is as sound now as it was fifty years ago.

This chapter ends with a few general remarks on fishing, both in big rivers and in smaller ones, which perhaps may be helpful.

Inexperienced fishermen often imagine that more expert performers have some deadly fly or secret lure that enables them to come in with two or three fish, caught as if by magic, on days when weather and water conditions appear to make fishing hopeless, and when their own efforts are a failure. The fact that the expert may be unable to tell them, apart from certain facts of time and place and lure used, exactly how he induced the fish to take only adds fuel to the fire, and makes them think that something is being hidden from them. So it is, but not in the way they suppose. On most beats there are one or two outstanding fishermen, who consistently catch fish under all conditions, and can frequently do it when most others can't. What is the secret?

Apart from outstanding technical skill and the use of appropriate tackle, there are three main qualifications in fishing which lead to conspicuous success. The first is certainly keenness – the overwhelming determination to catch fish in spite of all difficulties, and the will to persevere ('patience' is the wrong word here, 'persistence' is a much better one), as long as there is even a remote chance. The second qualification is experience – there is no more royal road to success in fishing than in any other pursuit. We all have to learn the long hard way, and in this lies much of fishing's fascination. Without doubt knowledge of the salmon's habits and behaviour under all different conditions, and of how to frame one's approach towards catching him, and his likely reaction in as many different circumstances as possible, are of the greatest value. It follows that the man who has caught salmon by thousands stands at high vantage over the man of hundreds, and he in turn over the man of scores (until such time as some unavoidable outside factor such as old age or physical disability may intervene). Though it doesn't infallibly work out this way, it does so too often to be worth arguing about. The beginner should therefore lose no chances of fishing every different type of river that he can, in as many different areas as possible. He may have one favourite beat or one favourite river, but outside experience is never to be despised – he should also lose no chance of watching or talking with fishermen more expert than himself.

Hand in hand with the gain of such widespread experience goes that of local experience of the water being fished at the time. For instance—Where are the likeliest taking places? Which pools fish best in any given height of water, or time of year? Where if anywhere can fish be caught in a rising water? Where are any bad snags? Answers to such queries should be firmly implanted in the mind to be remembered for another time. It is hard to exaggerate their importance; and one never stops learning, as rivers are constantly changing after every big flood. A fishing diary, well kept, is a great help towards recalling important impressions and facts, besides being a constant joy to the memory. Do keep one.

Another way in which experience tells is that beginners often do not realize how good the fishing is. Put it this way; if you examine details of a good fisherman's catch over a long period, it quickly becomes obvious that the majority of his fish are caught on certain good fishing days when there are plenty of fish and they take well. These days may be comparatively few in number, though they produce a lot of fish. In contrast there will probably be many blank days, or days of one or two fish only. But the good fisherman realizes well when he is 'in', and on such days he fishes hard and perhaps kills ten or twelve fish. He makes hay, in fact, while the sun shines and knows how important it is to do so. The inexperienced man on the other hand, when he is lucky enough to be fishing on a really good day, kills perhaps two or three fish with some additional losses, and then eases off, thinking he has done wonders. It would perhaps be unkind to tell him that actually he has done badly, and on such a day he ought to have taken three times as many fish. In fact he has failed to realize how good the fishing has been.

My final suggested qualification is perhaps the most telling of all, however, and it is best described as 'meticulous attention to detail'. Has not genius been described as 'an infinite capacity for taking pains'? So it is with fishing. When all other demands have been met, it is the man who takes most trouble over details who will score. For instance: Are his hooks needle-sharp? Is his nylon mono-filament strong enough and without wind knots? Are his knots sound? Is his backing long and strong enough? and is he sure it will run out to its full extent without a jam? Are the working parts of his reel well oiled? Is his gaff-point sharp, and his landing-net sound? Is his reel really firmly fixed to his rod? Has he taped his rod-joints, or otherwise made certain that they will not work loose and perhaps break while he is fishing? Has he got a spare rod immediately available if the one he is using breaks? (very awkward if this happens on a really good fishing day, with no other rod within easy reach). Are his waders leak-proof? and their soles so far as possible slip-proof? Did he examine his fly and retie it to his leader after a fish has been landed or lost? Hopefully always 'Yes!'

These are just a few of the hundred and one details about tackle to which an experienced fisherman will automatically attend. Equally, when he is actually fishing, no detail of his performance will be too much trouble. However difficult the wind his casting will be good, he will watch out for wind knots, he will fish particularly carefully over known good taking places, and quickly over the un-likely ones, watching all the time for indications of what the fish are doing. Are there new fish coming into the pool? Is there a good stock of fish present, or only a meagre one, or none at all? Would another pool be a better bet? Is the water steady, or falling, or rising? Is his fly or bait fishing properly and at the right depth and speed? Have any fish moved to him or touched him without being hooked? This list is endless, but correct answers to these questions are crucial.

Even though individually no one of such considerations may be of vital account, collectively their importance is overwhelming.

CHAPTER 31

Spey fishing

To a fisherman few excitements are comparable to that of arriving by train at a station such as Aviemore, or Carrbridge, and stepping out into the clear invigorating air of Speyside, or of arriving by car after a long drive north past the Cairngorms and down the Spey, with the prospect of fishing ahead. The first sight of the Spey itself speeding on its downstream course (and how large and powerful it seems!), the wonderful scent of the firs, the broom, and the heather, with Ben Rinnes, the Cromdale Hills, or possibly the distant Cairngorms in the background, all combine to produce a spirit of delightful and well-nigh intoxicating anticipation. If it is true that in fishing, as in other things, anticipation often exceeds fulfilment, this is not always the case, and how memorable are the occasions when the reverse happens!

Even if during these past twelve or thirteen years, as already pointed out, the wonderful Spey spring fishing has gone sadly downhill, so that anticipation may have become blunted, nevertheless hope springs eternal; and are there not memories of great triumphs in the past to bear one up? And has not the spring of 1978 performed a volte-face and proved the best for fifteen years? And, apart from the spring, has not the summer fishing been consistently good throughout past seasons, and even improved? Indeed there is still good hope for the future.

From 1948 to 1968 the author was lucky enough to have a lease of the Rothes beat throughout the season, thanks to the kindness of the late Countess of Seafield and the late Sir Brian Mountain. Thanks too to the unfailing hospitality of Major Sir David Wills, I have been lucky enough to have fished the lovely Knockando water every season since long past. In fact, thanks also to many other kind friends, I have fished at one time or another on every Spey beat from Tulchan to the tidal water near Spey Bay, and can only say that I have profoundly appreciated every minute of it. I still fish the Spey for a month or more every season, and live in hopes of long continuing to do so.

Spring fishing was undoubtedly at its best in the 1950s, but the summer fishing was also good then. Still more fish are caught nowadays in the summer, but the river is fished harder by many more rods than there used to be, which partly accounts for it. Our best season at Rothes in the 1950s we caught over 600 fish, fishing three rods as a rule, though sometimes four. This was a good total, seeing that the majority of these fish were caught before mid-June, and three-quarters of them on fly, while Rothes was considered a second-rate Spey beat at that time, and had only one bank. The largest fish I myself saw caught at Rothes during those twenty-one years weighed 38 lb and it was caught on May 14th 1955 in the Long Pool by the Earl of Stair. He landed it in under five minutes! There was snow all over the banks that day. Three fish of over 40 lb were caught by my friends during my lease – they weighed 43½ lb, 41 lb, and 40 lb. We also had two or three thirty-pounders most years. For the eleven years 1950–60 I see from my record book that we averaged 434 fish per season at Rothes. The whole Spey was fishing well then, with far more springers than at present, and our bags were in no way comparable to those on first-class beats such as Orton, Delfur, Wester Elchies, Carron and Laggan, Knockando, Ballindalloch, or Tulchan. There were about fifteen spring fish in the water then for every one during these late years (until 1978).

Certain memories of those days remain firmly planted in my mind. For example, otters were then far more in evidence than now. One often saw them when fishing, even in broad daylight. One summer at Delfur there had been a litter of them somewhere near the Haddie pools, and the young cubs with their parents used to play in the tail of the Big Haddie in the evenings, a fascinating sight. Occasionally in the spring one came across a fresh salmon of perhaps 10 lb or 12 lb lying dead on the bank, apparently unharmed except for a small piece of flesh eaten out of the back of its neck. This was always attributed to otters. How did they catch such fish in such a large river? They always seemed to choose the fresh salmon, and scorned the kelts. The ghillies often took such fish home to eat, and naturally found them perfectly good.

Another memory of otters was amusing. We were seated at the Long Pool hut one evening, looking across the river and watching a very expert Spey caster fishing down the opposite bank. He was wading some way out, and had already caught two salmon which he had laid out on the bank behind him. As we watched, an otter ran out from among the trees on the far side, took no notice of the fisherman who was facing towards midriver, seized one of his fish, and started to drag it away. The fisherman so far was quite unaware of what was happening, but when we shouted and pointed he turned round, left the water, and ran after the otter, who dropped his booty and made off. One wonders how our friend would have accounted for the disappearance of his fish had we not been there.

Another day I was fishing the Blue Stone at Aikenway, when I saw a head appear out of the water in midstream, about eighty yards below. I paid little attention, assuming it was that of an otter. Soon the head disappeared under the surface, only to reappear shortly at half the distance, and then submerge again. Ten seconds later a fully grown seal did a porpoise jump clear of the water, immediately opposite me – an amazing sight, as this was about fourteen miles upstream from the mouth of the river. This seal evidently penetrated much further upstream than this. He was later seen at Carron, and an unidentified 'monster' was also reported at Ballindalloch at the same time – little doubt of what it was.

Sea Eagle

A further notable occurrence was when my ghillie James Ross and myself saw a white-tailed sea eagle at Rothes. This enormous bird appeared from downstream and flew up the river on two consecutive days at a height of about 130 feet, mobbed by a swarm of gulls and other birds. He came up as far as the tail of the Long Pool, 150 yards below us, and on the second occasion stooped on a fish in the shallow water there. There was some tremendous splashing, but whether he caught his prey or not was not clear. Local bird experts suggested later that we had seen an osprey, but this bird was twice the size of any osprey, of which I have seen a number, and he did not make that semi back-somersault which ospreys make when about to stoop. He just put up his wings and dropped. I believe that an attempt was being made at that time to re-establish sea eagles on an island off the Shetlands. This one may have strayed from there, or else arrived from Norway; but he was never reported again.

The biggest fish which so far as I know I ever myself hooked in the Spey was in the tail of the Two Stones at Delfur, one May. This fish took a No. 6 double-hooked tail fly (I was using two flies), and he played deep and strong for some time, though without any fireworks. Eventually we saw the length of his back above the surface, and it took one's breath away. He was huge. I played him from the left bank for about three-quarters of an hour, when he dropped down the rapids into the next pool below, called Beaufort. All went well, and after an hour he was getting tired and was in the tail of Beaufort nearly half a mile below where I had hooked him. Several times he came to the surface and thrashed, though he never jumped out. At last he came almost to within gaffing range, and Allan my ghillie saw him clearly in the water and let out an appropriate expletive. Then he made one last run across the pool and was coming back tamely, so we counted our chickens as hatched. All at once while he was still in midriver there was a sudden nasty pluck, and the loose line came flying back to me with the gut broken at the top of the cast. Simultaneously a small fish of about 10 lb made two unbalanced jumps in midstream, while I stood on the bank helplessly. It did not take long to realize what had happened; as my big fellow was easing back across the pool, this second small fish had either taken or been foul-hooked by the dropper, and for a second or two both fish had been tied together after my cast had broken. So I lost two fish and two flies, when if I had not been using a dropper the chances of landing the big one were by that stage most promising. I put this big fish at over 40 lb; Allan later said it was over 50 lb, but I hope this was going too far.

There were more big fish in the Spey then than there are now. My great friend Colonel J. P. Moreton hooked an enormous one in Pol Arder on the

Lower Pitchroy beat in September 1954. He played it for an hour on a No. 6 fly and fine gut before the almost inevitable disaster happened, and it broke him. J.P.M. has caught at least six forty-pounders during his fishing career, so knows well what a big fish looks like; but this was by far the biggest he had ever seen. It had been seen jumping previously, and he and his lady companion saw it clearly while he was playing it, and several times. Once it swam round into shallow water quite close to them. They estimated its weight at nothing less than 60 lb, even allowing for it being red and weighing light, and it could have been heavier. What a tragedy!

There are many other such stories of big fish being hooked and lost in the Spey, often after being played for hours. It was always odds on losing such fish, if you hooked one, through one sort of mishap or another. Often one's tackle was just not strong enough to handle them, and the main difficulty was always to get them within gaffing range. Even when apparently played out, they just would not come in, and this applied to the mere thirty-pounders as well as the bigger ones. The strength of the Spey current is a great help to hooked fish, also the many boulders and snags in the rapids.

To cut short fishing stories and return to Spey fishing tactics, if you intend to fish in early spring, say from the opening on February 11th to the end of March, you should fish somewhere in the lower reaches, from Delfur down. The Spey is not an early river like the Dee or the Tweed. Occasionally after a warm and wet winter fish will be found in numbers higher up at the opening, but not often. As a general rule, unless you are content with only odd fish, early spring should see you low down the river. At this time of year both weather and water are certain to be cold, almost certainly colder than you anticipate, so be clad accordingly. Mittens are essential, also something over your ears. If you are wading, you must have long trouser waders, with thick stockings or socks underneath, but not so tight as to check your circulation which makes the cold worse. Even if you are fishing from a boat or off the bank, trouser waders are much the best protection against cold and wet (coupled with a short waterproof coat), even if they are tiresome for walking.

In the early part of the season bait-fishing is the most popular method, and it is without doubt easiest to catch fish this way. A casting rod of eight to nine feet, of split cane, fibreglass, or now carbon graphite, and one of the best types of modern casting reel, well oiled, are all that is needed. Wooden devon minnows, in varying sizes from two-and-a-quarter inches to three-and-a-half inches, are probably the best baits, with nylon monofilament trace and line of a minimum twelve pounds breaking strain, preferably stronger, and ball-bearings swivels.

With a light, wooden minnow you should seldom get snagged; nevertheless it will be a saving of time and baits if you carry with you one of the many effcient types of 'otter' or bait releaser. There is little to choose between the best types of these. Don't try to fish too deep. It is quite unnecessary to 'scrape the bottom'. When I started spinning years ago I was told that if I didn't lose two or three minnows in the bottom every day I wasn't fishing properly. This is nonsense, as anyone can prove for himself. What is more important in cold water is to fish slowly, with your bait still spinning freely.

If you are going to fish fly, a much more difficult task, you must above all appreciate that there is a world of difference between fishing in cold water in early spring, with a large fly fished slow and deep on a sunk line, and fishing in May or thereafter in warm water with a floating line and a small fly. The two methods are poles apart. Fishing early in the season you need a long rod,* if only to compete with the wind, and to cast as far as possible with a heavy line and heavy fly. I would suggest a rod of at least fifteen feet, or longer, and a fast sinking line. If the water is colder than about 44°F you will also find it an advantage to have a weighted body to your fly, which should preferably be a hair-winged tube fly type.† The length of your fly should not be vast, anything between two and three inches is about right, depending on the colour and temperature of the water. As to colours, it does not seem to make a great difference. Black, yellow, and orange, or a mixture of them, are as good as any. There is nothing better than jet black in clear water. Your treble hooks, needless to say, should be sharp as well as strong, and a sliver of carborundum stone in your pocket is useful for keeping them so. See that they are in proportion to the size of your fly – too big is clumsy, and too small will lose you fish. Your leader of nylon monofilament should be of not less than fourteen pounds breaking strain, preferably stronger to face up to general wear and tear.

Cast as long a line as you comfortably can, about 45° across and down is normally the best angle. Don't forget that a fish's reactions in cold water are apt to be slow, therefore fish your fly round slow and deep to give a fish plenty of time to register on it.

If you catch the bottom more than once, put on a lighter line or lighter fly. Above all, when the cast is fished out, and the line has straightened below you, remember to pull in three or four yards in a deliberate draw, before you clear the

*For remarks on length of rod see page 151.
†Such flies are difficult to cast well, and good timing in the cast is all-important. But they do hook and hold well, and the long rod and heavy line are a help in casting them.

line from the water to cast again. In cold water this is the deadliest taking moment, when a fish that has followed the fly round sees it change direction and move upstream in an apparent effort to escape from him.

If the pool is a wide one, and the fish are lying far out, you may be forced to use a boat to cover them – indeed this may be a welcome alternative to wading in sub-arctic conditions. A long line now becomes less essential, though it is still an advantage if it enables you to cover more fish. It also, as always, fishes slower and deeper.

The first indication you will have that a fish has taken will be a draw on the line. All that you have to do to hook him is to draw back steadily and deliberately, preferably with the rod sideways. The only way you are likely to miss him is by making a quick snatch, after the manner of a trout fisher. On no account allow yourself to do this. Keep quite cool and don't be excited.

You will always get a certain number of 'plucks' from fish that don't take hold, this seems to be unavoidable; but their number is lessened if you use the right tackle, and fish well. In early spring most of these plucks almost certainly come from kelts in any case, which are no loss; but if you have good reason to think that fresh fish are plucking, try a smaller fly, or fish the fly differently, either faster or slower.

Once your fish is hooked you can pull hard at him with strong tackle. Don't let him drown your line if you can possibly help it, and get him ashore as quickly as you reasonably can. Half a minute to the pound is not too short a time to aim at for this. In the cold water of early spring hooked fish are usually far less active than later on, and if fresh run they are often tired after their upstream journey. So don't waste any time with them, as the good taking time may not last long.

Spring on Speyside comes late,* in fact it is not till the second half of May that one can reasonably count on warm weather; and the change is apt to arrive suddenly, as it does in continental climates. In early May the water temperature is normally still under 45°F, and the usual cold snap early in May, known locally as the 'gab o' May', often brings frost and snow. It follows that the heavy tackle of early spring can often be used until well into this month, with weight of line and fly or bait modified as needed to suit lower water if the level drops. By May too the whole river should be as well stocked with spring fish as it is ever going to be, except that in the lower reaches from Orton down most of the fresh fish by now will be running straight through without stopping.

Once the water temperature rises to around 50°F or over, your tackle and

*Snow has been recorded in July on Speyside before now.

your method of fishing should change. Your rod length can drop to fourteen feet or even thirteen feet in very low water, but you still want to throw a long line, and you still want to have maximum control over the way your line and fly fish round. Your line should now be a floating or semi-floating one, so that your fly will fish close to the surface. The fly itself should be smaller in size, though unless you are fishing entirely for grilse, size 7 is quite small enough. Occasionally it pays to try a big fly up to two inches long or more, particularly in the half-light or in strong streams. Pattern of fly seems to make little difference, as long as the dressing is sparse; and soft black hair seems as good an ingredient in the dressing as anything. Hair-winged flies in general seem to be more attractive to salmon than the older feather-winged flies. As to hooks, I personally prefer double hooks or treble hooks rather than ordinary single hooks, as they seem to take a better hold. I definitely dislike the long-shanked fine wire low water single hooks, originally associated with greased-line fishing. Though I have caught plenty of fish on these, I have also lost on them what I think is far too many. If I use singles, I prefer round bend snecked hooks, as long as they are strong enough. These too seem to hook and hold well, and they are useful for droppers.

Your leader for floating line fishing should, as always, be of the best quality nylon monofilament, down to ten pounds breaking strain for summer conditions; it is never safe to go lighter, and twelve pounds is often better. As already pointed out, you may always have the chance of hooking a big fish. Your line and backing should as usual extend to at least 130 yards.

This tackle should be suitable till pretty well the end of the season, except that during the first day or two after a spate you may fish rather heavier and bigger. Late on, in September, nearly all the fish are red and prefer small flies, if they will take at all. The only chance of fresh ones is in the lowest part of the river.

Grilse start to arrive in numbers soon after the beginning of July, with a few pioneers in June. They can be caught in any part of the river, wherever they choose to lie, including right up the tributaries, but they are apt to be choosy takers. Ideally one should fish for them with light tackle and very small flies. But they often lie side by side with big salmon, which also like small flies then – and some of the biggest salmon runs are now in July and August. On balance it is better to use tackle that can handle sizeable fish at the risk of hooking fewer grilse, rather than the other way round.

Summer fishing on the Spey is much the same as on any other big river. There is no backdoor way to quick success. Even in low water it still pays to throw a long line in most places, and the neck and tail of the pool is apt to be the best place. On big Spey pools it is best to fish quickly, that is making two or three good steps between each cast, and only to slow up where the chances are more than ordinarily good. There may be a lot of water to cover, and not too much time in which to do it, so keep moving on.

Don't be afraid if, when you hook a fish, he runs you out a long way away on to your backing. If your tackle is sound and you have plenty of backing you should not lose him. Summer fish in a big river often go like scalded cats, and you cannot hold them. My first Spey ghillie, Willie Craik, used to say about playing fish, 'When *he* pulls, you let him run. But when he stops pulling, then *you* pull.' It was good advice. Playing a fish with the correct and varying amount of pressure is like having good 'hands' with a horse. If you see a hooked fish persistently kicking and splashing, it is likely he is being badly handled. Above all do try to stop your line being drowned, which is not always easy.

One last piece of advice on Spey summer fishing; when the weather gets bright and hot it pays, as in other places, to fish early and late. On the Aberlour free water, the enthusiasts are often catching fish at 4 a.m. – not that I am recommending so desperate an hour, but from 6.30 a.m. to midday is the best time, and again in the evening, if it is not too hot. The afternoon is better avoided, as it gives a much poorer chance.

I have said little about bait-fishing at this time of year. Well, you can catch fish readily on light bait tackle and on small or medium baits; but it seems a pity to use bait on such good fly water and at a time when fish take the fly well, and I prefer to leave it at that.

The Spey closes on September 30th, and during that month fresh fish are now only to be found in the lowest part of the river near Fochabers. It cannot therefore now be classed as a true autumn river, unlike the Tay, let alone the Tweed. Nor is there any need to consider a change of tackle or fishing methods during September, to cater for a back-end run at the end of the season. Ninety-nine per cent of the fish caught then have been in the river for a considerable time.

One only wishes that the autumn run of Victorian and Edwardian days (as well as the spring run) was still with us. Will it ever recur? Time alone will tell.

CHAPTER 32

Dee fishing

Much of what has already been said about Spey fishing in the previous chapters also applies to Dee fishing, particularly in the lower Dee, which is closer to the Spey in size. All the same, as already pointed out, there is considerable differnce in the character of these two rivers and the habits of their fish, which is surprising in view of their comparative proximity.

To recapitulate, the Dee has always been an earlier river than the Spey, both in start and finish. By February 1st its lower reaches can be well stocked with fresh fish, even to above Banchory, twenty miles upriver. It is virtually a spring river only, and few fish enter it after May, those attempting to do so, whether salmon or grilse, being hard hit by the nets (compare the Spey and the Tay, where the biggest runs are now in late summer). Its water is normally very clear, with peat stain only after spates, and then in no great amount. It has a clean gravel or rock bottom, and there is little or no pollution. Its current is less strong than the Spey's, but everywhere adequate from the fishing point of view, and it goes to form ideal fly water. The river as a whole is considerably smaller than the Spey, and almost all of it can be well covered by bank-fishing or by wading. Boats are only occasionally used, on the lowest beats. The top part of the river above Ballater is a stream of quite moderate size, especially in summer when the water is low; and it cannot fairly be classed as a 'big' river there, even though it often holds a lot of fish.

The average size of Dee fish is not large, 8–9 lb. Twenty-pounders and over are scarce, though there is always the chance of one.* Even thirty- and forty-pounders still occur occasionally; but the Dee could hardly be classed as a 'big fish river', and is less so than the Spey, Tay, or Tweed. On the other hand it holds a better stock of spring fish than any of them.

The beauty of Deeside surroundings has already been fully described; upper Deeside in particular, from Cambus o'May upstream, provides unforgettable scenery as one looks westward towards Lochnagar or the Cairngorms. Ballater is

*Fish of 20 lb, or over are in fact around 4 per cent of the total catch.

750 feet above sea level, and Braemar 1100 feet, so whoever is fishing in that neighbourhood has all the advantages of a fresh and invigorating hill climate, with its pure sparkling atmosphere.

For early spring fishing in the Dee, during the first six weeks of the season from February 1st, the best area is the lowest part of the river, preferably below Banchory. While the water remains cold, this is the part of the river which the fish prefer, and it can be well stocked even before the fishing season starts. Further upriver, early on, is chancy – there may be some fish, or there may not, depending on how open a winter it has been. The water in February and March is invariably cold, and seldom above 42°F in temperature. How can it be otherwise, coming as it does from the snow-covered hills of the headwaters, and with additional low-ground frost almost every night? Sometimes, when the frost is keen, the river will be full of the unpleasant substance known as 'grue', a kind of soft floating ice. If thick, this will put an almost complete stop to all fishing for the time being; though it usually clears off enough at some period of the day to make fishing possible, if only for a short time.

All the usual warm clothes, together with mittens, are an absolute necessity here as anywhere else at this time of year, and long trouser waders are best, not only for wading but also on the bank as a protection against cold and wet. See also that there is a good wind- and weatherproof hut on the riverside for your shelter, equipped with an efficient stove to warm it. That you will often be thankful for it is surely an understatement.

In early spring most Dee fishermen use bait rather than fly, and continue to do so till mid-April. Light wooden minnows are the present most popular lure, used on one of the many efficient light bait-casting outfits. That this is an easy and killing method of fishing, no one would deny . . . but it seems a pity that fly is not used more often on such lovely fly water. One famous beat at any rate uses fly only from the start of the season, and does well enough. If you do decide to use fly rather than bait at this time of year, your tackle and methods should be those recommended for the Spey (see Chapter 31), except that on the Dee you are less likely to be boating.

After mid-April however it is an understanding on the Dee that fly only shall be used for the rest of the season, and most beats follow this good rule. By this time in the clear water and rather shallow pools of the Dee, with the water becoming warmer, salmon begin to take notice of smaller flies down to size 6 or less, which would have failed to interest them earlier; and this tendency becomes more marked as the season progresses. Although fishing with a floating line and small fly is the easiest form of fly-fishing, it is nevertheless a most absorbing one, and it provides the added attraction that the fisherman almost always should see the rise of the fish to his fly. Incidentally, if you see a fish rise at your fly, and he does not touch it, which can often happen, do not at once cast over him again. Give him a few moments' grace to return to his lie, as he may have followed your fly for some distance, unbeknown to you, before rising at it. So restrain yourself; lady fishers, I have noticed, have great difficulty in doing this! So have men for that matter, and if you must cast again at once, shorten your line by about four yards and only after two or three casts let it extend to its original length. If the fish still will not take, and won't rise again, don't go on badgering him but leave him quiet, having made an exact note of where you rose him and where you were standing. Carry on fishing somewhere else, then after about half an hour or longer come back and try him again. You will often get him like this. One supposes he may have been left in the state of mind of an investor who has missed buying a good share on the Stock Exchange when its price was low; and who swears that if it ever falls to that level again he will wade right in. It does and he does, and similarly the salmon does; thus the fisherman scores.

By the time the season reaches mid-April or May your thoughts nowadays should turn to fishing further up the river, somewhere above Banchory and even up to Ballater. Your tackle and fishing tactics should be the normal ones for floating line fishing in the late spring – a rod of thirteen or fourteen feet if of fibreglass or split cane, or of fourteen or fifteen feet if of carbon graphite, is about right. Your leader can be of ten to twelve pounds breaking strain and your flies between sizes 4 and 8. Appropriate tackle for this sort of fishing has already been described as for the Spey in Chapter 31 so there is no need to say more here.

As the season advances towards the end of May and into June, you may do better above Ballater. Up here, in summer conditions and as the water drops, you will probably have to adopt 'small river' tactics – your tackle should be light, your flies small, sizes 6 to 9, and your nylon leader of nine or ten pounds breaking strain and no more. As to your rod, twelve foot has become the standard length for floating line fishing, as popularized by Mr Wood of Cairnton fifty years ago. It is time this precedent was set aside, because any length of rod can be effectively used with a floating line, and what should govern this length is mainly the size of the river and to a lesser extent the size of fly to be used, and the strength of any adverse wind. Please note again that a modern carbon graphite rod of fourteen feet is lighter than a split cane of twelve feet. I would myself prefer to use such a carbon rod for this sort of fishing, because it throws a better line, gives more control of fly and line in the water, and is lighter than a shorter cane rod. With a rod of this type you can also fish a fly down to almost sea trout size, if you keep the rod well up when a fish is hooked and play him lightly off the top joint. But I would be very happy also with a light 14-foot or 13-foot spliced split cane.

One advantage in fishing a smaller type of river is that there is much less chance of a hooked fish being able to drown the line, so there is in turn less danger in the use of lighter tackle. Indeed it has often been noticed that under similar and normal conditions the Dee will fish a fly one or two sizes smaller, with correspondingly lighter nylon, than will the Spey or the Tay.

Regarding waders, it will be found that as usual long trouser waders in most places are an advantage. Deep wading in fact is seldom necessary, but there are holes here and there, and it is more comfortable to feel that one has plenty of free-board. Once you know your beat well you may find certain places where thigh waders are definitely long enough, but short of that to have trouser waders is a wise precaution.

In the small pools of the upper Dee you will need to fish delicately and lightly, closer akin to the manner of a sea trout fisherman. You will perhaps move a shorter distance between casts, as the fish in these little pools may be more concentrated, and you will have to take more trouble to avoid frightening fish either by letting them see you, or by letting your line fall heavily on top of them. You will find Polaroid glasses helpful in spotting the presence and movement of fish.

As daylight lengthens you will be wise to fall back here, as elsewhere, on morning and evening fishing, leaving your water quiet during the afternoon. And don't over-fish the water. Unless fresh fish are coming in fast, for a pool to be fished twice during a day is quite enough, particularly if it is also being fished from the opposite bank. Resident fish soon become uncatchable if they are 'plastered'.

If you fish on through July into the back-end during August and September, you will most probably be fishing for stale red fish which will have been in the river since the spring. Are they worth catching? To hook and play them may give a certain amount of fun, but when on the bank, or rather the table, most of them will prove inedible. Yet these fish are of the greatest value as spawning stock, so it seems a pity to kill them. Would it not be better to put at least the black hen fish back into the river, in the same way as one returns kelts? This is the one notable drawback to the Dee, that as few fresh fish enter the river after May good fishing seldom lasts, even in the upper reaches, after June.

If you do fish in the back-end, however, you will usually find that stale fish take badly and are very 'dour'. If they are going to take at all during these 'dour' periods, they prefer a small fly of almost sea trout size. Sometimes nevertheless they will take well, particularly when the river is fining down after a spate, or when frost has dropped the water temperature by several degrees. When they are on the go in this way, size of fly seems of less importance, bigger ones as well as small ones being taken with equal avidity.

All things considered, however, if you want to fish at this time of year, you will definitely do better to disregard the Dee, and fish on one of the later rivers of which there are many, both on the east and west coast.

Little has so far been said about patterns of fly for the Dee. The colour scheme of the fly, provided it is not too garish, as usual seems to matter little, though as a dominant colour, in clear water, there is nothing to beat black. The dressing however is much better if thin and sparse. For big sunk flies, long straggling hackles or long hair wings, thinly dressed, after the manner of an Akroyd, an old Dee pattern, or a Garry from the Tweed, are best. For the floating line there are a swarm of well-known favourites, such as Blue Charm, Logie, Silver Blue, March Brown, Lady Caroline, Black Toucan, Shrimp Fly, Thunder and Lightning, and others. All are good if well tied, i.e. securely, neatly, and thinly. It is doubtful whether salmon make any distinction between such patterns. Why should they? Whoever has seen a hatch of Blue Charms or Logies coming off the river? Plain black hair is, as elsewhere, as good a dressing for a fly as anything, both in clear and moderately coloured water, provided it is soft and pliable and not stiff like a shaving brush. In thicker coloured water one imagines that orange or yellow hair may be better, but this is by no means certain.

In contrast to pattern, the size of fly definitely counts; and don't forget that in the salmon's eyes the size is that of the hook and dressing combined, not of the hook alone. In cold water it has already been said that the sunk fly should be large, two to three inches long. A tube fly with a treble hook is the best hooker and holder, but if you use a big 4/0 or 6/0 single hook be certain that the point is very sharp, and after a fish takes you must hold him really hard to start with, preferably from below him, to make sure that the hook has penetrated over the barb. As an experiment, you may find it interesting to put your big fly in the mouth of a dead salmon, and see how hard a rod-pull it takes to get the barb covered. You may be surprised.

In warmer water with a floating line, as already noted, one needs smaller flies in the Dee than in most other rivers. Personally I prefer small treble hooks, small double hooks (though not smaller than size 8), or small round-bend snecked hooks,* and I have little faith in long-shanked fine wire low water single hooks. But let every fisherman experiment to his heart's content, which is what makes fishing fun, and let him persist with the type of hook with which he has most success.

And so, finally, if you are going to fish the Dee, I wish you all success. You are exceedingly lucky to be on such perfect water amid such wonderful surroundings, assured so it seems of a massive run of spring fish. He would indeed be demanding who would ask for more.

*See remarks on Spey low water flies – Chapter 31.

CHAPTER 33

Tay fishing

A few basic facts should be borne in mind by beginners on the Tay, or by those whose fishing there has so far been limited. The first is that below Ballinluig, where the Tummel doubles its size, the Tay is a very large river indeed, much larger than the Spey, Tweed, or Ness, its nearest rivals. Consequently, and second, except in low water, the fisherman will usually have to fall back upon the use of boats in order to cover the water properly. Thirdly, there is a better chance of hooking a really big fish in the Tay than in any other river in Scotland.

Enlarging on these points – when one first takes a close look at the Tay, probably from one of its bridges at Perth, Kinclaven, Caputh, or Dunkeld, the first thing that impresses one about this river is not so much its speed, or the character of its rapids and pools, but its sheer volume and size. By British standards the Tay appears vast, and one wonders how on earth such a portentous flow can be properly fished. What one does not realize at first sight, however, is that fish seldom lie from bank to bank across its imposing width. It is much more likely that on one side or the other, or on both, smooth gravel extends on the bottom till near the middle of the river. Fish do not usually like to lie on a smooth bottom, so the good holding water may extend over only half or less of the river's width. It may be on one or other side of the river or else in the middle, according to the formation of the pool. This at once brings the effective fishing area down to a much smaller size. The same holds good to a lesser degree in any large river, such as the Spey or Tweed, where the actual good fishing area in a big pool may be relatively small, and it becomes a question of discounting the large areas of unproductive water, of discovering where the good areas lie, and of planning the most effective way of covering them, whether off the bank, or by wading, or by boating (even in the mighty Tay there are a few pools where the current comes close enough to the side to provide bank fishing, such as the March Pool at Meikleour, or Catholes at Stanley). How is this best done? In spring it may be difficult, because fish jump seldom when the water is cold, and thus do not give away the position of their lies. Kelts are apt to jump from time to time, which may be misleading. It is worthwhile learning to distinguish so far as is possible between the jump of a fresh fish and a kelt. Kelts look much thinner in the air, and their splash is more superficial. But if you see fresh fish jumping consistently in any one place it is odds on that some are lying there. You should also be able to 'read' the river to a fair extent, and judge from its appearance where salmon are likely to lie and to take. When water is cold in spring they prefer deep water rather than shallow, and a steady slowish current rather than a fast and broken one. It follows that the middle parts of a pool or the gliding water near the tail are usually the best places, particularly if there are a few big boulders on the bottom which give shelter against the current.

In summer fish are continually jumping, and there are no kelts from May onwards, so there is no difficulty in discovering the lies. A knowledgeable boatman, in any case, whether in spring, summer or autumn, should keep you well informed, and see that you fish in the right places.

In most parts of the river wading is really only practicable in low water. Make no mistake, there is no better sport anywhere than wading a well-stocked Tay pool in low-water conditions, when you can get well in, and cover plenty of fish. Even a moderate-sized fish of 10–12 lb can run you well out on to your backing, while an active one of 20 lb or more can go almost any distance. The problem of playing such fish when you are wading or on the bank is indeed a formidable one, especially where there is a fast rocky stream, and it gives the finest possible sport. But with a rise in water most of the wading places, disappointingly, go out; and a boat with or without a boatman is the only answer. If you choose to boat yourself single-handed in a light and easily manoeuvrable boat with a long rope and anchor, you will again have magnificent sport with plenty of excitement. But if you cast from one of the big Tay cobles with a boatman to control it, and an outboard motor to propel it, the whole process becomes easier in every way, i.e. there is no difficulty in covering the water, no essential need for a long line, less trouble with awkward winds, less difficulty in playing and landing fish, as your boatman can net the small ones directly into the boat, or put you ashore at the right moment to play the larger ones – and so on. If you feel therefore that you are entitled to a break and some easy fishing, go in the boat with a boatman. This can be a welcome relief from wading, you have a better chance of landing a thirty- or forty-pounder if you hook one, thanks to your boatman's assistance, and you will have the entertainment of your boatman's company with, it is to be hoped, a fund of racy local stories.

As to big fish and your chances of hooking them, and I am talking about thirty- and forty-pounders, such fish are always present somewhere or other in the Tay, and eventually you are sure to hook one. In addition, if you fish consistently, you will hook plenty of twenty-pounders. You must therefore without fail employ tackle strong enough to give you a fair chance of landing such fish. Light tackle of the sort adequate for the Dee or Tweed in summer will only lead to disaster here. All may be well if you use it in the summer exclusively for grilse and small salmon, but if you try to handle a big Tay spring or autumn fish with a light rod and ten pounds breaking strain nylon and small hooks, you are likely to be left wondering what has hit you.

In spring or autumn with big flies and baits there is no need to go lighter than sixteen pounds breaking strain nylon for your leader – twenty pounds is often better and safer – or, if the water is low and clear and your lure small, twelve pounds breaking strain is the very lightest you should dare go. Hooks of size 6 are small enough. Anything smaller will probably tear out, bend, or break. As to total length of line and backing, 150 yards is none too much, and there would be no harm in having more. For myself, I would not like my backing to have a breaking strain of less than eighteen pounds, and I would use either good quality monofilament for this, or else one of the American 'Dacron' types of braided nylon, very thin and strong. If my reel was not big enough to take this length of line and backing, I would lose no time in buying a larger one that would.

Don't in any way be discouraged by the normal clarity of Tay water, un-expected perhaps in so large a river. This is no deterrent to salmon taking, as anyone who has fished in the still clearer waters of Norway or Iceland will tell you. Fish like their water to be as pure as possible; fouling matter such as peat, road washings, sewage, or land drainage, does not so much stop them seeing the fly or bait as making them feel sick and therefore disinclined to take it.

Lastly, if you are going to wade the Tay, or boat it for that matter, don't forget that more fishermen are drowned in it than in any other Scottish river, and every year seems to produce one or more victims. So, you have been warned! *Absit omen.*

The Tay spring season opens on January 15th and 'spring' is certainly a mis-placed description. This is the coldest time of year, the very middle of it; and although the mean winter temperature of Tayside may be warmer than that of Speyside or Deeside, the result until about mid-March is certainly not apparent. The Tay fisherman has got to be prepared at this stage to fish in little short of arctic weather, with the usual accompaniments of frost, snow, ice, grue, sleet, or gale at intervals. If he gets sunny weather, or mild cloudy weather, he is lucky. It is not therefore surprising that, in January, February and March, most beats below Ballinluig fall back on harling. With fish scarce, and with the water in the 30°s F one could hardly expect otherwise, particularly as harling has been a traditional method of fishing the Tay as long as salmon have been caught on rod and line. So if you go to fish there at this time of year be prepared for your boatman to attempt to make you harl. He will tell you that you will catch more fish that way, which is probably true. But what he will not tell you is what a dull way of fishing it is for you (though not for him, as he is running the boat and really doing the main part of the fishing). Be warned, therefore, and on some beats boatmen like to continue harling right through April, even into May. My recommendation for what it is worth is that, unless you are well advanced in years or incapacitated in one way or another, you should avoid harling altogether. This can be done by fishing elsewhere (other than where harling is considered absolutely necessary), or by fishing at a time of year when you will catch your fish as well or better by casting, or else by insisting on casting from a boat, rather than harling, in any circumstances. This last puts you at risk of having a row with your boatman, always a disaster; so you may have to tread warily and be a good diplomat.

Towards the end of March the weather and the water should be getting warmer, although it is likely to be mid-April before the spring really makes itself felt. By now, if the water has fallen low enough, you may be able to cover some fish by wading. Also fish will take a big fly freely and you will catch plenty on fly if there are plenty there. My friends and I have proved this over and over again through a number of years, catching up to fifty or sixty in a week between four of us. But if you prefer to fish bait, you will no doubt do as well. Your boatman is almost sure to tell you that you are wasting your time with a fly, and the only way to convince him is to show him otherwise by practical results. If you don't know the water, he may even put you to wade in a place where it is impossible to cast far enough to cover fish with a fly, and then show you how easy it is with a bait, casting forty-five or fifty yards (thus implying that fly-fishing is a useless method). Of course, if you are to catch fish you must cover then properly; and if a boat is necessary for this, then a boat you must have, or else you will merely be confined to casting practice or to ghillie-ing for someone else.

For most of the Tay, April is the best spring month, though the second half of March can also be very good in the lower river. By May the weather should be much warmer; there is a lot of difference in mean spring temperature north and south of the watershed at Drumochter and the Devil's Elbow. By degrees the water will become warm enough for you to catch fish on a floating line and smaller fly, and you should be able to wade in more and more places. The run of salmon will thin out, and no doubt as the water falls the nets kill a larger proportion of the incomers. In fact, by about the third week in May the best of the spring fishing is definitely over, boats on may beats are taken off, and you need some good streamy water on your beat if you are to continue fishing with success.

No differentiation has so far been made here between fishing in the main part of the Tay below Ballinluig, and in the upper Tay above that point or in the Tummel. The two latter have flows of approximately similar size, and each of them being only about half the size of the main Tay downstream naturally falls into a different category as regards fishing conditions and methods. The Tummel, in addition, is now subject to sudden artificial fluctuations in water level, owing to the action of the Hydro at Pitlochry. This does not help fishing, so the upper Tay is the more attractive of these two rivers, and can be described as very pleasant medium-sized water. Its fishing is all by casting, either from the bank or by wading, and only occasionally from a boat. The best spring month in this part of the river is again April, and there is always the chance of a big fish here, or for that matter in the Tummel as well. But catches in general are never so large up here as they are on good beats below Ballinluig, and it is fruitless to expect them to be so.

For those who like it, there is also trolling to be had in Loch Tay from the start of the season onwards. I can say little about this form of fishing as I have never done it, only read or talked about it. Certainly a fair number of fish can be caught in this way, and spring in Loch Tay is the best time. It seems to provide a great deal of enjoyment for many fishermen every year, so good luck to them. The only piece of worthwhile advice I can give them, also to harlers, is to keep a firm grip on their rods so that a fish does not suddenly pull them overboard! This actually happened to the butler in a house where I was once a guest, and the rod was never seen again. Presumably he had laid it on the thwarts for the moment while he attended to other matters. Anyway, it was gone for ever.

In loch fishing I can see that there is plenty of skill in knowing the good fishing areas, according to wind and weather, also in the boat management. Presumably if one runs one's own boat, as opposed to having a professional boatman, it is likely to be more fun. Yet if one is lucky enough to have the alternative opportunity of good river fishing, is there any doubt where the preference of most of us would lie?

A brief mention now about fishing in the headwaters and tributaries. All this, except in the Tummel below Pitlochry, comes under the category of 'small river' fishing, needing appropriate tackle and methods, and thus bears little relation to fishing in the main Tay. The Lyon is probably now the best of the tributaries, though sadly lacking in water owing to the Hydro. The Tummel, although much bigger, does not now produce many fish except downstream of the Hydro dam at Pitlochry. Some fish are also caught in Loch Faskally above this dam. The Tilt and lower Garry are of modest account, although they do produce a few fish in late summer and autumn.

The Dochart holds some fish from May onwards, though in no great number, and apt to be stale by the time they have reached so far upstream. A lot of fish go up the Isla, and then up the Ericht and into its upper waters. This area is potentially good fishing ground, but for a long time, as already mentioned, has suffered from poaching and many forms of illegal fishing, which have largely spoilt it.

Angling on the Ericht was once good. Thomas Stoddart writing in 1853 said: 'The Ericht was at one time amongst the best in Scotland for rod-fishing. The Duke of Atholl, who was in the habit of fishing it regularly about forty years ago, often killed five, six, and seven salmon and grilse before breakfast.' Well, well, salmon were being caught in numbers in the Thames at that time, so the reader may think Stoddart's remarks a bit outdated; but if he goes to look at the Ericht, a delightful small river, with (salmon-wise) many assets, he will doubtless agree that with proper control it could be made first class once again.

The Almond is the only other Tay tributary where there is fishing worth mentioning, but owing to an attenuated flow it is only with the autumn rains at the back-end of the season that salmon ascend it. It is useless in spring, and although a useful spawning tributary, only produces an odd fish to the rod in autumn.

There is little more to be said about fishing in the Tay tributaries. The best of it in the Tummel, below the falls near Pitlochry, was submerged under a great depth of water when the Hydro Dam was built many years ago. Now there is little left of any note, at any rate for the time being, so any fisherman approaching these tributaries would be unwise to expect much, apart from fishing in some delightful surroundings.

Returning to the main Tay and its summer fishing in June, July, and early August, these are the 'dog days' on most beats. With the water at summer level, the run of salmon dwindles or is caught in the nets, which no doubt get the vast majority of incomers. Summer spates to help fish past the nets are rare, and the rod-catch of salmon during these months on most beats is small.

Grilse on the other hand are well worth taking into account. There is a good run of them from around the last week of June to early August, and it is these fish which are the making of the summer fishing. But grilse are very choosy where they stop to lie, and they run fast and far to the waters of their choice. One thing they look for above all, and that is streamy water. A Tay beat that does not have good streams will not hold grilse, and it is no use looking for them there.

A number of beats therefore are of little use in summer, if they only have the long deep steady running pools which salmon favour in spring. But a few of them such as Taymount and Islamouth have excellent streams, so do Kinnaird and Grandtully higher up the river, and grilse distribute themselves over such beats or push on further into the headwaters. If therefore you want to fish during the summer months, make sure that your intended beat is likely to hold grilse, which you can do from examination of previous records, or through enquiry from some reliable source. If it doesn't, you can be certain that your fishing will be disappointing.

Assuming therefore that you are installed on a good summer beat holding plenty of grilse, you are likely to have great fun. Wading rather than boating will be the order of the day, though if a boat is available you can use it if needed for you to cover lies that are out of reach by wading. The streamy parts of the Tay at low water afford most attractive fishing, and many small potholes and 'neuks' come into play for the first time. There is nothing more entertaining than fishing small pools in a big river. Early and late, in warm weather, will be the best times for fishing, as everywhere else; but there is no harm in that, and what could be pleasanter than the dawn hours of a subsequently radiant summer's day?

The choice of suitable tackle will present a problem, already touched upon earlier in this section. Which is preferable, to use light tackle, a fine leader and fly size 9 or 10 – the appropriate grilse tackle – at the risk of losing a big salmon if you hook one? or to use heavier tackle that will handle a bigger fish, but will lessen your bag of grilse? Advice on this is difficult, as it all depends on the circumstances of the moment. If there are few large salmon about, but plenty of grilse, light tackle is likely to be best; but if there are plenty of salmon, as well as grilse, so that the chance of one or the other is nearly even, heavier tackle would be an obvious need. You will have to make up your own mind on this, in accordance with prevailing conditions, and adapt your tackle accordingly. If it is of any interest, my own record book over several years of Tay summer fishing shows a proportion of five fish of 7 lb or less (i.e. in the grilse category), to one fish of 8 lb or more, including a few of 15 lb to 20 lb. In these circumstances my own effort at a compromise in tackle has been a carbon graphite rod of fourteen feet or a light spliced cane rod of thirteen feet, a suitable floating line with 120 yards minimum of backing, a monofilament leader down to ten pounds breaking strain, and small flies down to size 8, lightly dressed. The hook, if it is to be suitable for hooking and holding grilse, cannot be large, and should be of fine wire and very sharp. Small trebles are good, but I am inclined to think that a single small round-snecked bend is better. Such is my suggestion for tackle, and the reader may well ask, while granting its suitability for grilse, how it can be expected to hold big salmon on a long line in the rough rocky tumble of a Tay rapid? I confess I do not know a good answer to this, but at least it gives one a better chance than exclusively grilse tackle, such as an eleven foot rod, seven pounds breaking strain leader, and fly size 10. Apart from this, in Army phraseology, one just has to 'do the best one can'.

One special piece of equipment is useful for landing grilse or small salmon, and that is a light portable landing-net, that can be wielded by the fisherman single-handed. There are several different types of such net available; one with a solid metal hoop is best. This is not to say that beaching a fish is not a better way of landing it; but suitable beaches are not always available, in which case a landing-net is most useful. It is also useful for landing fish into a boat. It is, in contrast, a painful and clumsy business gaffing a grilse. Not only are grilse small, but they twist in the water like eels, making an exasperating target for a gaff-point; also being light they can sometimes jump off a gaff if they kick hard. In any case the wound made by a gaff spoils such small fish. Beaching or netting them is much better.

All the same, as already pointed out, never neglect to have a gaff available one way or another when you are fishing the Tay, even in midsummer. Was there not a fifty-one-pounder caught one July on a sea trout fly at Ballathie? How would you feel if you were by yourself and you hooked such a fish, or even a mere thirty-five-pounder, having no gaff to help you land it? Need any more be said?

There is little more to be added about summer fishing in the Tay. Throwing as long a line as possible, to the full capacity of your lighter tackle, is still an advantage, as is deep wading in most places. But apart from the fact that hooked salmon may run you out a far longer line than in other rivers, the process of fishing is little different from that on any other large river such as the Spey or Ness at the same time of year.

By the middle of August things begin to change. Boats are refloated, where they have been taken off, and the late summer or autumn fish, call them what you will, start to arrive. The nets come off on August 21st, and from then until the close of the rod season on October 16th the stock of fish gradually builds up. Autumn fish spread steadily throughout the river, although the biggest concentration is always to be found in the lower river from Ballinluig down. Good beats hold fish by the hundred, even sometimes by the thousand; and even if the less good ones hold them only in fifties the total stock is vast. Whether these fish can be classed as true 'autumn' fish of our grandfathers' days is arguable. There are nowadays plenty of fresh fish, many with sea-lice, caught in September; but during early October such fish become more and more scarce. Towards the end of the season in mid-October red fish close to spawning out number the fresh ones by about a hundred to one. Was it the same say seventy years ago? It is hard to tell.

The Tweed, the other great autumn river, is by comparison much later. In many years its autumn fish do not enter in numbers before mid-October, or even later if the water is consistently low. And fresh fish with sea-lice are still to be found frequently during November.

Not so in the Tay, however. Nevertheless if a Tay fish of perfect shape and colour, with sea-lice, and excellent to eat is caught during September (and there is no shortage of these), what is this but an autumn fish? So the whole matter ends by becoming a mere splitting of hairs, and the truth is simply that the Tay autumn run for reasons unknown comes in much earlier and ends earlier than that of the Tweed.

One thing is certain about Tay autumn fishing, and that is if you want to catch a forty-pounder, here and now is your best chance of doing it. There is no better 'big fish' river anywhere in Scotland. Only a few years ago a fifty-pounder was killed at Ballathie. If you are less ambitious and a thirty-pounder is enough for you, your chances are even better, there being no lack of these every season.

Going back to the start of the autumn fishing in late August and early September, you will probably find the water fairly low and warm. You will still therefore be fishing with smallish flies or baits, flies of sizes 4 to 6, a leader of about twelve pounds breaking strain, and a floating fly line. If rain comes, as it is sure to sooner or later, and the river rises, you may need to increase the size of your lure. I have already written at length about the advisability of a long rod, and ample supply of sound backing, so will not repeat this. But with the need to increase the size of your fly or bait, so the strength of your tackle should be proportionately increased throughout. Autumn weather is both unpredictable and changeable, varying from near summer conditions to rain, gales and cold. What is more, it fluctuates wildly from year to year, which increases the uncertainty of what to expect. Towards the end of September it is pretty sure that the water temperature will drop to 50°F or below, and in October it may go below 45°F. That is the nearest to a firm prediction that one can dare go; and the only sound advice one can give is that a Tay autumn fisherman should be prepared for anything, wading or boating, water high or low, temperature warm or cold, fish big or small, and that his tackle should be diversified accordingly. For example, in late August, as has already been shown, he is likely to need what is almost a summer outfit, while by October he may well be back to the sunk line, heavy flies, or big baits of early spring. Some beats late in the season will even have gone back to harling, so the wheel will have turned the full circle.

It would be hard to exaggerate the magnificent sport which Tay autumn fishing can give. The best beats are probably Redgorton, Taymount, Islamouth, Murthly, and Kinnaird; but there is also fine streamy water at Benchill and Stanley (though for some reason their catches are not so good). Low or medium water gives the most enjoyable fishing, especially when it is low enough for wading. Don't forget that a river as big as the Tay will never be too low for fish to run, particularly as there are no serious obstructions and no nets, in autumn, to take a toll. Even if a higher river makes wading impossible, and you have to fall back upon a boat, you should still have first-class sport. Most beats have something approaching a 6-foot range in fishing height, so only a flood can checkmate you.

That some beats on the Tay are not as good as others goes without saying (no names, no pack-drill!). But how can this be otherwise? rivers being as they are, like ladies, very changeable! If you rent a poor beat, and are disappointed afterwards, is it really anyone's fault but your own? Are not reliable records of previous catches always available if you ask for them? If they are not, you should be very wary. And if the excuse for poor catches is that the water has been 'lightly' fished, or words to that effect, as already made clear, you should be doubly wary. How many *good* fishings in Scotland are 'lightly' fished in this present day?

There is one inconvenience which may trouble you on the Tay, and that is when the Hydro at Pitlochry regularly causes an artificial rise in water level of one foot or more at some time or other during the day. This seems to happen during periods of high water and unduly wet weather. If your beat is well stocked with plenty of fish, such a rise may make little difference, since it has not so great an unsettling effect as a natural rise from well oxygenated rainwater. So enough of your stock will probably stay with you, and still take. But if you are thinly stocked your chances of sport after a rise like this may drop sharply.

Little is left to be said about this splendid autumn fishing. I should like to close with one story from my own experiences. Some years ago towards the end of September I was wading from the right bank of the pool called Sandy Ford at Islamouth, and was approaching its tail. The river was moderately high, so I was not wading far out, but all the same could cover plenty of fish where the water shallowed into the draw. I had just got past the brick bothy, if any of my readers know this building, when my fly was taken fairly close in. I was fishing with a white floating line, clearly visible, a No. 4 hook, and fourteen pounds breaking strain leader. For two or three minutes the fish hung there steadily, and as he was near the lip of the draw and I did not want to be taken down the rapids below I started to walk him up, keeping a steady pull on him. He followed docilely enough for about twenty-five yards which was what I wanted, and I hoped to get him further. But not so. Suddenly he took umbrage, whipped round, and headed off at top speed downstream jumping as he went. I saw a big fresh fish of around 28 lb, no monster be it noted but nevertheless a good one, as he tore the line off my reel. Soon he was away out into the middle of the draw, there was no holding him in that strength of current, and my white line disappeared fast into the Tay as my backing ran out. That was the last I ever saw of my line. I could not follow along the bank because it was overgrown with withies or saplings, so I staggered downstream in waist-deep water at topmost speed, my reel whirring furiously all the time. By the time I reached Davie's Stone where the stream began to slacken, I must have had nearly 100 yards of backing out, and I had long lost all direct touch with my fish. My backing now disappeared into the middle of the river, and was entangled in some snag about forty-five yards out. I got level with where it was fast, pulled this way and that way, made extempore otters, and did everything I possibly could but all to no avail. There was no boat anywhere near, and nothing further that apparently could be done. The evening was drawing in, so after twenty minutes I pulled till my backing broke, and walked the homeward mile with a reel three-quarters empty, feeling more defeated by a salmon than ever before or since. So far as I know no one ever saw my line or my fish again. The river rose six feet that night.

This is the sort of thing I mean by the modest understatement: 'Autumn fishing on the Tay can produce excellent sport.'

Greylags
at Meikleour

CHAPTER 34

Tweed fishing

'The Tweed is different' – all Tweed fishermen will know the implication and meaning of this phrase. It is not only the spell cast by this lovely river and its surroundings which enchants us, not only its historical background and its great fishing traditions, but above all and naturally its fishing and its fish.

Where for instance could one find pleasanter water than say at Floors on the middle Tweed, with such variety of pools from the fast-running narrow neck of the Ferry Pool to the long, deep dub of the Garden Wall and the Putt? Where could one fine prettier or streamier pools than the Mill Stream and Lovers' Leap at Rutherford, or the Orchard, the Red Stane, or the Doors at Makerstoun? – and there are plenty of other such happy hunting grounds.

And where could one find a prettier fish than the shapely Tweed springer, even if he is of moderate size? or the fresh run twenty-pounder, or larger, of autumn? Magnificent fish both of them, as anyone who has seen them laid out in numbers after a good day's fishing will confirm.

Indeed the Tweed has its own exclusive character, from the fast-running streams near Peebles to the long tidal flats below Norham. In this extensive stretch of river every type of fishing water is to be found – if it is true that its general rate of flow is slower than that of a highland river of the north, nevertheless over most of its course there is ample current to provide all that could be wanted for good salmon fishing.

An added attraction of the Tweed, as already shown, is the great length of its fishing season, and the intriguing fact that its best fishing is divided into two quite separate periods, spring and autumn. Ten months from February 1st to November 30th is surely a long season? But it should be realized that all the good fishing takes place during the first three-and-a-half months and the last two-and-a-half, with a four months' unproductive gap between. Spring and autumn fishing bear little relation to each other, are widely parted, and produce an entirely different type of fish. Does this not add to the Tweed's interest? Please don't say that it would be better if good fishing continued unceasingly through-out the ten months' season – you would of course be right, but no British river can fish well for so long a period as that, or even approaching it. (The Spey and Tay come nearest to doing so.)

Moreover the Tweed can provide fishing of a sort to cater for all types of angler, the young and energetic who prefer it the hard way, the middle-aged and not so active, and the elderly or incapacitated who can take it easy in a boat with a good boatman. When I am eighty I know that I shall not be able any more to wade the Spey or Dee, but I still hope to be boating with Charlie and Frank on Lower Floors and killing plenty of fish!

A word here on the subject of Tweed boatmen (there are no 'ghillies' on this river). The large majority of these are first-class men, born and bred on the Borders, patient and only too willing to give their 'rod' all possible help, whether moral or physical. It is no easy work rowing a boat all day in a strong current and perhaps a strong wind; and there is often a danger of these men overworking themselves in their anxiety to show their rod good sport, especially if they are getting on in years. It is worth remembering this, so on difficult days do give your boatman a break from time to time in any way you can. When fishing from a boat you are largely dependent on him for your success, so you would be well advised to look upon your day's fishing as a joint effort, and seek his co-operation on this basis. It will pay you time and again.

Tweed boatmen are expert with the long handled big landing-nets, to be found lying by most pools, and expect to land fish in no other way. Gaffs are illegal instruments in spring and autumn, being associated in the mind of the law with poaching activities, in fact it is illegal to bring them within one mile of the river. If a suitable beach is available there is of course no reason why you should not beach a fish as readily as have him netted, but as a matter of fact good beaches on the Tweed are rarer than on rivers further north. If you are wading and by yourself, you would be wise to carry a light portable landing-net, for use where a beach is lacking.

From the start of the season, for the first two weeks till February 15th, you will be confined to fly-fishing, with a big sunk fly (a tube is probably best) and a heavy line. You will most probably be boat-fishing, as the water is likely to be high and certainly cold, though you may be able to do some wading if it is low enough. Your best chance will be on a beat downstream of Kelso cauld. Although this obstacle to the passage of fish is not a difficult one, it is seldom that many fish run it so early in the year. By mid-March it is a different matter. Fly-fishing in early February is a chancy proposition; weather is unpredictable, and there are many hazards, such as low water, ice, and grue at one end of the scale, with high dirty flood at the other. Tweed spring fishermen pray for a mild winter, with a full and not too cold river during December and January which will bring a prolific run of springers into the river before the nets start on February 15th, and will continue to draw them in afterwards. If at the opening the river is running at a fair fishing height and is reasonably clear, and the weather is not unduly cold, you should do well with a sunk fly and continue to do well as long as such conditions last. Make hay while the sun shines, as the weather can do a volte face at this time of year. If you are unlucky, however, you may have a dirty yellow flood for days on end, or else find your water almost frozen over and full of grue. As a result you may get only two or three days' fishing, or less, in a fortnight. This possibility, grim and tantalizing in effect, has to be faced.

On February 15th and until September 15th, bait-fishing is allowed, and most fishermen, anyhow in the earlier part of the season, at once take it up. It is undoubtedly a more killing method than fly-fishing, until such time as around the first week of April when the water warms up enough for a floating line to be used. By mid-March fish should have travelled well upstream beyond Kelso, and all mid-river beats should be starting to kill their share. Needless to say spring comes earlier on Tweedside than further north. By the third week in April the best of the spring fishing is over on the lower river, and by mid-May further upstream. As a rule February and March are the best months below Kelso, and April above, but all depends as usual on weather and water conditions.

As to tackle and what is best to use, your outfit in early February should be similar to that described for Spey, or Tay, in early spring. You need for choice a long and powerful rod, mainly to cope with the formidable winds which often occur at this time of year. Tweed spring fish, under favourable conditions, are free takers and easily caught. There could be no easier fishing for beginners than this; and fish are often hooked from a boat on little more than a rod's length of line. But what is 'possible'* is not necessarily the best idea, and undoubtedly the longer the line, well thrown, the better.

You will also need the usual heavy sunk line to fish your fly deep. All sorts of patent contraptions have been invented to cause the fly to fish close to the bottom, 'deep sinkers' of one sort or another, sometimes of weird appearance. They can mostly be consigned to the refuse bin. A heavy line and heavy-bodied hair wing tube fly will do all that is required if you fish it in the right way, i.e. a long cast, time to sink, lead the fly slowly round through the current or pull it in

*Many things are 'possible' in fishing, if surprising. The best big river fisherman I ever knew once told me that he had experimented on the Tweed by attaching a large fly straight onto his dressed fly line, without any nylon, and quickly caught a salmon.

slowly if there is little current, and above all a slow draw in for three or four yards of line at the end of the cast when the line has straightened out. This last is the most deadly taking moment of all. You may find some difficulty in clearing a heavy sunk line from the water preparatory to making a fresh cast. If so, try making one or two false casts with a shortened line, having first pulled in by hand several yards of slack line which can be 'shot' with the next proper cast.

As to your leader and pattern of fly, even though the Tweed spring fish are small there should be no need to fish lighter than sixteen pounds breaking strain nylon. It may be well tested, as there are plenty of kelts at this time of year which take freely, and you may well hook big stale autumn 'kippers' in addition to fresh springers. Pattern of fly, as in other rivers, matters little; long hair wings of black, yellow, or orange are best.

With the advent of bait-fishing on February 15th you can choose any light and sound bait outfit that you like. You should have plenty of line or backing on your reel, whether you are fishing fly or bait, to allow for emergencies with a hooked fish. Though the Tweed is less demanding than the Tay or Spey over this, owing to its softer current, even so emergencies can happen, and in a big river it is safer to be well prepared. Baits themselves are of many different types. In years gone by Tweed boatmen would not look at you unless you fished a golden sprat. Nothing else would do, however foul-smelling was the bottle where it came from! Now wooden devons are all the rage, and very killing they are, or else their cousins, plastic devons. With these in various sizes, and a Norwegian spoon or two, not too bright, for coloured water, you can hardly go wrong.

It seems though that fashions in salmon baits are rather like those in ladies' clothes, erratic, exotic and expensive; and one wonders what will take the place of wooden or plastic devons 'when the fish get tired of them'? Your guess is as good as mine.

I prefer to make no comment on prawns, shrimps, plugs, or worms. I have long ago caught fish on all of these, but have no wish to do this any more, nor to encourage anyone else to do so.

Towards the end of April when the water warms up to around 48°F or higher, fly-fishing with a floating line and small fly becomes effective. Size 7 in flies is small enough, and a slightly bigger one may often be better. The strength of your leader can be dropped to ten pounds breaking strain, though to fish finer is risky. You are more likely to be wading than boating; long trouser waders are advisable in most places, though occasionally thigh waders may be adequate.

As the year passes on from May into June and July, hot summer weather descends on Tweedside, the water level falls, and fishing comes more or less to standstill. How different things were in bygone days! Scrope writing in the 1830s described the Tweed as being full of summer fish in the Melrose-Kelso area. Nowadays only if you live within easy distance and can get to the river after a rare but welcome spate, or if you fish in the early hours of sunrise can you hope to have success with summer fishing. You will have to be very cunning and fall back on all the most refined artifices of tackle and technique. Even then your bag is unlikely to be heavy, and if you catch a fish or two they will probably be stale ones. If you seek to discover the cause of this sad state of affairs, it seems that you need look little further than to water abstraction coupled with excessive netting. In fact on most Tweed beats during the midsummer months you can take it, sad to say, that as a general rule, in the words of Richard Franck (1657), you might as well go and 'angle for oysters'.

With the approach of autumn however the Tweed fisherman can prepare for the cream of his season's sport. The autumn fishing of present days seems a really good gamble, and at this present date is inclined to be still improving. It can start any time after early September when the first autumn rains cause the river to rise, and the nets being lifted on September 15th is an added help. With suitable conditions, i.e. with anything other than dead low water, autumn fish will continue entering the river right through to the end of the season on November 30th and after.* What is the best time in autumn for rod-fishing? It will probably be between mid-October and mid-November, and it is impossible to be more definite. So much, as always, depends on weather and water conditions; and what in autumn could be more uncertain? For instance in September and early October there is a definite risk of a prolongation of summer conditions, with continuing low water and no sign of welcome rain to bring a rise. In this case if fresh fish enter at all, they are likely to stop low down the river below Coldstream. Occasionally it happens that there is no rise in water till November, in which case you may be sure that only the lowest part of the river till then will produce any fresh fish. Towards the end of October and in early November the Tweed can also be full of fallen leaves from the many wooded slopes of its middle and upper reaches. After a windy day or night these can cause infinite annoyance, as one seems to hook one every cast. Beyond using a single-hooked fly, and trying to flick off leaves in the air rather than pulling in the line and removing them by hand, there would seem to be no remedy. In November too, as the weather becomes colder, fishing can be hampered by ice and grue,

*Very big runs of Tweed autumn fish have sometimes been reported in December, during the close season.

freezing low water, or alternatively by gales and porter-coloured flood, the latter a risk in October also for that matter.

Having listed these formidable autumn hazards, I at once hasten to say that if you find the river in good fishing order during the autumn, i.e. at a fair fishing height, neither in flood nor dead low, and reasonably steady and clear, you will surely find fish and should get first-class sport, with the one proviso that you are neither too far up or too far down the river, of which more to follow.

Where to fish is important. As has already been mentioned, below Coldstream is a good area in September and early October if the water remains low. New fish may have come in then, but remained close to the tidal reaches if there has been no rise in water to encourage them to run higher. Such a situation however is unlikely to last long. Most years there is a good autumn flood sometime in September, or at least in early October, which cleans out the bed of the river, and speeds the autumn fish well on their way upstream. They move upwards much quicker than spring fish, because their spawning time is closer; given the slightest encouragement, even a few inches rise in water, they are eager to push on. The best autumn beats lie at present between Kelso and Boldside. For some unknown reason, except at Hendersyde and Sprouston where there is a cauld across the river, the formerly good beats from Kelso down have ceased to fish well in autumn over the past several years. This is disappointing, and one hopes it may only be temporary as is quite possible, but it cannot be ignored. So if you have any choice as to where you fish in autumn, you would be well advised as things stand at present to operate somewhere upstream of Kelso cauld. Anywhere from there up to Boldside, where the Ettrick comes in, should produce excellent fishing. Upstream of Boldside is much more chancy, and you are more and more likely to catch stale red fish instead of fresh ones the higher you go upstream. There is only one time when this upper river is likely to be a better hunting ground, and that is when the water is so high as to put all the lower beats out of fishing order, but when the upper river will still fish. This can occasionally happen, making the upper river a useful last resort. The tributaries, as already mentioned, only fish well in high water after rain, so cannot be recommended with any approach to confidence.

Autumn tackle normally consists of a long rod, heavy line, and large sunk fly, exactly similar to that recommended on the Spey, Dee, Tay, or this river for use in early spring. As bait-fishing is banned from September 15th onwards, only fly tackle has now to be considered. Early in the autumn it sometimes happens that the water is still quite warm, in the 50°s F, in which case a floating line with a fly size 4 to 6 may be the best choice. Before long however colder weather is bound to arrive, and as soon as the water temperature drops below about 48°F one usually does better with the traditional Tweed autumn outfit of the sunk line and big fly between one-and-three-quarter inches and three-and-a-half inches long. The higher and colder the water becomes, the more one needs to fish deep and slow, until by late October or soon after one's methods are identical with those of early spring – the same long cast, the slow leading of the fly round, the same draw-in of line at the end of the cast, and the same unhurried sideways draw of rod and line against the weight of a taking fish – all such normal tactics of heavy sunk line fly-fishing come once more into play.

Do make sure as always that all your tackle is strong and sound from backing to hook-point, and to test it before you start fishing and not after. It is amazing how often people get broken by a fish, and only then give their tackle a good testing to find weak spots. Such spots can occur in odd places and funny ways. For instance I have seen an apparently perfectly sound reel of a reliable brand of monofilament, which had weak spots in it about every twelve yards. It would break easily at these places, but the rest of it was as sound as a cable. It lost its owner several fish through inexplicable breaks, before he diagnosed the trouble and jettisoned it. Autumn fish in the Tweed can weigh heavy, they pull hard, run hard, and can be dour and difficult to bring to the net. Don't handicap yourself by using weak tackle. Your leader for instance, when you are fishing sunk fly, should not have a breaking strain of less than sixteen to eighteen pounds. As to flies, as for other rivers there is nothing at present to beat a heavy hair-winged tube fly, black, orange, or yellow in colour, with a sound treble hook, sharp and not too small in size.

One final point about tackle – having said that a sunk line is a regular requirement, I would like to qualify this in the case of very low water that is too cold for a small fly. It is possible to get such conditions, and to have plenty of fish as well, if high water earlier on has brought them in but has lately fallen away. In these circumstances your best combination is a floating line, or a floating line with a sinking tip and a moderately heavy fly. The reason for this is to avoid catching the bottom or boulders on the bottom. Pools in the Tweed are seldom of great depth and often have outcrops of submerged rock. A heavy sunk line outfit, as used in normal conditions, can lead in low water to the fly becoming hitched up far too often.

Autumn fish are by nature good takers, provided they have not become 'potted' and if their attention is not distracted by rising or dirty water. What is more, they take well when the water is cold, far better when its temperature is 35°F–42°F than, say, 45°F–50°F. This does not seem to follow the spring pattern, when 50°F is a good taking temperature, but whatever may be the reason it is a fact. Even with very cold water near freezing point autumn fish will still take well during a limited period of the day, other things being equal. With such temperatures it is not usually of much use starting fishing before 10.30 a.m. or continuing after 4.30 p.m.; though the fun can wax fast and furious once it starts. You ought not to spend too long over lunch or any other distraction during good fishing time.

As to wading or boating, you may do as you please, depending on the type of water you are fishing coupled with the availability of boats and boatmen. The majority of fishermen seem to prefer boating, which is easier work. Some pools and some beats fish better wading, and some boating. At first, anyhow, it is probably best to follow the normal local practice as to which you do. If you wade you will find the going in the Tweed fairly easy compared to the Spey, Dee, or Tay. The bottom is usually less broken and the current less strong. Trouser waders in autumn are always an unmixed blessing, so never fail to include them in your kit.

One last tip, which can be valuable. If you are fishing in very cold weather, either in spring or autumn, your rod-rings can become filled with ice so that the line jams fast in them. There is a way to avoid this. Put out in as few casts as you can a fair length of line, but not more than you can lift, and throw without pulling in and shooting any. Keep your line at this length, continue fishing with it thus, and don't increase or shorten it. If you draw no line in through the rings, and don't shoot any, no drips of water will be drawn in with it to freeze there. The trouble will only start when you hook a fish that pulls your line out and through the water, and you reel it back. Try to keep your hooked fish as static as possible (easier said than done, no doubt!), or if you have a boatman he can keep your rings clear, once on the bank. Putting grease on them helps. Fishing under these conditions sounds pretty desperate, but in fact such icing does occur not infrequently during February or November; it is as well to know this method of combating it, as fish can take quite well even with it this cold.*

---

*The main requisite for this, of course, is that the air temperature should be at least as warm or preferably warmer than the water temperature. This fundamental principle in fishing is so well known that so far I have made no reference to it. But what is less well known is that it applies just as surely when the water is warm, right up to the 70's F, as it does when it is cold and near freezing (or at any intermediate temperature). With the air at two or three degrees colder than the water you will seldom get a fish to take, and as the gap in temperature widens your chances worsen. This applies everywhere and at all times in Britain; and the only place where it does not apply to anything approaching the same extent, so far as I know, is Iceland.

Little more remains to be said about this splendid Tweed autumn fishing. There is a wonderful fascination about it, partly because all other fishing is at a discount at this time of year, and partly because it is an unexpected thrill to catch fine silver fish so late in the season. An added excitement is that there are no legal nets operating, so there is always the possibility of an outsize run of fish; and there is no waiting as at other times of year or a weekend 'slap' on the nets – every day is a potential running day in autumn. Always too there is the chance of a big fish. I must admit that over the last twenty-two years my own biggest Tweed autumn fish scaled only 26 lb, but every year one sees or hears of much bigger fish than this being caught or lost by friends or acquaintances. Or perhaps one hears of double figure catches by some fortunate angler. All this combines to fire one's keenness, and aid one's perseverance. William Scrope wrote as long ago as 1843: 'Your fly, or its exact position, should never be lost sight of; and you should imagine every moment of the livelong day that an extraordinary large salmon is coming at it.' This dictum is no less true now than it was 136 years ago, and better advice for a salmon fisher would indeed be hard to find.

APPENDIX

A Description of the Flies Illustrated in
the Colour Plates

Spey flies *facing page 17*

1. *The 'Munro's Killer'*. A modern hair wing dressing named after the late J. A. J. Munro, who for many years operated a fishing tackle shop in Aberlour. It has been much used, first on the Spey, then on other rivers.

2. *The 'Black Pennell'*. The Black Pennell is not by origin a Spey fly, but has been found as useful on that river as anywhere for salmon in low and clear water, also for grilse and for sea trout. It is a simple and effective dressing and dates from the last century, being named after Mr H. Cholmondeley Pennell who compiled the *Salmon and Trout* volume of the Badminton Library. It is a useful summer fly and makes a good dropper when tied on a single sneck-bend hook as illustrated here.

3. *The 'Black Heron'*. A traditional Spey pattern, mentioned in *Autumns on the Spey* (1872) by A. E. Knox and described even then as being 'an old Spey fly'. The Black Heron with its long heron hackles and mallard wing is an excellent clear-water fly and is still often used in present days.

4. *The 'Arndilly Fancy'*. Another modern hair wing dressing, named after a good Spey beat, and much used there.

5. *The 'Delfur Fancy'*. This handsome fly, named after one of the best and most prolific Spey beats, was invented in the late Victorian era. It was one of the first built-wing flamboyant patterns to challenge on the Spey the supremacy of the former traditional and more sombre dressings. Of these latter there were many, such as the Black Heron (No. 3 *above*), the Lady Caroline (No. 7 *below*), the Gold Riach (No. 8 *below*), the Purple King (No. 9

below), together with others such as the Gold and Silver Speal, the Green and Black King, the Dallas, the Lord March, the Miss Grant, the Elchies Fancy and the Carron Fly to name some of them.

6. *The Black Tosh*. This was one of the earlier hair wing tube flies and was invented about the year 1957 by Mr E. Ritchie, a well-known ghillie for many years at Delfur. Ritchie got the hair for this fly from his dog Tosh, and named the fly accordingly. He always insisted that the hair should be pure black, though in fact other colours are good also. Flies of this sort, together with their smaller-sized counterparts such as the Stoat's Tail, have bid fair to oust the older types of feather-winged flies.

7. *The Lady Caroline*. An old Spey dressing, dating back to the last century and named after Lady Caroline Gordon-Lennox, daughter of the then Duke of Richmond and Gordon at Gordon Castle. It is described by Sir Herbert Maxwell in 1913 as 'a fly of very ancient type, named after a lady still with us'. The Lady Caroline is a useful low- and clear-water pattern, still popular and often used.

8. *The Gold Riach*. One of Knox's 'old Spey flies', described in *Autumns on the Spey* (1872). Spey fly-dressers then had a special and peculiar style of tying. The dressing was sparse, with a simple mallard or teal strip-wing tied short to lie close to the body. Sober colours as used in these flies were formerly preferred until the brilliant hues of Blue Chatterer, Golden Pheasant, and other exotic birds, together with brightly-dyed hackles introduced from Ireland in the 1860s gradually came to predominate.

Modern anglers might well prefer the older,

less showy types. These traditional Spey flies look remarkably lifelike in the water, and their long hackles, when working in a stream, greatly resemble the whiskers of prawn or shrimp. There was a type of fowl, known as the 'Spey Cock', specially bred by keen tyers to produce the type of hackle; and it is a curious and unique feature of Spey tying that the body hackle was wound in the opposite direction to the ribbing tinsel over the berlin wool, hardly a secure method of tying, one would have thought. Heron hackles were also much used and to good effect. Another curious feature was that the broad tinsel round the body was often wound the opposite way to the gold or silver thread, to produce a 'cross gartering' effect.

9. *The Purple King*. The same remarks apply as for the Gold Riach (No. 8 *above*). The Purpy, as it was known, was one of the most popular flies at the end of the last century and is still sometimes used. There was also a Green King, a Red King and a Black King amongst old Spey flies.

Dee flies *facing page 49*

1. *The Blue Charm*. This is perhaps the best known and most successful of all the Dee flies, a clear-water fly much favoured by Mr A. H. E. Wood of Cairnton, the inventor of the greased line method of fishing. It was during the 1920s and after that Mr Wood made this fly so popular, but in fact the pattern dates back to long before that time. It is given in *The Salmon Fly* (1895) by Kelson as an established dressing.

Mr Wood did not ascribe any particular merit to the Blue Charm, apart from the fact that it was basically a dark fly and so gave him an alternative choice in colour to the brighter Logie or Silver Blue, which he also liked. But he did rightly emphasize the importance of clear- and low-water flies being lightly dressed, as the Blue Charm is, or should be.

If the proof of the pudding is in the eating, the Blue Charm has certainly been a most successful fly, as it is not far off 100 years old now

and is still one of the most popular patterns for use anywhere.

2. *The Logie*. Another Dee fly, also given in *The Salmon Fly* (1895). This pattern was also liked by Mr Wood of Cairnton, though he preferred his special type of long-shanked fine wire single hook instead of the double hook here shown. The Logie is a well-known fly, best in low water, which like the Blue Charm has had a long and successful career. It is still widely used.

There is a famous 'Logie' pool at Dinnet on the Dee, so probably the fly was named after that; but 'Logie' is a common name in Aberdeenshire, Angus and Perthshire.

3. *The Silver Blue*. Kelson in *The Salmon Fly* (1895) describes this fly as a popular pattern on the Dee at that time. It was another of Mr Wood's choices for greased-line fishing and in fact has always been a popular pattern both for salmon and sea trout, and still is. Its bright colour scheme makes it a favourite fly for sunny weather.

4. *The Jeannie*. An excellent fly for clear water, well-known and popular everywhere. This again is a Dee dressing, according to Kelson, and was invented at some date prior to 1895. The Jeannie was also used by Mr Wood of Cairnton in the 1920s and after.

5. *The Shrimp Fly*. This is not necessarily a Dee pattern, but has been included here as a good clear-water fly, useful on the Dee as on other rivers. It is a popular dressing of comparatively recent origin. There are several different variations of this fly.

6. *The March Brown*. This again is not necessarily a Dee pattern, but is simply a glorification of the well-known trout fly of this name. The March Brown is one of the very few salmon flies which are a deliberate imitation of a natural fly. The March Brown hatches in abundance in the rivers of N.E. Scotland during the spring and both salmon and more often kelts can be seen taking it. The origin of the artificial imitation is probably very old indeed. The artificial however is by no means dependent on the presence of the natural fly for its success in taking fish and is a

good clear-water fly anywhere, at any time, often used. Mr Wood, to win a bet, is said to have used nothing but a March Brown throughout a whole season on the Dee and still to have caught more fish than any of his friends.

7. *The Gordon*. An old traditional Dee fly and no nineteenth-century Dee fisherman would have allowed it to have been missing from his fly book. The Gordon is an elaborately dressed built-wing pattern no doubt effective enough in high water. The technique in the old days was to fish with one rod only, say sixteen feet, and to go down a pool first with a plain fly, like the Akroyd, then with a more fanciful fly such as a Gordon, and finally, if these failed, perhaps with a gudgeon, using the same outfit throughout. Subsequently, the fisherman would move to another pool and go through the same process there.

Sir Herbert Maxwell says of the Gordon in 1913, after giving its dressing: 'In tying this or any other salmon fly, tackle makers often make the mistake of putting too much feather in the wing. It is far better to fish with a fly rather bare and thin than with one overdressed. The Gordon originally came from Deeside, but if I were limited to the use of one pattern in any river, this is the one I would choose, for it is the only fly for which, when harling the Tay with three rods astern, each with a different fly, I have fancied that salmon show a preference. It is an excellent fly on any size hook, and for all fishable conditions of water or weather.'

Modern fishermen would surely accept the first part of Sir Herbert's contention, but be doubtful about the second part. If the Gordon were to be used in low water nowadays, it would certainly have to be made much sparser in dressing.

In the old days most pools used to have a 'salmon stane'. The simple guide to water height was that, when the 'salmon stane' was covered, the pool was fishable, but when it was clear, the pool was too low to fish, either with a Gordon or an Akroyd (No. 8 *below*), or anything else.

8. *The Akroyd*. A Dee 'strip-wing' fly, invented by Mr Charles Akroyd of Brora, about 1880. The peculiar features of the strip-wing flies are the two cinnamon turkey wings tied close to the body, alongside it, and in penthouse fashion, separated; also the slim body, with the jungle cock cheeks tied in downwards and alongside the throat hackles. (Other flies of similar strip-wing type are the Glentana, the Tartan and the Jock o'Dee.)

Sir Herbert Maxwell, writing in 1898, says of this fly: 'It may be taken as the type of the old fashioned Dee fly dressed on a very long shanked hook. There are endless modifications, the long heron hackles, both black and gray, being a conspicuous feature, and they used to be traditionally finished off with a teal or pintail hackle at the shoulder. It is difficult to get feathers long enough in the fibre to wing these long hooks, and it was an ancient practice to tie in a second pair of wings half way down the body. Flies so dressed swim very nicely.'

The Akroyd was sometimes alternatively dressed with a pure white wing, and sparse dressing was always considered one of its most desirable attributes.

It is not a fly that one would choose for use in thick or coloured water; but in clear waters like those of the Dee it has proved its value over a long period, used in any appropriate size.

As early as 1850 such strip-wing flies were dressed on a special type of Dee hook, often as large as 4/o or bigger, with an extra long shank.

9. *The Mar Lodge*. This fly is named after a former royal residence on upper Deeside and dates from Victorian times, being described by Sir Herbert Maxwell in 1896 as a 'very tasteful fly of modern repute in the Aberdeenshire Dee. Best used in large sizes.' The Mar Lodge is a fully dressed built-wing fly, typical of the late Victorian era, no doubt successful enough when used in the high water of spring or autumn. The dressing is complicated to an extent where it would be difficult to fine it down sparsely for use in smaller sizes in low

water. The middle third of the body of this fly, being of black floss silk ribbed with thin silver tinsel, interposed between two sections of flat silver tinsel, is a unique feature occurring in no other fly.

Tay flies *facing page 77*

1. *The Nicholson.* A traditional Tay pattern, but its origin and the reason for its name are unknown. A fully dressed built-wing pattern, it involves a complicated tying, and is something of a work of art.

It is illustrated in Earl Hodgson's *Salmon Fishing* published in 1906, so presumably was in use in Victorian times.

2. *The Dunkeld.* This is the only Tay fly which has persisted in popular modern use, but it is better known in its abbreviated form for sea trout and brown trout, rather than as a fully-dressed salmon fly. The essentials of the Dunkeld however, the mallard wing and jungle cock eye, the orange and jay hackle, and the gold tinsel body, are bound to be an effective combination for salmon, particularly if dressed sparingly for use in clear water.

3. *The Silver Grey.* Although this fly is not by origin a Tay fly, it is universally popular and effective. It was in fact invented by James Wright of Sprouston on the Tweed in the mid 1860s, but would be as useful on the Tay as anywhere else. The silver grey is remarkably lifelike in general colour and appearance.

4. *The Black Dog.* In his book *Salmon and Sea Trout* published in 1898 Sir Herbert Maxwell describes the Black Dog as being a 'modern version of a very old Tay pattern. Black used to be the prevailing tone, but gay colours have been added to keep it abreast of the fashion. It is used as a large spring pattern.'

This dressing appears to have little or no connection with Macintosh's Black Dog of 1808, illustrated in the Lonsdale Library, *Salmon Fishing* and copied from *The Driffield Angler* of 1808.

Kelson in *The Salmon Fly* (1895) describes the Black Dog as 'an old standard of my father's and a useful high water fly'. This

would probably have dated the dressing back to the 1840s.

5. *The Hairy Mary.* A popular modern hair-winged fly, originating some twenty-five years ago, the Hairy Mary is not in fact a Tay fly. Its invention is ascribed to Mr Reidpath of Inverness and is one of the earliest hair-winged flies. A useful fly anywhere in low and clear water, it has a number of different variations according to the type of hair with which the wing is made. The wing here illustrated is of grey squirrel's tail.

6. *The Benchill.* Named after the famous beat on the lower Tay below Stanley. This is another elaborately-dressed fly, typical of the later Victorian style. This fly is also illustrated in Earl Hodgson's *Salmon Fishing* (1906). In their larger sizes these elaborate Tay flies would doubtless have been 'harled' in spring and autumn. They were tied sometimes on hooks as big as 8/0.

7. *The Red Drummond.* This fly was named after a leading Perthshire family which has always owned fishing on the Tay. Earl Hodgson illustrates this fly, but its origin is unknown.

8. *The Popham.* This fly in fact did not originate on the Tay, but would be as useful there as anywhere else. It is one of the most elaborate of all built-wing dressings, dating back at least to the start of this century. Its main feature is perhaps its complicated body in three different sections veiled with Indian crow feathers. It affords a fine example of the fly-tyer's art.

9. *The Green Highlander.* Not a Tay dressing, but a popular fly anywhere in the North. It is one of the few salmon flies with green as its predominating colour.

Tweed flies *facing page 113*

1. *The Silver Wilkinson.* A well-established built-wing pattern, with a bright colour scheme enhanced by the magenta and blue hackles. The Wilkinson has achieved success everywhere, and is still widely used.

It was first tied in 1859 by the Rev P. S.

Wilkinson, who invented it particularly for use on the Tweed. Mr Wilkinson originally named this fly the Silver Belle and it was only later that its name was changed. Messrs Farlow still have the original fly in their pattern book.

One of the earliest silver-bodied flies, it soon became, with the Jock Scott, a *sine qua non* on the Tweed and boatmen at one time were chary of any other patterns being used. It was on a Silver Wilkinson that the record Tweed fish of $57\frac{1}{2}$ lbs was caught by Mr Pryor at Floors in 1886. Also it was on a small Wilkinson that Mr Brereton caught his fifty-five-pounder at Mertoun in 1889.

2. *The Lady of Mertoun*. This is an example of an old Tweed pattern, no longer in use, which Scrope in 1843 describes as being one of his most successful flies. The dressing, even at that date, was probably an old one. Note the abbreviation of the hackles and the sombre colour scheme. (See also the Toppy, No. 8 *below*.)

3. *The Garry Dog*. One of the first hair-wing patterns, invented and first used on the Tweed in the 1920s. It was named after the inventor's dog Garry, and the hair for the wing was found from this animal. This pattern has proved effective, particularly in cold or coloured water. It is still widely used, tied in orthodox fashion or as a tube fly, and has served as a prototype for many other types of hair-winged flies.

4. *The Thunder and Lightning*. One of the best known and most frequently used salmon flies up to the present day. This fly has had a long successful innings, as it was invented by Jas. Wright, the famous tyer of Sprouston on the Tweed, in the mid 1850s. Though originally meant for the Tweed, it has been equally successful elsewhere; but owing to its comparatively sombre colouring, it is best when used as a clear-water fly. For this purpose, there is no better pattern.

The contrast of the black silk body and its gold ribbing, with the bright orange body hackle and the blue jay at the throat, also the plain mallard wing with its cheeks of jungle cock, is a pleasing one; and the name evolves readily from the colour motif.

5. *The Durham Ranger*. This is another well-known creation of the celebrated Jas. Wright of Sprouston. The story goes that about 1860 a party of English fishermen arrived from Durham to fish on the Tweed and this fly was specially tied for them to use. Its immediate success lead to its being christened with the name which it still bears.

The golden pheasant tippet wing of the Durham Ranger shows up in colourful fashion which leads to this fly being considered a good one for heavy or coloured water, though for low clear water it may seem too showy.

There are various modifications, such as the Black Ranger, the Red Ranger and the Silver Ranger, all with the same golden pheasant tippet wing. It is doubtful whether the salmon find any difference between them.

6. *The Blue Doctor*. The 'Doctor' series of flies was another of the productions of James Wright who flourished as a fly-tyer in Victorian times and was the inventor of so many of the well-known flies which we still use.

There are three varieties in the Doctor series, the Blue, Black, and Silver Doctors, all of which are still popular, though the last two are the best known.

The red head is a prominent feature of these flies. A Blue Doctor was responsible for the killing of a fifty-one-pounder on the Awe in 1907 by Dr C. Child.

7. *The Jock Scott*. This is without doubt the best-known salmon fly, both inside and outside the fishing world; and although it has now largely fallen out of use, it has probably killed more fish than any other pattern. The Jock Scott certainly possesses a most attractive harmony of colours and is a true showpiece of the fly-tyer's art. It was tied in elaborate detail, as apparently was thought necessary in Victorian times and it is a most difficult fly to tie really well. The reader may be surprised at the number of birds, both exotic and commonplace, the feathers of which are used in the dressing of a Jock. Here is a list of them: Golden Pheasant, Ostrich, Toucan, Indian Crow, Turkey, Peahen, Florican, Bustard, Peacock, Teal, Mallard, Gallina, Summer

Duck, Jungle Cock, Blue Chatterer, Macaw, Swan (dyed), with ordinary cock or hen hackles (dyed).

The inventor of this fly was John (nick-named 'Jock') Scott, fisherman to his name-sake Lord John Scott, on the Tweed. In 1845 his lordship was making a voyage across the North Sea to Norway on a fishing trip, and Jock Scott was accompanying him. To pass the time during a rough passage, Jock occu-pied himself in tying flies, and this pattern was the main outcome. Apparently it did well in Norway and after Lord John's eventual death, Jock was employed as a part time fly-tyer by Mr Forrest, the tackle maker in Kelso. One day, the fishermen from Bemersyde came into the shop and invited Mr Forrest to come up and try for some fish which he knew were there. Mr Forrest did so and caught three on this fly which Jock had tied for him. He was delighted and christened the fly Jock Scott after its maker and so it has remained ever since.

It was with a Jock that General Home killed his fifty-one-and-a-half-pounder in Birgham Dub in 1902, also Mr Howard St George his fifty-one-pounder in the Tweed in 1921. Many other notable fish have been killed on it.

There are several variations such as the Blue Jock Scott, the Claret Jock Scott and the Silver Jock Scott, but none are so attractive as the original.

8. *The Toppy.* Another of Scrope's favourite flies dating back to the early nineteenth century (see Lady of Mertoun No. 2 *above*). The Toppy may still occasionally be seen in use. Tweed flies of early Victorian times, like Spey flies, seemed all to be fashioned in compara-tively dull hues, prior to the introduction of the more gaudy types of dressing from Ireland. An amusing paragraph in Scrope's *Days and Nights of Salmon Fishing* (1843) reads:

> Concerning these flies I will note one thing, which is, that if you rise a fish with the 'Lady of Mertoun' and he does not touch her, give him a rest, and come over him again with the 'Toppy', and you will have him to a certainty and vice versa. This I hold to be an invaluable secret, and is the only change that during my long practice I have found eminently successful.

Apparently the fishermen of that day also had their foibles!

9. *The Silver Doctor.* See Blue Doctor No. 6 *above.*

Other well known Tweed flies are the Kate, Greenwell, Silver Grey and White Wing, amongst others.

INDEX